ACTING INCA

PITT LATIN AMERICAN SERIES
John Charles Chasteen and Catherine M. Conaghan, Editors

ACTING INCA

INCA

Identity
and National
Belonging
in Early
Twentieth-
Century
Bolivia

E. GABRIELLE
KUENZLI

University of
Pittsburgh Press

Published by the University of Pittsburgh Press, Pittsburgh, Pa., 15260
Manufactured in the United States of America
Printed on acid-free paper
10 9 8 7 6 5 4 3 2 1

Library of Congress Cataloging-in-Publication Data

Kuenzli, E. Gabrielle.
Acting Inca : identity and national belonging in early twentieth-century Bolivia / E. Gabrielle
Kuenzli.
    pages   cm. — (Pitt Latin American series)
Includes bibliographical references and index.
ISBN 978-0-8229-6232-8 (pbk. : alk. paper)
   1. Aymara Indians—Bolivia—Ethnic identity.   2. Aymara Indians—Bolivia—
Government relations.   3. Aymara Indians—Bolivia—Politics and government
4. Bolivia—History—Federal Revolution, 1898–1899—Social aspects.   5. Bolivia—
Politics and government—1879–1938.   I. Title.
F2230.2.A9K84 2013
305.898'324084—dc23   2013008037

This book is dedicated to the Incas Hijos del Sol theatrical guild of Caracollo, Bolivia, and in particular to the actor Lucho Montaño, in recognition of their dramatic representation of the town's and the nation's past.

CONTENTS

wish to thank my generous mentor, Larry Glickman, and my colleagues in Latin American history, Michael Scardaville, Martine Jean, and Matt Childs. Several foundations supported and made my research possible; I thank the FLAS Fellowship Program, the Fulbright CIES Foundation, the National Endowment for the Humanities, and the University of South Carolina. I also thank my students who took my course in modern Latin American history; their real interest in the significance of the Liberals' construction of a lengthy and drawn-out legal process to ultimately condemn the Aymara war veterans reminded me again how important processes are, both in archival documents and in teaching. A group of people in South Carolina who have made this state a wonderful home deserve special mention; to Elise Matthews, Tatjana Matthews, and all my friends and mud-run partners at KORE Wellness, thank you for your support, humor, talent, and friendship.

I thank my friend and roving technical support advisor Errol Tisdale and copy editor Bruce Bethell for all their work on the manuscript. Final thanks go to the University of Pittsburgh Press and in particular to the acquisitions editor Joshua Shanholtzer and to the editors John Chasteen and Catherine Conaghan for all their attention and effort in producing this book.

Working with the Incas in Boliva, researching in Caracollo, and watching them present their play was a fascinating experience. I thank the Inca guild members for their immense talent and real dedication to narrating the nation's Inca past each August 6, on Bolivia's birthday. I owe special mention to the former president of the Incas and my compadre, Lucho Montaño. His tireless dedication to the Incas, his real interest in helping construct the guild's past, and his passion for history made him stand out. The prefecture and the Oruro courthouse also supported my research, granting me access to their archives. The specialist on the history of the Civil War of 1899, the late Ramiro Condarco Morales, generously spent many an afternoon with me at his house in La Paz, discussing the Aymara participation in the war. "C'est magnifique!" he would exclaim when he found the discussion especially interesting. Robert Smale, the only other foreign researcher working on Oruro's past during my stay in Bolivia, was good company in the multiple archives. Nancy and Silvio Fernández's family gave us our home away from home in Oruro. The Workshop of Andean Oral History (Taller de historia oral andina), with which I was affiliated in the early stages of the project, provided important feedback on my work. In Sucre, Dr. Marcela Inch granted me access to the documentation at the National Archive, and the staff was, as always, wonderful to work with. Maria del Rosario Barahona Michel was an excellent research assistant and a very good friend. Pascale Absi, a French anthropologist researching in Bolivia, engaged me in hours of conversation regarding Incas, anthropology, and history with great humor, earning her the permanent label of friend and Inca aficionado.

When I returned to Bolivia in 2010 to continue research, I stayed in La Paz. The La Paz Archive (Archivo de La Paz) had useful collections and was a very cozy and hospitable environment, which I attribute in great part to the archive's excellent (now former) director, Rossana Barragán, and many of the La Paz historians who worked there, including Pilar Mendieta, Pablo Quisbert, Ximena Medinaceli, Eugenia Bridikinha, and Maria Luis Soux. Ivica Tadic, at the Costa de la Torre Archive, was a fountain of information and very helpful with my research. The graduate students Luis Sierra, Tasha Kimball, and Carmen Soliz were great company and conversationalists in La Paz.

This book recognizes the important negotiation between local communities and political parties in the nation-building process, which often manifests itself through unexpected mediums. Local intellectuals, who often find themselves limited by the parameters of and access to written historiographical debates regarding the nation's past, take recourse in alternative sources, such as public festivals and theater, to engage politics, "recast" national identity, and participate in the narration of their nation's history.

ACTING INCA

INTRODUCTION
Indian Problems,
Indian Solutions

On March 29, 1899, in the midst of a civil war pitting the Liberals against the Conservatives, the Liberal Party supporter and Aymara indigenous community leader of Peñas, Juan Lero, received a letter from a neighboring Indian community leader. Its author confirmed support for the Liberal Party and a willingness to coordinate military efforts among Bolivia's highland indigenous communities on behalf of the Liberal leader, General José M. Pando. "I write to inform you," stated José Maria Galligo, the community leader of Guayllani, "that here we are ready to take up the railroad tracks and fight against Alonso [president of Bolivia and head of the Conservative Party]. Please tell us on which day we should mobilize. We await your reply."[1] This correspondence illustrates the network of indigenous community leaders that developed in the second half of the nineteenth century in Bolivia. These leaders played key roles in defending their community lands, in petitioning the government, in brokering political alliances, and in testifying in courtrooms. Cesiliano Gallego, the Aymara community authority of Merque Aimaya, assured Juan Lero in April 1899, just days before the end of the civil war, that the people of Merque Aimaya would also lend their support to the Liberals' final push for victory. "I got your letter . . . in which you told us to prepare our community," he wrote. "We are ready for tomorrow; wait for us and we will bring honor to Pando's forces."[2]

1

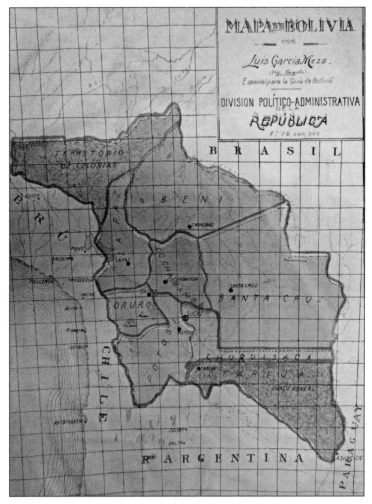

FIGURE 1. Mapa de Bolivia por Luis Garcia Meza, division político-administrativa de la república, Ministerio de Colonización y agricultura 1908. Courtesy of the Geography and Map Division of the Library of Congress

These letters between Aymara leaders, or *caciques apoderados*, illustrate that the Aymaras' support for the Liberal Party was both widespread and coordinated through indigenous leadership; it permeated many communities in highland Bolivia in the corridor between La Paz and Oruro extending south toward Peñas and Challapata and into the Department of Potosí.

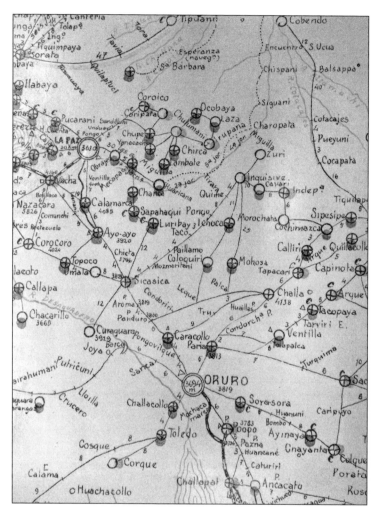

FIGURE 2. Mapa General de la República de Bolivia por Luis Garcia Meza, 1909.
Courtesy of the Geography and Map Division of the Library of Congress

Aymara support for the Liberal cause is explicit in the letters just cited
and remained evident throughout the last days of the civil war, which ended
in April 1899. Esteban Ari, an Aymara supporter of the Liberal Party, referred
to "the reign of justice" that he believed the party's rise to power would
bring.[3] Ari's comment indicates that real hope for political change existed
among Liberal Party supporters living in small communities throughout the

highlands, and they continued to reiterate their support for the party after the civil war.

The shift of power from the traditional elite of Bolivia, who owed much of their fortune to the rich silver mines of Potosí and to the fertile valley lands, to the highland-based Liberal Party in La Paz was especially significant in terms of redefining regional clout and political power in favor of western highland Bolivia. The Conservative Party concentrated political authority in the capital seat of Sucre; the Liberal Party fought for a federal model for the Bolivian nation. Capitalizing on the emerging tin boom in western highland Bolivia that would dominate the nation's economy in the early twentieth century, the Liberal Party headquartered in La Paz, a city perched at approximately 12,000 feet whose proximity to the tin mines made it home to a new "tin baron" elite. As General Pando and his faction attempted to consolidate both economic and political power in highland Bolivia, they reached out to the dominant regional population, the Aymara indigenous group, for military support. Rather than portray the Aymara-Creole alliance in support of the Liberal Party as a union of convenience, I suggest that this working partnership profoundly shaped the nation-building project in early twentieth-century Bolivia.

Understanding the Reverberations of the Civil War of 1899 and Early Twentieth-Century Nation Building

From December 1898 until April 1899, highland Bolivia was the site of a civil war that ultimately led to the rise of the Liberal Party and the transfer of the majority of the government from Sucre to La Paz. The highland Aymara indigenous group played a key role in this transformative process through the alliance between Aymara communities and Creole politicians. Rather than obtain their leadership position through lineage claims, the indigenous leaders acquired influence through their experience and their communities' trust in them.[4] These caciques apoderados fought attempts to privatize communal land as a result of the Disentailment Law of 1874, which proclaimed the division of collectively owned lands; they also represented community interests in court and filed numerous petitions on behalf of their constituencies. By the time the civil war broke out, these indigenous community leaders had at least one decade of experience in petitioning subprefects for land and labor rights; working in Bolivia's archives in search of land titles; and negotiating with national politicians, as is illustrated by the relationship between Pando and the principal cacique apoderado, Pablo Zárate Willka, which existed prior to the onset of the civil war.[5] Opposed to the Conservative Party regime's implementation of the disentailment law, and attracted by the benefits of a federalist system, the Aymara population sought a political alternative to the centralized government system supported by Conservative Party politicians, who ordered surveys of communal lands in preparation for their privatization in the 1880s.[6]

Although Liberal Party politicians initially justified the war as a means to secure a federal system of governance that would grant greater regional autonomy, this original basis of contention became overshadowed by the dominant factors of race and region. The towering peaks of the Andes Mountains, which characterize western Bolivia, offered an inhospitable environment that was often perceived by turn-of-the-century intellectuals as an impediment to attracting desirable foreign immigrants, since they could not withstand the region's cold climate and low oxygen levels. Intellectuals also identified the predominant Indian population in the highlands, the Aymaras, as a contributing factor in creating the "uncivilized" environment of La Paz.[7] During the war, newspaper articles decrying the savagery and primitiveness of the Aymara population created an image of La Paz and the highlands as a dangerous frontier zone where "savagery and civilization" repeatedly bumped against each other because of their uncomfortable proximity. Documents authored by the cacique apoderado Zárate Willka indicate that he attempted to ameliorate racial tensions shortly before the end of the civil war. He envisioned the "new Bolivia" that would emerge under Liberal Party tutelage as a more racially tolerant and inclusive nation. In "Proclamation of Caracollo," a circular dated March 28, 1899, that he sent throughout the highlands, he spoke of the "regeneration of Bolivia" that was taking place through the transformative experience of the civil war, in which indigenous people and Creoles were fighting together to defend their political ideals. Zárate Willka reminded Bolivians that the Indians should respect the Creoles and the Creoles in turn should respect the Indians: "We are all of the same blood, we are all children of Bolivia, and we should love each other like brothers."[8]

Zárate Willka's words would eventually ring hollow in the ears of the new Liberal Party politicians, who were eager to distance their victory from the Aymaras' wartime support. After the war had ended, these politicians would fight the Aymaras in courtrooms, criminalizing their participation in the Civil War of 1899. The new regime opened a series of legal hearings designed to investigate whether the Aymara population had even supported the Liberal Party during the military campaign. Prosecutors in these proceedings, such as the Peñas and Mohoza trials, branded the Aymaras' participation in the war as a race war against the Creole landowning population, and the fleeting alliance between Aymara communities and the Creole politicians quickly dissolved. The Aymara leaders Zárate Willka and Juan Lero, who had played pivotal roles during the civil war, insisted that they had not authored any race war and that they had mobilized on behalf of the Liberal Party.[9] Despite these claims, legal authorities found the Aymaras in question guilty of heinous and violent acts, which served to distance and marginalize the Aymara population and to identify them as enemies of the nation. The Civil War of 1899 thus ultimately led to a deepening of racial divisions between the Indian and Creole populations.[10]

The Aymaras' participation in the Civil War of 1899 is therefore often remembered as an Aymara-led race war or, more recently, as the formation of an autonomous Aymara movement, which reveals that the racial divides exacerbated during the nation-building era are still not resolved. Some historians concede that the Aymaras and the Creoles initially allied themselves, but few are willing to claim that this alliance continued toward the end of the war or following it, stating instead that the Liberal Party's victory, pronounced on April 10, had not met the expectations of their Aymara allies.[11] According to this interpretation, the Aymaras continued to fight for their own political agenda and against the Creole landowning class and the Liberal Party.[12] Recent revisionist narratives written since the 1970s have emphasized the Civil War of 1899 as the foundation of Aymara ethnic movements in the twentieth and twenty-first centuries.[13] The "Zárate Willka Rebellion of 1899" plays a prominent role in a new historical consciousness that underscores the neocolonial conditions prevalent in Bolivian society and seeks to decolonize historical narratives that marginalize indigenous peoples and their pasts. Aymara organizations today often define their political struggles as the culmination of the "Zárate Willka Rebellion" and articulate their demands for Indian autonomy as a continuation of the caciques apoderados' demands in 1899.

A separate line of scholarship recognizes that although the judges criminalized the former Aymara allies who participated in the civil war, the modernizing potential of the highland indigenous population remained important to Liberal politicians and intellectuals.[14] These studies suggest that the rejection of mestizos, or mixed-race populations, common among intellectuals at the turn of the century meant that Indians were a more "redeemable" population than the mestizos.[15] The indigenous population could be "improved" and "civilized," so that it might constitute the backbone of the labor market for the new modernizing highland capital city and serve as a regional symbol for this era's highland-based nation-building project.[16] These accounts, however, fail to explain how the Aymaras, accused of race war and branded as savage in the legal proceedings that had criminalized their participation in the civil war, could be quickly transformed in the national imagination as crucial to the nation-building project. Moreover, traditional historical narratives and revisionist Katarista historiography have both reproduced stark divisions between Creoles and Aymaras, although for very different reasons. Both versions obscure the alliance between Aymaras and Creoles in support of the Liberal Party in 1899, and neither investigates the important possibility of a working relationship between the Aymara and the Creole populations at this time. Paradoxically, the historical statements used as evidence that the events of 1899 gave rise to an autonomous Aymara movement led by the caciques apoderados or that they constituted an Aymara-led race war against the Creole elite generally come from Ramiro Condarco Morales's book *Zárate, el "temible" Willka: Historia de la rebelión indígena de 1899.* Condarco Morales's detailed study, which recounts the Civil War of 1899 and, in particular, the alliance between Aymaras and Creoles, bases the majority of its conclusions on testimony presented by the prosecution in the Peñas trial. In using Condarco Morales's book as a primary source to decolonize the historical narrative of 1899, the revisionist Katarista historians are inadvertently relying on the testimony of the prosecution and its witnesses, reproducing the voice of the agents of oppression rather than the words of the Aymara defendants.

My study revisits the multiple ways the Aymara population participated in national politics in late nineteenth- and early twentieth-century Bolivia and, in doing so, shaped the nation-building project. The analysis extends beyond the civil war, bridging the nineteenth and twentieth centuries and connecting the Aymaras' participation in that conflict to the liberal nation-building project of the early twentieth century. The Creole politicians in the Liberal Party did distance themselves brusquely from the Aymaras after the war, but this does not necessarily negate the earlier political alliance that Aymaras and Creoles forged in the name of liberalism. In addition, the reality that highland Bolivia was home to a predominantly Aymara population shaped the national discourse under the tutelage of the Liberal Party; it sought to justify moving the capital to the highland region, which was characterized by low oxygen levels and a high concentration of Indians. The Aymaras' role in the civil war may have ended tragically in the courtroom, but this does not imply that their desire to engage the nation did as well. The Aymaras' continual engagement with liberal Creoles' national discourse and constructions of Indian identity becomes evident first through their alliance with the Liberal Party and then through the Aymara elite's construction of a "preferred" Indian identity that resonated with the liberal project. Using the previously neglected testimony of the Aymara defendants during the Peñas trial, this study demonstrates that cross-cultural, multiracial collaboration between indigenous communities and national political parties are as much a part of the Aymara past as are autonomous Indian movements.

In discussing the Aymara participation in the Civil War of 1899, I refer to the two groups that constituted the alliance at issue as "Aymara" and "Creole" so as to separate constructions of race and racism from associations with political movements. Former studies on the civil war have employed the words *Aymara* and *liberal* to discuss the tensions within this alliance. While these studies focus mainly on the question of an Aymara-led race war, the Aymara/liberal binary implies that the conflicts were both racial and political; accusations of race war seemed to preclude a full consideration of the Aymaras' views on liberalism and on political change. Employing the terms *Aymara* and *Creole* permits an analysis that posits both Indian and Creole supporters of the Liberal Party; some shortcomings, however, remain. As will become evident, political and social divisions did not always align neatly with constructions of racial difference. Manuel Rigoberto Paredes, a man of Aymara origin who spoke Aymara and Spanish, was also a politician, an author, and an active member of the Liberal Party; he illustrates the rise of urban Indian intellectuals in La Paz during the early twentieth century. The fact that Aymara individuals acted both as complainants and defendants in the Peñas trial complicates any dismissal of the Aymaras' support from consideration as adherents of the Liberal Party. The terms *Aymara* and *Creole*, then, cannot fully capture relations between race and politics in early twentieth-century Bolivia, but this terminology does offer a corrective to the racial and political binaries implied in the earlier usage.

The Civil War of 1899 and its aftermath highlight key tensions in Bolivia's nation-building process, which was characterized by paradoxical efforts among Creole intellectuals to construct an ideal "Indian" identity as emblematic of the nation and the national past yet simultaneously to marginalize the actual Aymara population. Intellectuals took up the themes of civilization versus barbarism to glorify the past Inca civilization, which they contrasted to what they perceived to be the lamentable state of the Aymara population in the early twentieth century. The Incas had been the conquerors and the nation builders; the Aymaras had been subsumed within the Inca Empire and had never developed such a sophisticated civilization. Constructions of a "preferred" Inca identity, however, did not remain solely in the hands of the Creole intellectuals. Instead, the early twentieth-century Aymara elite in the highland town of Caracollo adopted an Inca identity following the civil war to avoid the stigma of being Aymara, which was seen as an unacceptable form of Indianness, and to seek national inclusion in ways that an assertion of Aymara identity would have prohibited. In this case, Creole intellectuals, pressed to address the "Indian question" because of the Aymara participation as the allies of the Liberal Party in the civil war, opened up spaces for national belonging through their rhetorical inclusion of a socially constructed Inca identity. These spaces were filled by the highland Aymara elite, who adopted an Inca past into their genealogy. For example, in the predominantly Aymara town of Caracollo, which served as a strategic site of support for the Liberal Party during the war, the local Aymara elite performed theatrical representations of the Inca Empire, which resonated with the Liberals' promotion of the nation's Inca past in the early twentieth century. In the play, the Aymara past (or the Uru or Guaraní past, for that matter) prior to Inca rule is rendered invisible.

Liberalism, Race, and Nation Building in Bolivia

Framing the Civil War of 1899 as an instance of Aymara support for the Liberal Party and understanding the subsequent early twentieth-century constructions and performances of Inca identity as a discourse of national belonging invites new lines of inquiry and understanding regarding constructions of race, Indian identity, and nation building. Scholars have previously approached the field of race and modernity in Indo-America by analyzing the categories of Indian, Creole, and mestizo identities. The first contribution of my study is a deeper investigation of the category of "Indian," which allows us to see differences crucial to understanding the multiple spaces "Indians" held both discursively and sociopolitically in Bolivia. From the point of view of nation building, not all Indians were created equal. As Rebecca Earle, David Brading, and Alexander Dawson have demonstrated, preconquest empires might be refigured as illustrious precursors of postindependence nations even as present-day indigenous majorities were marginalized, subordinated, and denied (either de jure or de facto) the benefits of citizenship.[17] In Bolivia this panorama was all the more complex because the indigenous majority there comprised multiple and nested communities, reflecting linguistic, regional, and cultural divides shaped and reshaped over many centuries of political and economic transformations. Historically, the Aymara population (also referred to as Kolla) was organized into separate kingdoms that asserted dominance over other ethnic groups in highland Bolivia until the Incas conquered them in the late 1400s, subsuming them within the Inca Empire. Colonial resettlement programs and rotational labor drafts to the mines were only the beginnings of larger patterns that blurred associations between region and ethnic identity on a quotidian basis.

In the late nineteenth and early twentieth centuries, Bolivia's political discourse did not strive to respond to these complexities of ethnic identity but rather intended to reorder the physical and political landscape through the racialization of the highland region where the rising Liberal Party was headquartered. Within the Conservative Party, some Creole intellectuals, such as Mariano Baptista, claimed that the Aymara forces mobilizing throughout their mountain environment reflected the impassivity of the Andes peaks in their very nature; the Aymaras were hard, severe, unchanging, and resistant to progress.[18] The carefully crafted Inca image, in contrast, described as whiter and more "civilized," was meant to imbue Bolivia with a promising and emblematic past that defined national identity and cast Bolivia's majority indigenous population in a progressive light. Since the historical context negated any outright glorification of the Aymara, the Inca became the axis within a liberal discourse designed to address questions of progress and race. Inca leaders, such as the last sovereign ruler of the empire, and sacred archeological sites became integral parts of liberal intellectuals' visions of national identity, modernization, and progress, representing a "civilized" Indian past that contrasted with the "barbarous" Indian present.

The liberal Creoles' discourse in the postwar era marked an important shift in the national narrative; for the first time, writers aligned with the Liberal Party cautiously included the Aymara population within the national historical narrative and cast them in a progressive light. The ancient Aymaras received recognition as the ancestors of the glorified Incas. In this context, the "Bolivian Inca" had an important ancestor, the Aymara. These intellectuals' careful construction of the Inca image disparaged the contemporary Aymara population but did recognize the ancient Aymaras as the relatives and predecessors of the Incas. In establishing this evolutionary connection between the Aymaras and the Incas, such intellectuals maintained preferred constructions of Indian identity at the core of Bolivian national discourse. Rather than adopt a discourse of mestizaje, as happened in Mexico, or attempt to marginalize the issue of race, as occurred in Cuba with the idea of racelessness, discourses of national unity and racial improvement in Bolivia tended to remain within the broad category of Indianness itself.[19] These liberal intellectuals may have deemed the Indian race a problem, but the spectrum within the category of "Indian" served as an indicator for the broader civilizing process designed for Indian improvement from "Aymara" to "Inca." Although the majority of the indigenous population was deemed unfit to receive the benefits of citizenship in the early twentieth century, constructions of Indian identity remained at the heart of national discourse in Bolivia.

Second, my work moves beyond Creole imaginings of nation to consider the ways in which indigenous people engaged the intellectuals' appropriation and promotion of an Indian past. Using theater as one of my historical sources, I investigate how the local Aymara elite in the historically Aymara highland town of Caracollo refashioned and adopted an "Inca" identity in the wake of the civil war. During the tin boom of the early twentieth century, theater constituted a hallmark of modernization, rivaling the importance of the Roman Catholic Church during the colonial era in its capacity to moralize, civilize, and instill patriotism in its audience. This local cultural manifestation serves as a source to inform our understanding of larger national political processes. Capitalizing on the intellectuals' promotion of the Inca as the "acceptable" Indian identity, the Aymara elite constructed and performed an Inca identity by acting in the drama of the conquest and representing the confrontation between Incas and Spaniards.

The construction and performance of the Inca image and past served as a discursive means through which the local elite and national intellectuals remapped the boundaries of national belonging and of Indianness, identity, and race within the emerging Bolivian nation. Previous scholarship, such as that of Nathan Wachtel and Raquel Chang-Rodríguez, has associated local community-level promotions of Inca imagery or theatrical performances of the Inca past with indigenous rebellion or with a collective desire to return to an Indian past.[20] In contrast, the Caracollo Inca play served as a means to negotiate the Indian presence within the liberal political project. Theatrical performances of the Inca past in Caracollo serve as an intriguing source for the study of local constructions of an Inca identity in early twentieth-century Bolivia. My analysis of the play, which originated shortly after the Civil War of 1899, is informed by scripts, masks, costumes, the historical context, and the oral histories of contemporary Inca actors, which all underscore the centrality of constructing an Inca past in the historical narrative of Caracollo. In highlighting the fall of the Inca Empire and the arrival of the Spaniards, the Aymara actors render the Incas as the only Indian protagonists in the play. The exclusion of their own Aymara past prior to contact with Europeans, coupled with the promotion of the Incas as the only Indian protagonists in the play, reflects a turn-of-the-century trend that directed the nation's attention away from a non-Inca indigenous history.[21] Again, the local Aymara elite adopted an Inca identity after the war to avoid the stigma of being "Aymara"—an unacceptable form of Indianness—and to mobilize for national inclusion. Appropriating and promoting an Inca past allowed the local Aymara elite to consolidate power on the local level as well as to claim a space for themselves as "progressive Indians" within the nation in ways that an assertion of an Aymara identity would have prohibited.

Third, this study explores what it means to construct and adopt an Inca identity in a geographic area that was located on the fringe of the Inca Empire and that has historically been home to a large Aymara population. By considering what "acting Inca" has meant in Caracollo, situated at the Inca periphery both historically and discursively, we can better understand the fluidity of significance in adopting an Inca identity as well as its resonance across time and space throughout the Andes. The racialization of the Bolivian highlands as a predominantly Indian region was evident in the statistics of the 1900 census, whose directors, Manuel Ballivián and Luis Crespo, estimated the national population to be 51 percent Indian. The valley regions of Cochabamba and Chuquisaca (where Sucre is located) appeared to have Indian populations well below the national average, with respectively 23 percent and 39 percent of their populations defined as Indians. The highland departments of La Paz and Oruro were well above the national average, with majority Indian populations of 76 percent and 68 percent, respectively.[22] Not only did the valleys have lower Indian populations, but they were also historically associated with the Quechuas, the descendants of the "gentler and more civilized Incas," who supposedly, as the census directors state, "further developed the Aymara civilization, making it great."[23] In legitimizing their rule and their region, Liberal politicians thus faced challenges both quantitative, in terms of the region's large Indian population, and qualitative, in terms of the historical significance associated with the more "primitive" Aymaras. The Inca image and past were key to Liberal Party politicians' and intellectuals' transformation of western Bolivia into a beacon of national progress.

This study offers a reassessment of Bolivian intellectuals' early twentieth-century designs of nation, which were shaped in part by the actions and political initiatives of the very Indians the intellectuals sought to categorize, define, and contain. I attempt to show that conversations regarding the "regenerative potential" of the Indian race took place through constructions of different Indian identities. The highland Aymara elite opted to promote an Inca past via theatrical presentations and narrations beginning with the historical watershed marked by the might and fall of the Inca Empire, silencing the pre-Inca Aymara past, and doing so, I contend, because adopting an "Inca" identity following the civil war allowed them to seek national inclusion in ways that asserting an Aymara identity would not have permitted.

Finally, given the strength of the contemporary Aymara political movements in Bolivia today, my reassessment encourages us to rethink the history of the Aymaras' political initiatives. Their attempts to include themselves within the nation as supporters and allies of the Liberal Party in the early twentieth century suggests that Aymara political initiatives have not all been premised historically on resistance to the nation. Rather, Aymara communities have elaborated a broad spectrum of political projects of both inclusion and exclusion vis-à-vis the nation at distinct historical moments. As the Aymaras continue to engage and negotiate concepts of nation in the twenty-first century, they have converted "Indian politics" into "national politics" in Bolivia.

The Civil War of 1899 in Contemporary Bolivian Politics

Part of what motivates this study of the past is the Civil War of 1899's relevance to constructions of identity and nation in the early twenty-first century. In contemporary Bolivia, the legacy of this conflict incites both regional and racial debates. Browsing the extensive inventory of pirated DVDs at a street stand in La Paz, I came across the 2009 production La Guerra Federal, a film about the civil war made by the former president Carlos Mesa Gisbert and Mario Espinoza Osorio.[24] Having paid five bolivianos (less than a dollar), I was curious to see what the mass appeal of 1899 might be. The film renders images of the past immediately relevant to viewers by explicitly connecting the late nineteenth-century events to contemporary Bolivia and to the repeated cries for political and regional autonomy that in 2008 came from the eastern departments of Bolivia, whose inhabitants were eager to loosen their ties to the larger Bolivian nation. That year, as national unity was splintering under President Evo Morales and several departments defined an autonomous status and a new relation to the Bolivian nation, cries of race war were once again heard. From the perspective of the eastern, "non-Indian" departments, the Aymaras were "on the attack again." This time, however, mandates emphasizing social equality to rectify the historical exploitation of the Indians came from the presidency rather than from the geographical or political periphery.

The film depicts the Creole-Aymara alliance in the Civil War of 1899 as degenerating after the Liberal Party's victory, with the Aymara indigenous forces then initiating a race war. Mesa Gisbert underscores the historical social abyss between the Indian and Creole populations and between regions in Bolivia through direct references to the civil war. The film highlights two main aspects of the war: the deterioration and dissolution of the initial alliance between Creoles and Indians that led to the Indians' ostensible "race war" and the Liberal Party's failure to instigate a federal system of governance as originally intended. Mesa Gisbert, who narrates the film, states:

> Bolivia in the twenty-first century has to prove to itself that it is possible, without violence, and without blood, to overcome the challenges and integrate [the nation] and make it more inclusive. The indigenous world is the protagonist in the twenty-first century. The world "beyond the Andes" is, in the twenty-first century, at the forefront [of this process]. If we exchange the word "federalism" for "autonomy," we see similarities, and we need to respond favorably . . . and not repeat the dramatic historical errors. I hope that what happened in 1898 and 1899 can serve as a reference point [for the present] so that we can construct a better nation.[25]

In illustrating the Aymaras' historically menacing role in 1899 and juxtaposing it with that of Evo Morales, currently president of Bolivia and also Aymara, Mesa Gisbert implies that the specter of race war continues to exist among the Creole population. Power dynamics have shifted, and the Indian stands at the center of the nation rather than at the periphery. Roles may be inverted, but the question of regionalism and of regional governance, expressed through a discourse of racism and of racial intolerance, continues to plague the nation and, as the question of departmental autonomy indicates, to threaten its very existence.

The cartoonist Kjell Nilsson-Maki also underscores the mounting racism in Bolivia and the Creole population's alarm at being governed by an "Indian president." In the cartoon "Indian Warrior" (see fig. 3), President Morales's "Indian" features are exaggerated by the cartoonist with the addition of feathers to underscore the menace of the "Indian warrior." This twenty-first-century comic suggests the current racialization of political dissonance in Bolivia; Evo Morales's presidency has introduced a series of reforms that many of his political opponents viewed as an "Indian threat."

Yet the predominance of indigenous politics, including Aymara politics, in Bolivia today should not surprise us. President Evo Morales and the many rich Aymara political currents that fuel Bolivian political debates in many ways represent a continuation of the Aymaras' struggle for citizenship rights.

FIGURE 3. "Indian Warrior," a cartoon by Kjell Nilsson-Maki showing Evo Morales. Reproduced by permission from www.CartoonStock.com

However, the contemporary political arena also reflects the centrality of an Indian identity in ambivalent historical national discourses—in this case, an identity best defined through the practices of Creole liberal intellectuals and the Caracollo Aymara provincial elite in the early twentieth century—that kept the Indian question at the center of the national agenda.

1 THE AYMARA IN THE CIVIL WAR OF 1899
Enemy or Ally of the Liberal Party?

From December 1898 through April 1899, Creole and Aymara indigenous forces allied themselves with the Liberal Party in an effort to seize leadership of the country from President Severo Alonso and the ruling Conservatives. On April 10, 1899, the Liberal Party defeated the army and took control of the nation. This Creole-Aymara alliance, then, helped transfer power from one political party to another. Moreover, the rise of liberalism and the wartime experience itself promised social and political change. As the war neared its end and the Liberal Party's victory drew close, Pablo Zárate Willka, a *cacique apoderado* (Aymara community authority) who supported the alliance between the Liberal Party and Aymara leaders, articulated his vision of Bolivian society under liberalism in the "Proclamation of Caracollo," dated March 28, 1899, which circulated widely among the highland offices of provincial governments. Addressed to each individual canton or provincial capital in the highland region and emanating from the general command in La Paz, Zárate Willka's missive outlined the changes to be implemented as a result of the war. Directing his message at all residents and the landowners in favor of federalism and the Liberal Party, Zárate Willka underscored how the war had created common ground for Creoles and Indians in the name of the Bolivian nation: "All the indigenous people and the whites rose up to defend the Republic of Bolivia from the disgusting traitor Alonso." He continued: "With great emotion, I order all the indigenous people to respect the townspeople and not to abuse them, since the indigenous people rose up in combat [against the Conservatives] and not against the townspeople. In the same way, the whites or townspeople should respect the Indians because we are all from the same blood, we are all children of Bolivia, and we should love each other like brothers."[1] Zárate Willka not only emphasized this newly created common ground between Creoles and Aymaras but also quelled any suspicions of race war, underscoring the two groups' shared status "as children of Bolivia." In referring to the common identity of all Bolivians, Zárate Willka attempted to level the colonial legacy of stark racial divisions and envisioned a modern nation of "Bolivians." The war, according to Zárate Willka, would produce a greater sense of national unity and cooperation between Indians and Creoles and thus minimize racial strife.

In the aftermath of the war, Liberal politicians, judges, and authorities repealed federalism and minimized their former alliance with the Aymara communities, criminalizing them as proponents of race war intent on attacking the Creole population of Bolivia. Yet the way through which the Liberals condemned the Aymaras reflects important developments in the postwar context. Rather than immediately condemn the Aymaras for leading a supposed race war, individuals within or aligned with the Liberal Party employed the legal system to resolve the situation. The new government committed considerable time and human resources in this project, putting the accused Aymaras on trial in several legal proceedings that lasted from one to four years; the "objective" legal system would restore public order. José M. Mendoza, a lawyer for a complainant in one of these trials, underscored the judiciary's importance in maintaining social structure: "The vigorous maintenance of the justice system is crucial. Moral standards, the social order, and the unity and strength of the nation depend on it. Even the smallest deviation from the maintenance of justice would mean for us a return to a state of savagery and primitiveness."[2] The Peñas trial, examined in this chapter, lasted from 1899 until 1903, during which time complainants accused Aymaras of looting, theft, and murder and of challenging Bolivian national sovereignty by establishing an Indian government under the cacique apoderado Juan Lero. The judges were charged with disconnecting the Aymaras' wartime support from the Liberal Party's victory, which they did by underscoring the supposed desperate state of the "primitive" Aymaras, whom they found to be very much in need of the "civilizing forces" of liberal tutelage. Paradoxically, the Aymaras' participation in the Civil War of 1899 earned them the right to a legal process that would ultimately marginalize them from the Bolivian nation.

The new government spent the years following the civil war investigating the actions of Aymara communities and leaders during the conflict. Lawyers and judges collected hundreds of pages of testimony from the accused Aymaras. Of special interest were the caciques apoderados, whose role in national politics had become increasingly visible in the last third of the nineteenth century because of both the Disentailment Law of 1874, which privatized corporate Indian landholdings, and their communities' participation in the civil war. On July 20, 1900, the judge in the Peñas trial addressed the cacique apoderado Zárate Willka: "Explain your role in the innumerable crimes the public attributes to you; that taking advantage of the pretext of the revolution, you raised the flag of genocide and destruction against the landowners you call c'aras."[3] In his refutation of the charges, Zárate Willka, the foremost Aymara leader and Liberal Party ally, located his actions squarely within that faction's war effort. He stated that he was not in or near the town of Peñas around April 10, the day of the Liberals' victory. "As one of the foremost auxiliaries of the Liberal army," Zárate Willka stated, "I was [in Oruro] with Colonel Pando, fighting the conservative forces, who were well armed and could have killed me, which ultimately would have been better than the position in which I now find myself, jailed and accused of many crimes, and all because of my great sacrifice and service to the nation. I am not educated enough to fill volumes with all the positive services I have carried out for the benefit of state institutions and in the name of the patria boliviana."[4]

Despite Zárate Willka's eloquent refutation of the charges, the attorney for the prosecution, José M. Mendoza, underscored the Aymaras' alleged savagery in his description of their supposed barbarous acts, attributing it to their "innate character": "Indians are greatly satisfied by vengeance. . . . This is not the first time that the Indians have displayed their fierce character, which they have possessed since time immemorial."[5] District Attorney Ballongalvarro agreed with Mendoza; he described the cacique apoderado Juan Lero, of the community of Peñas, as "the fierce caudillo" and cautioned against the dangers of a literate Indian: "Lero has some level of education[;] he knows how to read and write, and it is he who conserves the traditions of his race. He probably preserves latent memories of Tupaj Amaru and other indigenous leaders."[6] Indian education would prove a controversial topic in terms of improving and "civilizing" the indigenous population. In the eyes of the district attorney, educated Indians might read and write, but their nature would remain inherently savage.

In 1901, when a verdict was finally reached in the Peñas trial, thirteen of the accused Aymaras were sentenced to death, and dozens of others were banished to the cold and desolate but mineral-rich Salinas de Garci Mendoza for an unspecified period of time.[7] Upon learning that legally only three of the accused Aymaras could be sentenced to death, the judge revised the decision accordingly, and the numbers sent to Salinas de Garci Mendoza increased.[8] The process of revising the final sentence took over a year, yet the ultimate decision hides as much as it reveals. A careful consideration of the unexplored Aymara defendants' testimony indicates that the accused Aymaras acted on behalf of the Liberal Party. Opposing sides in the civil war had been defined by political persuasion rather than racial identity.

Largely using the hitherto unexplored source of the defendants' statements, this chapter will consider Aymara participation in the Civil War of 1899 and its significance to contemporary Bolivian society as well as to turn-of-the-century Latin American historiography.[9]

Historiography of the Civil War and of Indians in Nation Building

Beginning in the 1970s, scholars working within a new current in Bolivian history that sought to reclaim and to rewrite the Aymara past turned their interest to the Civil War of 1899. Eschewing traditional historical narratives, which often treated the Indians' participation as the actions of an uncritical mass that served the interests of the ruling elite or as a product of Indian ignorance, highland historians created a revisionist narrative that formed the bedrock of the Aymaras' autonomous political struggle. This revisionist historical narrative emerged in the late 1970s in support of the Katarista political movement as the nation began to emerge from an epoch of military dictatorships. Aymara organizers, such as Jenaro Flores and Macabeo Chila, offered new leadership as the heads of departmental labor unions in La Paz and Oruro.[10] Urban La Paz youth took an interest in their Aymara past and founded organizations such as the "Fifteenth of November Movement" in the late 1960s. This leadership and these institutions connected rural and urban Aymara communities as they responded to repressive state politics and worked to claim a space for themselves within the nation. The Katarista political platform rooted itself in the Aymara experience as a response to neglect from both the state and labor unions. Through the Katarista movement, dissidents protested political repression, insisting on wresting control from the military regimes and opening the system for both democratic elections and the revalorization of the nation's majority indigenous population.

Katarista historians, such as Silvia Rivera Cusicanqui and the members of the Workshop of Andean Oral History, including Esteban Ticona, Roberto Choque Canqui, and others, strengthened Indian political and cultural organizations with their revisionist narratives of Aymara history. A product of its historical context and of the Aymaras' political marginalization, Katarismo as a movement and as a historiographical genre resisted a state that had formerly cannibalized the Aymara past. According to this narrative, Aymara protagonists, such as Tupac Katari, Zárate Willka, and Juan Lero, fought back against a neocolonial state that challenged communal land tenure and oppressed the indigenous people. Rivera Cusicanqui's watershed publication *Oppressed but Not Defeated: Peasant Struggles among the Aymara and the Qhechwa in Bolivia, 1900–1980* (1987) successfully historicized Aymara rebellion by demonstrating that acts of resistance were part of a broader political platform of resistance rather than spontaneous or "irrational" outbursts. The Katarista narrative, as Nils Jacobsen notes, charts a history of strength rather than weakness, showing the indigenous population to have confronted the challenges presented by Creole and mestizo authorities by "stepping outside the frame of reference prescribed by the colonial and republican regimes."[11]

The Katarista historian Esteban Ticona, for example, underscores Zárate Willka's dedication in pursuing an Indian-based political agenda in the civil war. He argues that although Zárate Willka's initial support was "decisive" for the Liberal Party's victory, the Aymaras abandoned the war effort: "The indigenous masses realized that they should develop their own position against the q'aras on both sides, liberals and conservatives alike. For this reason, in Peñas, the leader or cacique apoderado of Peñas and of Tapacarí [Juan Lero] organized an Indian government."[12] Katarista historians have constructed a narrative that repeatedly underscores the importance of an Indian-based political agenda that could redress the Aymaras' political marginalization. These accounts of Aymara history—and national history—have made important advances in portraying the Aymaras as central political protagonists in the nation's history. Yet recent revisionist Aymara historiography may have silenced alternative or competing Aymara histories. Specifically, testimonies of the accused Aymaras in the Peñas trial suggest that the alliance between the Aymaras and the Liberal Party was an earnest effort to effect change in national leadership and political systems and to improve race relations in Bolivia, an idea echoed in Zárate Willka's previously cited "Proclamation of Caracollo": "We want to see the regeneration of Bolivia[;] all the indigenous people and all the whites will rise up to defend our republic of Bolivia."[13]

Many of the recent revisionist historians, intent on recovering the Aymara experience in the Civil War of 1899 so as to establish a background and historical context for autonomous resistance to state oppression, cite Condarco Morales's seminal book *Zárate, el "temible" Willka* (1965) instead of going directly to the trial records themselves.[14] This book is both intriguing and polemic; Condarco Morales was the first scholar to seriously consider the possibility of an earnest alliance between the Aymaras and the Liberal Party in the civil war, which he ultimately claims unraveled as the Liberals' victory fell short of meeting the goals of the Aymaras' political agenda, causing the Aymaras to initiate their own war. A careful reading of the Peñas trial documents, however, indicates that Condarco Morales relied a great deal on the prosecution's affirmations of race war to confirm the shift from alliance to antagonism between Creoles and Aymaras. The accused Aymaras' testimony rarely supports his conclusions. Because Condarco Morales simply cites the trial, the year, and relevant page numbers, it is also difficult to tell whose words he employed as evidence. In my analysis, I clearly attribute the ideas and words to the relevant speakers and authors so that readers know which statements come from the complainants and which come from the defendants. A careful identification of the sources reveals the complexity, if not the impossibility, of labeling the Aymara participation in 1899 a race war. As Aymara and non-Aymara complainants squared off against Aymara defendants, political persuasions, rather than unified race-based movements, drove their testimonies.

According to the primary testimony from the Peñas case, the Aymaras on trial vigorously denied that they had launched any sort of autonomous Indian movement or established an Indian government challenging Bolivian national sovereignty. The accused Aymaras tied their claims to the honorable status of their role as supporters of the Liberal Party in the war. While the outcome of the civil war did deepen racial divisions between the Creole and Aymara populations, it also generated stronger ties between the Aymara and the Bolivian nation, as claims by Aymara war veterans attested. The legal definition of citizenship in Bolivia indirectly denied the majority of the indigenous population the benefits of this status, for it established a series of requirements, including literacy, employment, and a minimum income level.[15] The Aymara war veterans attempted to circumvent these requirements in claiming a space within the nation through their military service to the Liberal Party precisely during the nation-building era, when the scope and definitions of citizenship, identity, and modernity under a liberal government were regular topics of debate among Bolivian intellectuals. As a result, the aftermath of the civil war introduced a period of ardent struggle to negotiate and redefine the scope of inclusion within the Bolivian nation under Liberal tutelage.

As the examples in this chapter suggest, Aymara protagonists mobilized both inside and outside traditional political parties in ways that have substantially shaped the nation, of which the Aymaras are in many ways coarchitects. The Civil War of 1899 began during a period of more inclusive social and political practices, which was followed by an effort to close those openings as the war came to an end. In the process, however, new social actors emerged to engage concepts of nationalism and national unity, and in doing so, they refashioned the definition of national belonging to claim their space within Bolivia.

The Bolivian Context before 1899

The participation of Indians in Bolivian national politics and struggles did not suddenly come about in 1899. We should therefore view that year within the larger trajectory of indigenous people's participation in national conflict and consensus. To appreciate the full historical range of Indian mobilization, we must look at the obvious tactics of revolts and wartime alliances, as well as beyond armed conflict to the more subtle instances of legal appeals.

Dependent on the indigenous contribution as the major source of national revenue, the government was reluctant to break up the kinship-based community lands, or *ayllus*, prior to the 1860s, but the recovery of the silver mines facilitated new possibilities. In 1860–1869 Bolivia's average annual production of silver increased to 344,435 marks and leaped to a prosperous 1.6 million marks per annum in the 1890s.[16] The peak of the nineteenth-century silver output occurred in 1895, when production reached 2.6 million marks. The indigenous contribution also continued to increase, but it now made up a smaller percentage of total national revenue.[17] The nation no longer depended as heavily on the indigenous tax as it had previously. Progress-minded national politicians could now literally afford to address the problem of the indigenous communities' practice of collective landholding.

In 1866, in an effort to stimulate production in the agrarian sector, President Mariano Melgarejo proclaimed the end of indigenous communities' collective land tenure, announcing that the land belonged to the state and that native Andeans would now have to pay for the right to farm the tracts. Official governmental publications claimed that the land had become sterile under indigenous management.[18] Overnight, ayllu community members faced the real threat of being transformed into landless peasants. In 1870 isolated responses developed into a defiant movement directed against the edict of President Melgarejo, who sent in troops to repress the communities of Huaicho, Ancoraimes, and Taraco. Between November 2 and November 5, the Bolivian army killed roughly 2,000 indigenous people.[19] Increased

FIGURE 4. Luciano Willka. Reproduced by permission from Archivo La Paz

opposition against President Melgarejo led to his overthrow by the year's end, and a law was passed invalidating the sales and usurpations of indigenous lands that had occurred as a result of the 1866 decree. In addition, the Bolivian government recognized indigenous leaders allied with the oppositional forces, such as Luciano Willka (fig. 4), who received the title of sergeant and was permitted to wear the Bolivian military uniform that corresponded with his rank as visible proof of his service to the country.[20]

As an indigenous ally of the incumbent government, Luciano Willka enjoyed recognition and privileges that were not extended to Indian soldiers during their alliance with the Liberal Party in the Civil War of 1899, yet little is known about his life and politics. The apparent favorable official response to the participation of Indian allies with respect to Luciano Willka contrasts with the more negative attitude displayed toward Zárate Willka in 1899, which suggests that the image and representation of Indians as allies of Creole leaders changed dramatically in the late nineteenth century. The dapper figure of Luciano Willka commands attention and respect; the military uniform immediately identifies him within the scope of national symbols and political factions. In contrast, Zárate Willka (see fig. 5), peering up at the camera in his indigenous dress, is not easily identified as a national hero. Rather, to the many late nineteenth-century La Paz inhabitants who fervently preferred not to acknowledge that the Aymaras made up the overwhelming majority of the region's population, Zárate Willka may have represented more of a political threat, causing his support for the Liberal Party to be repeatedly challenged.

The government, increasingly more independent of the Indian tax, again decreed the end of community landholdings as expressed in the Dis-

FIGURE 5. Pablo Zárate Willka and his army. Condarco Morales states that this photograph is from Arthur Chervin's collection (see Arthur Chervin, *Antropologie bolivienne* [Paris, 1908]). Chervin claims that Zárate Willca is the figure in the middle, but Condarco Morales does not believe this. There are several photographs of Zárate Willca, but whether the man pictured here is Pablo Zárate Willka remains in dispute. Reproduced by permission from Archivo La Paz

entailment Law of 1874 (La Ley de Exvinculación de 1874). This law permitted the sale of all ayllu land not being actively farmed; it also attempted to promote private property among indigenous farmers. The decree was couched in a rhetoric of citizenship, suggesting that the indigenous people would be incorporated into the nation as individual small farmers. In addition, a newly levied universal property tax (the *catastro*) effectively raised taxes for indigenous peoples by 20 percent.[21] In practice, the 1874 decree often served to open up more land for investors to purchase and develop, because community members often lost control of their parcels during the titling transactions.

The desire for estates was particularly acute on the altiplano. La Paz comprised the largest population in Bolivia: 42,849 people according to the census of 1846.[22] The city was burgeoning thanks to the new railroads that connected many of the country's cities and towns to one another and opened them all to external markets to the west. As the commercial center of the nation, La Paz attracted migrants from all corners of Bolivia, generally eager to turn a profit. Many of the rising *paceño* entrepreneurs, locked out of the mining monopoly held by the Sucre Valley elite, jumped at the chance to acquire the altiplano land made available by the 1874 decree.[23] The effects would continue well into the following century. In 1846 there were 716 communities and 500 haciendas in the altiplano region; by 1941, that had shifted to 161 communities and 3,193 haciendas.[24] Communities were broken up, and the land disappeared into the hands of often anonymous investors, especially in the highland region. Erwin Grieshaber estimates that of the 7,616 land sale contracts registered in the Department of La Paz between 1881 and 1920, only about two dozen were annulled, with the lands being returned to Indian communities.[25] However, indigenous leaders were working within the legal channels in the late nineteenth century and made inroads, albeit small ones. They were not simply leading revolts from the political periphery. It should not come as a surprise, then, that as tension between Conservatives and Liberals escalated toward the end of the nineteenth century, indigenous people continued to insert themselves into the electoral process and threw their support behind the Liberal Party. The era of formal political parties in Bolivia began in the 1880s, with Elidoro Camacho founding the Liberal Party in 1883 and Mariano Baptista establishing the Conservative Party around the same time. The ruling Conservatives began implementing the Disentailment Law to privatize community lands. The Liberals emphasized federalism and promised a change in power, thus replacing the oligarchic silver elite of Sucre.

The caciques apoderados mobilized throughout the 1880s and were able to gain concessions from the Bolivian government. In 1883 they obtained the legal concession of the Ley Pro-indiviso, which protected Indian community lands by establishing ownership through colonial land titles. They also managed to slow down the legal process of land purchases by giving indigenous people more time to appeal and contest the acquisitions.[26] These concessions, however, were not enough; Indian lands were lost at alarming rates throughout the altiplano. Violence escalated as the military responded to rumors of discontent. In 1885 troops entered and crushed resistance to the division of community lands in both Omasuyos and Sica Sica.[27]

The caciques apoderados focused their demands on land and education for the Aymaras. In the 1880s indigenous people repeatedly refused to comply with the *revisita*, or visit from the tax commissioners, who inventoried landholdings so as to assess taxes, a process that often preceded land sales. In 1885 the caciques apoderados from the departments of La Paz, Oruro, and Potosí petitioned the government to annul land sales and call off the land surveys. Dissatisfied with the government's lack of attention to the request, the indigenous population began organizing throughout the highlands.[28] The cacique apoderado Zárate Willka typified this new kind of social actor emerging in the late nineteenth-century context.

Zárate Willka appears in documentation from the 1890s as an *originario* of the ayllu Collana of Machacamarca (i.e., descended from its original families), in the province Sica Sica, located in the Department of La Paz. More specifically, he was from the community of Imilla-Imilla, where a monument honoring him was erected in the 1980s. In 1882 Zárate Willka was twenty-two years old and married to Dorotea Mamani; the couple had two children. By 1894 he had already established himself as a community leader; records of negotiations identify him by name and by title, "*apoderado general.*"[29] As the historian Mendieta Parada observes, by the time the Civil War of 1899 had commenced, Zárate Willka was an experienced leader who traveled throughout Bolivia and was used to forming alliances with caciques apoderados and urban politicians alike.[30] Correspondence between Colonel Pando and Zárate Willka from 1896 indicates that a political alliance between the two leaders was in place prior to the outbreak of the civil war.[31] In one letter, Zárate Willka informs Colonel Pando of the alliances among indigenous peoples, caciques apoderados, and some landowners that were forming in the countryside, identifying them as favoring what he terms "our side."[32] This suggests that Zárate Willka and Pando's working relationship antedated the war, as do the caciques apoderados' efforts to organize in the countryside on behalf of the Liberal Party by developing alliances that cut across race and class lines. In the letter, Zárate Willka also tells Pando of the land struggles between indigenous people and landowners, and he informs Pando that they face great persecution from the Conservative authorities, thus connecting the problems associated with land tenure to the Conservative Party. His emphasis on these conflicts over land suggests that Zárate Willka was hopeful that his relationship with Colonel Pando might bring about an alternative to the implementation of the Disentailment Law. He also revealed widespread support for Colonel Pando among Aymara community leaders by sending Pando greetings from "el indígena Copacabana" and others.[33] In closing, Zárate Willka asked Pando to leave him a letter detailing any political updates for him to pick up at Pando's home in La Paz.[34] This letter suggests Zárate Willka was collaborating with Colonel Pando to benefit the Liberal Party prior to the Civil War of 1899; it also indicates a degree of familiarity between these two leaders.

Far from being disconnected from politics, late nineteenth-century caciques apoderados utilized legal channels and supported the Liberal Party to effect change; the rise of the caciques apoderados and the alliances they created were intimately tied to the rise of liberalism in Bolivia. The very act of seeking answers to their demands within the national arena indicates that the caciques apoderados were constantly engaging their governmental representatives.

In 1889 twenty-four caciques apoderados, including Zárate Willka, Lero, and others who would play central roles in supporting the Liberal Party during the civil war, asked the president of Bolivia for his assistance in curbing the actions and attitudes of provincial state representatives in dealing with their indigenous constituencies. The community leaders stated that they had met to discuss how to address the weighty "personal contribution" tax and were accused by local authorities of plotting a rebellion.[35] Citing their rights as expressed in Article 4 of the Constitution, which conferred the right to hold meetings, the community authorities appealed to the president to enforce the republic's laws. Revealing an excellent knowledge of the decrees governing the Bolivian nation, Diego Caricari and Feliciano Espinosa, the two principal authors, stated that their meeting was not an exhibition of deviant behavior according to Articles 1, 2, and 3 of the penal code. Yet the community leaders had been made to endure a trial and imprisonment for an extended period of time until, "as clear as the light of midday, [their] innocence was proven and the slanderous nature of the accusations was made clear." Caricari, Espinosa, and the other community authorities underscored their heightened sense of patriotism in writing to the president:

> Far from the crimes that they imputed to us, the most sacred thing to us is the Constitution of the Republic and those who hold the reins of government. In spite of our ignorance, we know the benefits of constitutional order. . . . We know that only in this way [with the protection of the national constitution] will equality, progress, subsistence, and abundance reign[;] in this sense we are idolaters of [national] order and its innate de-

fenders. It is the prefects, judges, and subprefects who do not understand; they look at us tediously, they forget about our meetings and concerns and tell us that we are impertinent no matter how reasonable matters are. So many things have been forgotten . . . and they look at us as if we were savage beasts.[36]

By the time the highland community leaders wrote this letter in November of 1889, their case had been resolved and they were no longer imprisoned. The important point here, however, is that they appealed to the head of the nation to make him aware that local representatives were not responsive to community petitions and issues and that these authorities abused their constituencies. Caricari and the other community leaders asked the president to insist on competency from local governmental representatives so that they did not spend the nation's time and money in vain; they also asked that the prefects, subprefects, and judges treat the Indian population in a "humane fashion."[37] Distinguishing the problematic local entities of government from the president and the nation, Caricari and the community representatives cited their rights under the national constitution and appealed to the president himself to ensure just treatment and a fair process of appeal on the local level. Adept at presenting their concerns to local government, the caciques apoderados did not hesitate to appeal to the president or other persons of authority when they felt thwarted or dismissed on the local level. Also important to note is that the community leaders denounced the prefects', subprefects', and judges' cries of Indian rebellion, which represents one of several antecedents of unfounded accusations of Indian mobilization prior to 1899.

One of the politically important regional centers where the caciques apoderados and the community members supported the Liberal Party well before the outbreak of the civil war was Colquechaca, the site of a Liberal Party branch headquarters as early as 1887.[38] The tin-mining center of Llallagua-Uncía was another important source of support for the party. Miners at both location succeeded in promoting the party's agenda throughout the countryside because Llallagua-Uncía and especially Colquechaca were important centers lying on regional routes of migration, with people coming there to work at the mines and then returning home. Religious activities, too, helped circulate information, for colquechaqueños made pilgrimages to the shrine of Quillacas, located on the distant shores of Lake Poopó, as well as to the shrines of Surumi and Panacachi.[39]

Highland support for the Liberal Party manifested itself via the voting process. Whether or not they qualified to vote, many indigenous people traveled to the city to join the festivities honoring the party's victory in the La Paz municipal elections of 1891. Journalists estimated that approximately 1,000 indigenous people made the trip to the city to celebrate the Liberals' victory.[40] Liberal politicians also reached out to the indigenous population, soliciting their support in the 1896 election, pitting Pando against Severo Alsonso, and then again in 1899, when the Aymaras served as the wartime allies of the Liberal Party.[41] Even though many Aymaras could not vote, they constituted a visual and vocal majority of support that indicated Indian enthusiasm for the party. Through both its federalist discourse and, at least in part, these new bases of political support that it had cultivated among the indigenous population, the Liberal Party presented itself as an alternative to the current Conservative regime, whose officials were busy carving up communal landholdings. The multiple ways indigenous people responded to the mounting confiscations of their lands in the second half of the nineteenth century indicate that they were very much involved in national politics prior to the civil war.

Liberalism shaped indigenous people's political views as well as their actions. In Macha, for example, after community members had unsuccessfully petitioned the subprefect to halt the land commissions, community members from Macha, Pocoata, and Sacaca rose up and protested the land reform surveys. As they directed their frustration at the land commissioners residing in Macha, the protestors cried out "¡Viva Camacho!" in support of Elidoro Camacho, the founder of the Liberal Party, leading officials who documented the events to describe them as "plebeian and completely liberal people."[42] The residents of Macha attempted to alter national procedures and practices of land tenure related to the Disentailment Law of 1874 in ways that did not threaten or reject the nation, as their cries of support for liberalism and Camacho reveal.

In 1896 Pando, the leader of the Liberal Party, sought the help of the Aymara population to defeat the Conservative candidate Severo Fernández Alonso in the presidential elections. The Bolivian historian Pilar Mendieta states that cries of "Tata Pando!" rang out across the altiplano as the Aymara expressed their preference.[43] Facing such opposition, Alonso barely defeated Pando in the elections. The latter man's appeal to the indigenous population and their enthusiastic response were thus already cause for alarm among the Creole urbanites of La Paz, several years before the Aymara would take up arms. The La Paz newspaper El Comercio reported: "To convert [the Indians] into a political instrument in support of a political party is like using a double-edged blade, [which can be] useful against our enemies today but can wound us tomorrow. They will not convince us that any political party would rely upon their support; we prefer to believe that this is only the work of political shysters."[44]

In 1898 overwhelming popular support for the Liberal Party continued, stretching from La Paz to Challapata. As representatives of the Liberal Party traveled across the altiplano, returning from a trip to Sucre, they were met and accompanied by 5,000 enthusiastic community members.[45] Isaac Campero described his group's reception: "In Caracollo, Panduro, Sicasica, Viacha, [and] Ventilla the multitudes surprised us, cheering [for the establishment of the Federal Committee]. It seemed as if nobody stayed home."[46] One soldier, stationed on the altiplano just before war broke out, in December, wrote to his family describing the warm welcome the Liberal Party army received on arriving in Caracollo. He recalled that the lights shining from all the houses offered a glowing welcome to the troops. Community members displayed great enthusiasm for the cause and greeted the army with cries of "Long live the Federation!"[47]

Within the indigenous population, the rising Liberal Party seemed a desirable political alternative.[48] Sinclair Thomson and Forrest Hylton suggest that Aymara communities may have seen Pando as an ally because he had participated in overturning the presidency of Mariano Melgarejo, who had attempted to privatize communal landholdings in the 1860s.[49] Opposed to the Disentailment Law and attracted to the benefits of a federalist system, the Aymara population sought a political alternative to the Conservative politicians, who had implemented the division of indigenous communal lands throughout the 1880s. A demoralized Conservative soldier stationed in Oruro lamented the Aymaras' enthusiasm for his enemies' cause and his own side's plight: "The battalions Sucre, Olañeta, and 25 de mayo had their weapons and ammunition confiscated in Caracollo; they have asked to return to Sucre. In the night the inhabitants [of Oruro] walk cheering Pando. Our army is not properly armed."[50] This soldier had no doubt that the Liberal Party enjoyed widespread support, even in Oruro, a city that supposedly served as a highland base for the Conservative army. Colonel Pando was able to garner such support for the Liberal Party because the indigenous population sought to bring about political change in Bolivia through this alternative political party, making the cooperation far more substantive than an alliance of convenience.

Pando's ability to recruit heavily among the Aymaras of the altiplano sprang in large part from the fact that a significant portion of the Aymaras supported the Liberal Party in local and, later, national elections and pushed for the change its electoral victories might bring. Zárate Willka clearly articulated this desired change in his "Proclamation of Caracollo," which suggested that a more integrated social order might emerge from the wartime experience and with the rise of liberalism.[51]

Significantly, once the Liberal forces proclaimed victory, doing so on April 10, 1899, Pando entered the city of Oruro together with Zárate Willka, visually confirming the alliance between the Liberal Party and its Aymara supporters. Both regular and irregular Liberal troops entered Oruro, whose residents celebrated Indian and non-Indian soldiers alike as heroes. After the festivities, Colonel Pando and Zárate Willka both slept in the prefect's palace,[52] an event that symbolizes the extent to which the wartime experience attenuated the racial, ethnic, and regional fragmentations plaguing Bolivian society and promoted national unity.

Prior to the civil war, however, Pando had expressed his reservations regarding the inclusion of the Aymaras under the Liberal Party's political umbrella. On May 6, 1896, he wrote to Cesareo Zalles, the prefect of La Paz: "I just got the message that the Indians from the communities of Palca have met and plan to visit me. If I send them a message or meet with them, it will signify my role as their leader, which is not part of the political agenda of the Liberal Party. I write to tell you of this situation and to ask you to take care of it in whatever way you think is best."[53] Pando's subsequent opinion does not seem to have changed much regarding his Aymara allies. During the war, he took advantage of opportunities to distance himself from the Aymaras and to align himself politically with the Creole elite. On March 4, 1899, he wrote to President Alonso, his enemy, expressing fear of a pending race war led by the Aymaras. He entreated Alonso to negotiate an end to the war so that they could cooperate in facing this coming race war, which he perceived to be imminent:

> Everyone is aware of the internal ills this war is creating, especially the inevitable race war initiated by the indigenous race. We need to work together to end this civil war so as to be able to present a united front to quell the Indian revolt. It is the honorable thing to do and I hope you will be amenable to this plan. . . . The Indians are initiating a war motu propio against the whites. Taking advantage of the war context, they will become strong. Even if we unite our troops against the Indians in this moment, we will barely be able to control them. It seems incredible that you are not aware of the great danger we are in.[54]

The Aymaras were aware of Colonel Pando's ambivalent stance and confronted him on several occasions. On March 3, 1899, just before he wrote the letter in which he asked Alonso to privately negotiate an end to the war, Pando left Sica Sica at two in the morning and headed toward Oruro, which was under the control of President Alonso. He took only one man with him, an individual with the surname Monasterios, who had recently been traveling between the Conservative and Liberal camps. Pando was intercepted en route by "el indio Villka," who was more than likely Zárate Willka, leading five hundred Aymara soldiers, who knew of his mission of betrayal. Willka stopped Pando and said, "You're not content with all the sacrifices we've made for you, and now you're going over to Alonso's side, and you'll leave us hanging. You will not continue one step farther." After intense negotiation, Pando was allowed to continue only to Caracollo, a Liberal Party stronghold thirty-seven kilometers north of the city of Oruro, and the Aymaras followed Pando there. Monasterios was allowed to continue on to Oruro, while Pando waited in Caracollo. On his return trip, Monasterios was interrogated several times by Aymara soldiers before he returned to Pando. After Monasterios and Pando talked, Pando wanted to send Monasterios back to Oruro with a response. The Aymaras refused to let him pass. Pando was forced to return to La Paz and to communicate with President Alonso via a cable.[55] Zárate Willka and the Aymara forces' suspicions were confirmed with the March 15 newspaper publication of the letter exchange between Pando and Alonso. Pando had indeed gone to negotiate the end of the war with Alonso. In the published letter, Pando branded the Aymaras as proponents of a pending race war rather than as his allies.[56]

On April 20, 1899, suspicions regarding Colonel Pando's allegiances again ignited. The authors of a letter signed by "la comunidad," who were fighting on behalf of the Liberal Party, wrote to Pando to say that they knew he had been assisting the "alonsistas," that is, the Conservative soldiers supporting President Alonso, in the aftermath of a battle. The letter writers provided concrete examples by listing the names of alonsistas who had benefited from Pando's interventions, informing Pando that the Indians suspected him and that they were reluctant to take further action on behalf of the Liberal Party. In closing they wrote, "Choose, Sir. Then we will serve you."[57] The letter, written ten days after the Liberals' victory, dispels the assertion that an autonomous Indian movement existed after April 10. The letter indicates that "la comunidad" was well aware of Pando's torn allegiances and his ambivalence toward his indigenous allies; the Aymara supporters of the Liberal Party were critical of Pando and addressed him directly with their concerns instead of following his orders blindly. The letter focused on Pando's ambivalence, and the concerns it expressed increased following the war because of a series of decisions that rightly fueled doubts in the minds of his former wartime allies.

Immediately after the war, in an effort to discredit the sacrifices that indigenous soldiers had made for the Liberal Party, the major newspapers and the party's news bulletin both published a flurry of articles stressing the Aymaras' absence from the final battle. Seeking to cast the party's victory as having resulted from the dedication of Bolivian regular army battalions loyal to the Liberal Party cause, and minimizing the support of the Aymara irregular forces, the newspaper articles repeatedly informed the anxious public that the Indian troops had attended the battle only as reserve units that primarily cared for the mules.[58]

Despite public pronouncements that the Liberal Party did not owe its ascendancy to the Aymaras, it was an awkward triumph at best. Instead of fostering liberal political ideals and instigating a federal system, the Liberals' triumph was overshadowed by a troubled discourse of race and citizenship. For the new Creole elite, moreover, the battle was not finished. Although the Liberal Party had won, it had done so only by depending on massive indigenous participation, making the victory an apparent contradiction. These fervent instigators of European-style progress seemed to have taken an evolutionary step backward to win. In their view, they had enlisted and relied on the most "backward" members of society to push forward. The Indians had been their allies for progress. Not only was this a discomforting fact, but the party's Creole elite had been tainted in the process. The party's victory drove the Indian question more pressingly to the forefront of national debates, demanding limits and explanations in the construction of Bolivian citizenship and identity. Yet both before and after the war, many Aymaras fashioned themselves as supporters of the Liberal Party, as the following analysis of the trial reveals.

The Peñas Trial

The tensions between the Liberal Party Creoles and the Aymaras who had supported their army came to a climax in the Peñas trial. The nine volumes of trial documents contain claims made by the prosecution and its witnesses, who alleged that the accused Aymaras had opportunistically engaged in killing and looting, as well as the defendants' rebuttals. The prosecution accused indigenous people of killing landowners and established residents in Peñas and sacking their houses and properties. Furthermore, the prosecutors stated that the crimes were neither politically motivated nor connected to the civil war, and they claimed that certain residents of Peñas, Urmiri, Huancané, and the surrounding villages took advantage of the war context to attack their enemies. Many witnesses claimed that the reported Indian tumult was motivated by vengeance and the Indians' savage nature and that the violence purported to have occurred took place as part of a race war that the Aymaras had initiated. The complainants divorced the alleged Indian crimes from the civil war while portraying themselves as champions of the Liberal Party and of civilization. Many of them claimed that not only had the Aymaras sacked their properties and killed their loved ones, but they had set up an indigenous government in Peñas with Juan Lero as president, Feliciano Mamani as *intendente*, Ascencio Fuentes as judge, and Lázaro Condori as governor. The other Aymaras implicated were accused of being Lero's ministers and military personnel.[59]

The Aymaras' denials are not surprising. The accused were held for months and even years in dark jail cells and denied adequate food or medical attention. Nicanor Quispe, Mariano Muruchi, Eusebio Colque, and José Manuel Apaza petitioned the court for medical attention on August 19, 1900, stating that they had been jailed on suspicion and by that point had been held for seventeen months with no resolution. The men suffered from leg sores that would not heal. Nothing in the existing documents suggests that their sores were treated.[60]

Even if they survived the austere prison experience, these Aymara men still had the arduous job of trying to prove their innocence, an effort often hampered by insufficient Spanish-language skills, poor translation, bad health, and economic hardship. In mounting their defense, however, they articulated surprising links between their actions, the rise of the Liberal Party, and their claims to national belonging as supporters of that party.

The Prosecution: Constructing the "Savage" Aymara

Manuel Rivera, a prosecution witness, insisted that an indigenous government had been established in Peñas and that it was tied to a race war: "The first big step Juan Lero took towards fomenting the war against whites and mestizos was the formation of an indigenous government."[61] Mariano Sánchez, the interim local authority of Huancané, similarly implied that the violence was racially motivated by claiming that the Indians of Peñas had acted with "excessive vengeance" against the town's privileged residents.[62]

Oscar Bravo, the subprefect of Paria, echoed the claim that a race war was occurring in Peñas and the surrounding region. In his report to the prefect of Oruro on April 24, 1899, he stated that the Indians ("la indiada") entered the town and took landowners and other established residents prisoner. He also insisted that these bandits sought to kill all landowners and anyone else they perceived to be an enemy. Bravo identified Juan Lero (parenthetically calling him the "gobernador cacique") as the leader, whom he arrested along with thirty-seven other men.[63]

Representing the indigenous mobilization as a race war, the prosecution and its witnesses divorced the purported Indian uprising from the Civil War of 1899. Mariano Condori, for example, made an important reference to the timing and sequence of events in stating that the Aymaras took advantage of the context of the war to stage their uprising. He purposely framed the "revolt" as not pertaining to the numerous battles but rather as occurring outside the legal framework of the revolution. Like many others, he carefully and repeatedly separated the civil war from the violence alleged to have taken place in Peñas and Urmiri. As a self-professed admirer of the "brilliant triumph of the Liberal Revolution," Condori portrayed himself as a great patriot and the Aymara soldiers as a menace to the nation.[64] In carefully contrasting the glory of the civil war to the alleged barbarous crimes of the "Peñas revolt," he emphasized that these two events were in no way connected. The "Peñas revolt" and the civil war, as well as the membership of the participants and their goals, were portrayed as oppositional by their very natures.

The trial turned centrally on determining whether the events of the Peñas region could be proven to be part of the Liberals' war effort against the Conservatives. On the one hand, if the Aymaras on trial could prove that the events of Peñas had occurred in support of the Liberal Party, then they would profit from the Amnesty Law of October 31, 1899, which would lessen any sentence if they were found guilty. By accusing the indigenous people of Peñas of having perpetrated a race war, on the other hand, the prosecution created a sharp contrast between the legitimate civil war and the Indians' activities, a move that could render the amnesty law inapplicable to the accused Aymaras. If the prosecution succeeded, the accused Aymaras would be treated as common criminals.

As the court case continued, the prosecution continually tried to prove that the Aymaras were incapable of and unfit for participation in national politics. On February 20, 1900, after nine months of testimony and debate, the district attorney announced that the hearings were going to be reorganized. The court was to reconvene in Peñas to gather additional physical evidence and testimony. The Peñas case was not immune to the late nineteenth- and early twentieth-century practice of eugenics and its associated notions of congenital moral deficiency, since the district attorney announced that measurements of the defendants' skulls were to be taken. This study was intended to gather evidence concerning the developmental and mental limits of indigenous people by measuring their head sizes, data that would be used to severely question their participation in the construction of the nation and national politics.[65] Based on these "new" sources of evidence, which were gathered within a month, the district attorney composed a recommendation. Referring to the Aymaras in question as "uncivilized hordes," he claimed:

> It was not political passion, always dangerous for Indians, that made the Aymaras take action. No, the Indian is very far from understanding the obligations of citizenship. It doesn't really matter to the Indians which political party wins. The Indian leaders made the masses understand that if they killed and robbed members and supporters of the Conservative Party, the Liberals would support their actions. The Indians took action to take over lands that did not even belong to them, to avenge old conflicts, and to unleash their savage instinct. Politics played absolutely no role in their mobilization, and we know that the subprefects and local authorities [corregidores] made them cheer in support of Colonel Pando. It is important to remember that the Liberal Party had little to offer the Aymaras of Peñas and Urmiri.[66]

The district attorney continued, accusing the Aymara of perpetrating a race war under orders from Juan Lero.[67] His opinion was supported by international scholars' findings that indicated the Aymaras to be biologically inferior. In 1903 a French team of scientists, referred to as the Crequi-Senechal mission, arrived in Bolivia to study skulls found in the Tiawanaku archeological ruins and compare them to those of the indigenous population living in Bolivia. Arthur Chervin did not travel to Bolivia, but he received and analyzed the data. Combining the skull measurements of the accused Aymaras with their photographs, Chervin attempted to assess the data in terms of Bolivia's capacity for progress and modernization. Again, the Indian was at the center of the debates on Bolivian modernity. Many of the photographs of the Aymaras he analyzed show individuals accused of murder, looting, and theft in conjunction with the civil war. In many of these pictures, taken by the French research team, the Aymaras are disheveled, carry various artifacts that associate them with manual labor, and peer uncomprehendingly at the camera.[68] These photos served as an external, "scientific" confirmation of the Aymaras' ostensibly uncivilized nature. Chervin's findings were not favorable. Given Bolivia's large Indian population, the French anthropologist ultimately recommended increased race mixing if the nation was to progress.

The French team thus expressed pessimism vis-à-vis the Aymaras in terms of their genetic endowment, and Ballongalvarro, the district attorney, doubted that education could do much to improve them. Pointing to the literate Juan Lero, who was accused of having led the Indian rebellion and government, Ballongalvarro stated that an educated Indian was not an asset to the nation but rather a threat. It was Juan Lero who knew how to read and write, and as was mentioned earlier, the district attorney feared that he conserved the traditions of the Indian race, such as the memory of Tupac Amaru and other Indian leaders.[69] Ballongalvarro's statements had important consequences for the outcome of the Peñas trial, yet the district attorney also more broadly addressed the role that Indians would occupy in Bolivian society in asserting that education would not suffice in raising them to the level of citizens. According to Ballongalvarro, Indians are inherently vengeful, violent, and uncivilized and, whether literate or illiterate, would not be assets to the nation.

Whereas Lero was considered dangerous because he possessed a certain degree of education, many accused Aymaras became targets of abuse because of their lack of education. Some unnamed authority (the handwriting suggests a contemporary of the events) went through the trial records and counted the number of individuals in the Peñas trial who did not speak Spanish, marking their testimonies with a red pencil and making comments in the margins of the documents. This individual stopped tallying the number of monolingual Aymara defendants at thirty-four, though more would follow and give their testimony in Aymara.[70] Moreover, sometimes the documents themselves address the issue: "As neither the plaintiffs nor the defendants know Spanish, the judge has called Manuel Andia to translate."[71] Of those listed as monolingual, many were local political authorities within their communities. Mariano Ari, José Manuel Sequera, and Mariano Moruche were all alcaldes, or mayors, and Mariano Ururi was a cacique apoderado. The discussion of language served not only to depict the Aymaras as ignorant but also to invalidate the prestige and authority of the mayors and local representatives. After all, how could urban national authorities effectively communicate with local representatives if Spanish, the national language, was not a possibility? Most important for this epoch, the discussion of the supposed monolingual alcaldes cast them as uncivilized and disconnected from the state.[72] The underlying message in the documentation of the local authorities' monolingualism suggests that if they did not know Spanish, they could not grasp national politics. Furthermore, if the local authorities did not even speak Spanish, what was the deplorable state of civilization among the common community members?

While it is not possible to know whether the tally of monolingual Aymara speakers dates from the early twentieth century, as I suspect it does, ethnic identity and language were certainly prevalent factors in the outcome of the Peñas trial.[73] The judge and jury appear to have given less weight to defendants whose testimony had to be translated from Aymara to Spanish, failing to treat their accounts as crucial evidence in the decision-making process. In this context, Juan Avendaño, a lawyer representing the accused, complained of improper legal procedure in the trial.[74] Avendaño claimed that many of the defendants were forced to testify without the aid of an interpreter (he provided a list of them), with the result that their testimonies were declared invalid. Avendaño's repeated demand that these testimonies be taken again with the help of an interpreter fell on deaf ears.

The illiterate as well as the literate Aymaras posed challenges to court representatives. On the one hand, there was a large group of uneducated, predominantly monolingual Aymara speakers, many of whom could not even sign their names to their testimonies. On the other hand, there was Juan Lero, an educated Indian who was accused of having applied his skills and knowledge to challenge national sovereignty. According to the prosecution, neither the literate nor the illiterate Aymaras were fit to understand or receive the benefits of citizenship.

José Mendoza, a lawyer for the prosecution, pointed out the instructive role the Peñas trial was to play in promoting the concepts and practice of civilization and progress in Bolivia:

> The vigorous maintenance of the justice system is crucial. Moral standards, the social order, and the unity and strength of the nation depend on it. Even the smallest deviation from the maintenance of justice would mean for us a return to a state of savagery and primitiveness. Private property, honor, and civilization depend on the preservation of the moral and legal codes of society. Every trial is an opportunity to maintain these standards, every sentence a lesson to society. There is no better way than through the legal system to repress violence generated by antisocial sectors of society or to reinforce social stability. . . . Not only is the Bolivian public alarmed by the crimes committed, but also all of America waits anxiously to see the outcome.[75]

The outcome of the Peñas trial was to be symbolic of Bolivia's future. Progress would prevail, order would be restored, the "Indian problem" would be blamed for the shortcomings, and the Creoles would claim their victory. The trial reflected the political climate at the beginning of the twentieth century, which was especially hostile toward the concept of indigenous citizenship. As was mentioned earlier, thirteen Aymaras, almost one third of those accused, were condemned to death in the sentence initially handed down on January 25, 1901.[76] Angry appeals, heated debates, and legal statutes reduced this order. In the final sentencing, pronounced on February 27, 1902, three men were to suffer capital punishment.[77] The others were assigned ten years in jail, to be followed by banishment to the town of Salinas de Garci Mendoza for an unspecified period of time.[78] A careful reading of the court case, however, reveals a surprising amount of information regarding the role that the Aymara defendants envisioned for themselves in national politics. The accused Aymaras identified themselves as supporters of the Liberal Party, and in doing so, they challenged the narrow and exclusionary boundaries of national belonging.

The Defense: The Aymaras' Claim to Inclusion

During the Peñas trial, many of the accused Aymaras of Peñas, Urmiri, Huancané, and the surrounding region refuted the charges and denied that they had sacked properties. They stated that they had acted on behalf of the Liberal Party and within the confines of the civil war; in short, they claimed political motivations. Several community authorities attested that the Aymaras of the Peñas region had acted as allies of the Liberal Party: "Out of support for Colonel Pando," they stated, "the Indians rose up as patriots."[79] Francisco Sequera, a worker from Peñas, similarly indicated that the events of Peñas had been politically motivated. Through an interpreter, Sequera told the jury that he had served as a guard under the orders of Gregorio Chaparro, who had instructed community members to kill all the alonsistas.[80]

On February 21, 1899, when Casimiro Ortiz, who worked in Peñas, was asked where he was during April 12–13, 1899, he replied that he had been in Añahuayani, "controlling the roads." The examiner then asked: "Do you know who was involved in the killing, theft, and destruction of property in and around Peñas and Urmiri?" Ortiz replied that he knew nothing in regard to murders or looting. The examiner then pointedly asked: "How many times have you been accused of committing crimes?"[81] He offered no follow-up questions and did not bother to ask why Ortiz had been engaged in such an activity. Rather, the examiner only pressed for the names of individuals who might have been involved in the supposed looting and grasped for circumstantial evidence to implicate Ortiz in the matter by asking him how many times he had been previously accused. The records of the Peñas case show many cases where witnesses provided snippets of important information that, if pursued, could have revealed the intentions of the accused Aymaras, but such testimony was routinely silenced.

Even though the Aymara defendants and witnesses were never asked about their reasons for engaging in certain political activities, much less about their party affiliations, a surprising body of testimony suggests that the "rebels" of Peñas were not angry, vengeful hordes of Indians but rather simply soldiers fighting for the Liberal Party. Francisco Chaca, for example, is one of many defendants who inserted his party affiliation and political motivation into the questioning process. When asked who killed Hilarion Rivera, Celestino Vargas, and the others who lost their lives during the period in question, Chaca replied: "I have no idea who was involved in the violence. I only went to Challapata with my townspeople to celebrate the liberals' victory at the train station. We left around four to return to our homes."[82]

Mariano Gregorio, Diego Gregorio, Pedro Valencia, and Francisco Chaca, members of the ayllu Ilave-Chico, located in the canton of Challapata, accused the prosecutors Isaac Chungara and Joaquin Mamani of pursuing them out of political hatred rather than in response to specific crimes: "Isaac Chungara and Joaquin Mamani, who supported the Conservative Party, have accused us of crimes out of political hate[;] they have not only accused us, but they have also indicated that all the residents of the ayllus of Challapata are also guilty of the crime of having celebrated the liberals' victory."[83]

Despite the prosecution's efforts to minimize any profession of political motivation for the events in Peñas through a careful choice of questions in the examinations, again and again the Aymaras on trial inserted testimony that revealed that political persuasions had motivated their participation in the civil war. Elias Atanacio, a resident (vecino) of Peñas, stated that he and his comrades went to Machacamarca "looking for the Conservative soldiers."[84] Mariano Muruchi, another resident of Peñas, provided the following testimony: "The only thing I know is that all the Indians met in Lero's house to organize an attack on President Alonso's army."[85] Manuel Jachacollo, who worked on the hacienda Jachacocha, located in the vice-canton of Venta y Media, was another who claimed that the actions in question were politically motivated: "Manuel Choquecalla came to Juan Mitma's house to tell us that it was necessary that we help him round up the Conservative soldiers who were in Challa Apacheta and that if we did not help him, then we were Conservatives too."[86]

Juan Lero himself, described in the trial record as married and working in Peñas, argued that his actions had nothing to do with a race war.[87] A man of respect within the indigenous community, Lero lived outside Peñas proper on a small farm; the cacique apoderado was not one of the notable vecinos possessing a house on the main plaza and did not identify himself as a vecino. Zárate Willka, Lero, and other community leaders had exchanged letters detailing when and how to mobilize local troops on the Liberal Party's behalf, and these communications support Lero's statements. On March 20, 1900, Juan Lero received a letter from Zárate Willka, who, citing his own authority and that of Pando, told him to mobilize the community of Peñas in the name of patriotism and on behalf of Pando and the Liberal Party. Zárate Willka's words plainly reveal a political motive: "Patriotism demands the abnegation of its people in the name of the great cause that will bring about the regeneration of Bolivia."[88]

Despite such proof that his actions constituted legitimate wartime activities on behalf of the Liberal Party, Lero was taken prisoner, accused of naming himself president of an Indian government and of orchestrating the violence said to have occurred in Peñas. In refuting the charges, he provided his attorney a list of questions to be used during interrogation; in answering them, Lero would have been able to link the ostensible "Indian uprising" to the Liberal Party. According to existing documentation, Lero's questions seem not to have been used in the courtroom. At the trial, Lero stated that he was on his farm, Añahuayani, during the days in question. He said that he did not name himself president and that he had only put forth Ascencio Fuentes's name as corregidor, as the Indians had asked him to do.[89]

On September 30, 1899, Lero, in conjunction with Mariano Choque, Antonio Condori, Mariano Ururi, and other detained Peñas residents, had their lawyer, Daniel Barriga, write another series of questions and cues to be used in the trial to prove their innocence. One such cue, for example, placed all the events in question within the context of the civil war: "State whether it is true that the crimes imputed to us . . . are exaggerated or false, and that [the actions in question] were carried out within the context of war by the irregular army of Pablo Zárate Willka and in defense of the attacks on us by Alonso's supporters."[90] The existing documents indicate that these, too, were never entered into the legal proceedings.

Letters between Lero and other local authorities in the surrounding region indicate their close political connection and coordination with respect to Lero's efforts to mobilize the Aymaras in Peñas in support of the Liberal Party. A letter addressed to Lero and dated March 28, 1899, confirms that the community of Chayanta was ready to block the railroad tracks and fight against Alonso: "Tell us what day we should be ready, and we will all come."[91] Another letter addressed to Lero, this one from Guayllani, states that the whole department of Potosí would fight with Colonel Pando. "I write to inform you," stated José Maria Galligo, a community leader of Guayllani, "that here we are ready to take up the railroad tracks and fight against Alonso. Please tell us on which day we should mobilize. We await your reply."[92] On April 3, 1899, Lero sent a message to the local indigenous authorities, or *hilacatas*, of Machcamarca, informing them of progress in organizing support for the Liberal Party. Lero indicated that all the communities from the valleys to the altiplano were going to take part in destroying the railroad lines and fighting against Alonso, including the communities of San Pedro, Toro Toro, Sacaca, and Chayanta.[93] Pastor Salazar of Quillacas wrote a letter on April 5, 1899, confirming that people in that community were ready to block the railroad and that some communities had already begun to do so. "We will wait for Pando's orders to begin," Salazar stated.[94] Lero's correspondence, often written on bits of paper, many of which are badly damaged, has survived and is buried within the trial documents. Not only do the letters indicate that Lero and other community members did in fact organize on behalf of the Liberal Party, but they contain no mention of race war. However, these documents do express firm support for the Liberal Party and an expectation that, if victorious, it would bring the changes needed to end abuses against indigenous communities.

When testifying, Lero repeatedly insisted that he knew nothing about any murders. He stated that when he heard that crimes had been committed, he called all the Indians together and told them that they should not kill but rather organize themselves into a delegation to express their complaints.[95] Not surprisingly, the examiners did not ask Lero about his affiliation with the Liberal Party. The proceedings were investigating an Indian revolt; the concept of the Aymaras as participating in that party simply did not exist in the minds of the judges in 1899.

Despite this correspondence gathered for the trial, which establishes that Lero supported the Liberal Party during the civil war, the prosecutors and the judge branded him as the leader of an indigenous government responsible for violence and killings in the region. Lero's health deteriorated during his long wait for the court's decision. In 1900 Lero petitioned the judge for release because of poor health. "The prisons should be for punishment and not for prolonged suffering," began Lero. "At my advanced age and with the rheumatism from which I suffer, you are slowly killing me in this cell."[96] The request fell on deaf ears. Juan Lero died from chronic dysentery on June 12, 1901, before a decision was made regarding his case.[97] Yet Lero's statements in the primary court documents of the Peñas trial suggest that he considered himself to be an ally of the Liberal Party rather than an enemy of any national political party.

There were to be no indigenous heroes from the revolution. Rather, the Liberal Party regime's legal authorities filled the jails with indigenous prisoners, thus eliminating Aymara political leaders and converting them into public enemies responsible for Bolivia's lack of progress. The Creoles' agenda meant to depict the accused Aymaras as savages.

As Lero did in both his testimony and his correspondence, the defendants offered testimonies in which they clearly declared their support for the Liberal Party, which tends to vitiate the claim that the Indians were pursuing a race war in Peñas. Moreover, the presence of Aymaras as both complainants and defendants in the trial challenges this claim. On June 7, 1899, Zárate Willka testified that the Indians were neither fighting a race war nor even forming a united front. Instead, he suggested a more politically and socially complex terrain: "I have no idea who gave the orders for any assassination[;] the Indians are blaming me only to save themselves."[98]

Despite the common belief that the Aymaras attacked Creole landowners, the testimonies include further evidence that undermines claims of race war. Key among these documents are the testimonies of the Aymaras who claimed to have suffered losses in the events of April.[99] The local landowning elite was not necessarily white, nor were the *patrones* the only group filing charges against the indigenous people of Peñas, which indicates that any damage or violence was not directed specifically against the Creole elite. For example, Felisa Choque's husband, Isidoro Quispe, described as an *"indígena"* and originario of Peñas, was reportedly killed in that town during the course of these events. In her statement against Lero and his Aymara forces, Choque reported that several people did not file charges out of fear: "If about half of the relatives of those killed in the Peñas events have presented their cases before the court, there still are many who have not pressed charges out of fear of the rebels, many of whom are living in the surrounding hills of Peñas."[100]

Similarly, Leonarda Sequeda, identified as an indigenous woman of Peñas, claimed that Lero and his men were responsible for the death of her husband, Lázaro Quispe, an indigenous man of Peñas. According to Sequeda, the ostensibly criminal acts committed by Lero's band were directed at a much broader population than just the Creole elite: "They took advantage of the context to act upon old conflicts and disagreements that existed between them and their equals [indigenous people] as well as between the rebels and the notable residents of several towns."[101] Andrea Escobar, another indigenous woman of Peñas, similarly lost her husband, Martin Centeño, an originario who was killed during the events in question; Escobar affirmed that indigenous people committed crimes against other Aymaras and attributed the conflicts to local politics rather than racial strife. She claimed that the indigenous people among the complainants were attempting to use the event to claim land that was not theirs. In addition, Escobar affirmed that the Aymaras who refused to support Lero's movement suffered abuses and losses as a result.[102]

While Felisa Choque asserted that certain individuals did not file charges against the indigenous "bandits" of Peñas out of fear, others claimed that they did not do so because of economic hardship. Camilo Graviel and Francisca Humire, both of Peñas, lost their relatives, Francisco and Benito Graviel, in the events of April. They went to see Telmo Beltrán to file charges against Lero and his Aymara army, but Beltrán was charging forty bolivianos for legal fees, a steep sum for the two. Graviel and Humire asked the district attorney to talk to the intendant in Challapata about the high cost of filing charges, so that atrocious crimes such as these would not go unpunished.[103] This and similar evidence suggests that, besides not constituting a race war, the April movement in Peñas was also not motivated strictly by class strife. Camilo Graviel and Francisca Humire were not people of authority or position in Peñas. Rather, they were humble people who claimed to have been affected by the violence and were struggling to pay the fees for filing charges.

Less commonly, some defendants held that the events taking place in Peñas during April were a matter of local authorities attacking their enemies. Pedro Sequera, Nazario Choque, and Aquilina Davalos claimed that Lero, a group of mayors, and some caciques apoderados plotted against their enemies, including the corregidor Mariano Ortiz.[104] Nazario Choque testified that Feliciano Mamani gave the orders to capture both his father, Toribio Tomás, and his brother Balentín, as well as to imprison Manuel Urmiri, Juan Quispe, Crisosto Flores, Bacilio Choque, Apolinar Condori, and Gregorio Alegria. He also claimed that the four mayors served as accomplices in transporting the prisoners to Lero's house.[105] According to this interpretation of the events, local power struggles motivated the acts. And yet this account does not satisfactorily explain the diversity of the supposed victims unless we assume that each case involved a personal conflict.

The Peñas trial constituted an important and protracted struggle in which local Aymara participants—and the nation—sought to define local events, but the documents suggest that some officials were less concerned about the internal dynamics of the case and simply used the proceedings to limit the role of Indians within the nation-building project undertaken by Liberal Party politicians. I have already mentioned, for example, the bald rejection of untranslated testimony, which ultimately disfranchised many witnesses. In another issue that arose toward the end of the trial, it became apparent that there were at least two and perhaps three people named Mariano Choque who had been attempting to prove their innocence.[106] While the court was attempting to distinguish these individuals, one of them escaped from jail.[107] Despite the lack of clarity, one of the remaining two was subsequently found guilty and assigned the death sentence.[108] This Mariano Choque fervently argued that he was not the guilty Mariano Choque and appealed the sentence up to the day of his execution.[109]

Many other gross irregularities occurred during the trial, which complainants as well as defendants pointed out. For example, Isaac Chungara, an indigenous man who lived in Challapata and was one of the most aggressive individuals on the prosecution's side, criticized the authorities for not responding properly to cries for help. "The authorities acted as if it was a simple civil dispute that was not worth their time," Chungara stated.[110] Similarly, Timotea Troncoso, a seamstress and resident of Urmiri who accused Aymara defendants of killing her husband and child, observed that the Indians were indeed barbarous but that the judges were incompetent and misusing the legal system and that the lawyers were doing bad things as well.[111] Troncoso later stated that people were being taken to testify without the proper legal summons.[112] Seeking redress for the killing of her husband and son, Felipa Atauchi, a worker and resident of the farm of Tuturpata, located in the Peñas area, tried to specify that she had accused only Juan Lero, Teodoro Morochi, Facundo Chaparro, Apolinar Gonzales, Santos Leon, Octavio Capurata, Manuel Herrera, Mariano Rios, Victor Chaparro, Miguel Quispe, Francisco Torres, and Mariano Ari, but not others among the defendants.[113] These complainants' statements of discontent suggest a broad concern with legal protocol in the trial.

The complainants thus variously claimed that the April events of Peñas were a race war instigated by the Indians, a class war, and an attack instigated by corrupt authorities. Yet the previously cited testimonies suggest that none of these explanations adequately accounts for the diversity of the victims (or of those pressing charges, for that matter). No single paradigm is able to fully explain what happened in Peñas or completely illuminate the composition of the complainants and defendants according to traditional social divisions. The documents do suggest that a significant majority of the Peñas events were politically motivated and involved local clashes that resonated with and increasingly became expressed as differences between support for the Conservative Party and support for the Liberal Party and were directly related to the Civil War of 1899. Support of the two major political parties cut across divisions of race and class, forming new coalitions that can account for the victims' diversity. In particular, the presence of Aymaras on both sides calls into question the accusation of an Indian-led race war.

Yet even more direct evidence connects these events to the war and to Aymara support for the Liberal Party. Local authorities, including Lero and Mariano Ari, the mayor of Urmiri, composed a document from jail on June 7, 1899 ("on ordinary paper instead of on legal stationery," as the authors clarified most apologetically), that explains what happened that April in Peñas.[114] This document casts the indigenous people as supporters of the Liberal Party, places the events of April within the context of the civil war, and explains the fighting as a response to continued acts of aggression by the Conservative army and local landowners. The way in which the events are described, along with the way indigenous people portrayed their participation in national politics, is striking and most valuable in understanding the Aymaras' involvement in the civil war. The accused clearly state that they rose up "as patriots" in support of Colonel Pando and at the request of "don Billcas," that is, Zárate Willka. The scenario the detained Aymaras paint is one of political conflict between Liberals and Conservatives. The authors claim that as they were attempting to leave Peñas to go to Caracollo, which was the designated meeting place for the Liberal Party forces, the "corregidor alonsista," Mariano Condori, and other Conservatives in Peñas tried to take them prisoner to prevent them from assisting Pando. They fought several skirmishes with the Conservatives before they reached Caracollo. They claimed that the looting that took place in Peñas was done by angry Conservative hacendados, specifically, Pacífico Morales, Efenio Heredía, Sinforiano Aragandoña, Mariano Condori, Adolfo Bargas, and Miguel Choque, among others. In addition, they stated that they had suffered repression at the hands not only of Conservative Party supporters in Peñas but of authorities from nearby towns who traveled to Peñas to punish them. Among those they named were Mariano Condori, Marselino Barrira, Isaac Chungara, Mariano Poque Choque, and the corregidor of Huancané. According to the document, the Conservative allies "entered [Peñas] with four soldiers" and struck the defendants each "one hundred times with a stick"; it added that "they hit a woman too." The document further asserted that the problems continued after war ended: "The corregidor of Urmiri punished a young man from the Liberal Party out of vengeance and sent him to Oruro as a prisoner." The authors closed by calling for justice: "We have all suffered as a result of this combat. Now Mr. District Attorney, we ask and beg in the name of God and in the name of the Virgin of the Mineshaft, that real justice be carried out."[115]

According to Lero, Ururi, and the other authors of this document, any mobilization that took place in Peñas occurred for the good of Bolivia in favor of the Liberal Party as part of the civil war. The events in Peñas did not occur spontaneously but were part of a coordinated effort of support for the party, and, following the victory, a planned pursuit of and additional skirmishes with the defeated Conservative soldiers. If crimes did occur, they were instigated by the Conservative army, which abused Liberal Party supporters in Peñas by killing their livestock and sacking their houses. According to the local authorities, the Conservative forces recklessly plundered communities both during and after the war.[116]

It is not hard to believe that as the tides turned against the Conservatives and railroad tracks were destroyed, cutting the troops off from provisions, Conservative soldiers would have sacked Aymara communities. Reports decrying the Conservative army's actions appeared repeatedly in the press. An article from the Liberal Party publication El Boletín Oficial, which was reprinted in the La Paz newspaper El Comercio, illustrates such accounts: "The aggressive acts [that the Conservative army] committed against the Indian race, . . . the occurrences of theft, murder and of all kinds of violations, . . . have provoked sobering results. . . . The Indian race was forced to respond out of defense, not only out of their violent instincts. . . . The sad results, which we sincerely lament, were a direct result of the violations of the Conservative army."[117]

A few days earlier another article regarding abuses committed by Conservative troops had appeared in El Comercio. The author insisted that the Conservative soldiers had pushed the passive Indians to their limits: "The Indian uprising . . . was provoked by the abusive acts of the Conservative army, which, not content with committing all kinds of acts of violence against the poor Indian families, went to the extreme of hunting them like savages. . . . Such atrocious acts have provoked the otherwise passive and inoffensive character of the Indian race. . . . However, the [Liberal] government has taken every precaution to repress the Indians' anger."[118] Creole politicians in the Liberal Party created a discourse of blame that enabled them to avoid responsibility for the Aymaras' responses to these repeated attacks or to justify the use of harsher methods of repressing their indigenous allies. Nonetheless, the repeated examples of abuse suggest the extent to which Conservative soldiers damaged indigenous communities during the war.[119] The Oruro newspaper La Libertad regularly publicized personal experiences of loss and abuse that indigenous people suffered during the war. Not only did the Conservative soldiers leave a large number of dead and wounded in their wake, but they were responsible for a considerable amount of sacking. Lorenzo Limachi, who claimed he had been a victim of the Conservative troops, provided the following itemized list of seized goods:

> 128 sheep of high-quality wool production
> Two loads of white quinoa
> 12–18 lbs. of onions
> A lasso
> 8 chickens[120]

The imprisoned Aymaras portray themselves as political agents—and as victims of the Conservative army—embroiled in the politics of both the community and the nation, with their decisions having been shaped by the civil war. The problems that existed between the accused Aymaras and Mariano Condori, Isaac Chungara, and the other complainants arose precisely from differences in political persuasion. The violent actions in question were not those of Indians intent on initiating a race war, as the prosecution claimed. Rather, they were generated by the Aymaras' political convictions as part of the civil war. Moreover, the Aymaras of Peñas did not behave as unranked soldiers of an auxiliary army. They were not satisfied simply to engage in battle with the opposing forces when ordered to do so. As the imprisoned Aymaras stated in their document, they waited in the train station in Pazña with the intention of taking President Alonso captive. When they did not find him there, they went to Urmiri in an effort to capture the head of the nation themselves.[121]

Despite valiant efforts to convince the judge—and the nation—that the Aymaras had acted as patriots on behalf of the Liberal Party in the Peñas region, the authorities in the trial gave this document strikingly little attention. Although there is ample evidence corroborating certain parts of the Aymaras' explanation, the document was ignored and simply filed with the proceedings' other papers. The only person to engage this version of history, which portrayed indigenous people as aware and active participants in national politics, was Daniel Barriga, the defense lawyer. On September 27, 1899, Barriga issued a series of statements to be entered into the proceedings. He urged the court to recognize the actions of the Aymaras as politically motivated efforts in support of the Liberal Party.[122] Yet neither the Aymaras' document nor Barriga's statements received a hearing in the trial. Politically motivated and aware Aymaras simply did not exist for the judges.

Honor, Citizenship, and the Peñas Trial

The Republic of Bolivia's laws established several criteria for citizenship, conferring it only on individuals who were male, could read and write, earned a minimum income or owned land, and worked as something other than a servant. With the birth of the republic, moreover, the indigenous population was no longer recognized by the separate series of laws that had governed the Indians during colonial times. The new laws thus denied citizenship to the majority of the indigenous population by establishing these limiting criteria, severely undermining their ability to exercise civil rights within the nascent Bolivian republic. In addition, the state issued charters that neglected to specifically protect them.[123] The principal means by which indigenous people could gain any rights was to claim a space within the nation, which they attempted throughout the nineteenth century by asserting an honorable status. For example, in one court case that dates from the mid-nineteenth century, an indigenous hatmaker pressed charges against a vendor regarding past debts. The vendor countered the hatmaker's accusations with four counterarguments designed more to remind the hatmaker of his inferior status as an Indian than to address the complaint. He stated that, among other things, the hatmaker "came from such a low class of people that he was barely visible to others, since his class was made up of unknown, questionable people, '*miserables*,' with no real role in Bolivian society."[124] By referencing the hatmaker's class, the vendor attempted to delegitimize his very right to file a legal grievance. At the same time, the hatmaker's demands on the vendor indicate that indigenous people were contesting the narrow limits of national belonging within which they lived. While Bolivia's legal codes defined the categories of citizen and noncitizen, the courts often became sites of contestation as indigenous people sought both to defend themselves and to advance their own cases. Indigenous plaintiffs and defendants appropriated the discourse of honor to support their statements and to lend legitimacy to their claims. In 1846, in refuting murder charges against him, a young man stated that he wished to call witnesses to testify that he was an "honorable individual who had been an obedient son, raised by his mother."[125] In another case, an indigenous individual accused of robbery brought forward witnesses to confirm his honor. These people spoke to his untainted honor as an individual whose parents had "provided him with a moral education and housed him from birth until the present." As a result of his upbringing and honor, he stated, he had no real needs that would lead him to steal.[126]

Debates over national belonging intensified after the civil war. In the Peñas trial, both the prosecution and defense linked their statements and actions to the war and to national politics. At its core, the trial was a debate over definitions of citizenship and the formation of the nation. Most of the Aymara war veterans charged in the trial insisted that their service to the nation be recognized, while the prosecution accused the Aymaras of having instigated a race war. Constructions of race and honor created clear distinctions that established difference even within the indigenous population. Aymara complainants and Aymara defendants employed the discourse of honor through their oppositional constructions of "good" and "bad" Indians in an attempt to claim a space within the nation for themselves as supporters of the Liberal Party.

Mariano Condori, who stated that his son had been killed in the tumult and that his possessions had been stolen, attempted to incorporate the civil war into the already exclusive set of criteria that defined claims to an honorable status.[127] In first praising the Liberals' war effort and then contrasting it with what he claimed was the subsequent indigenous uprising, Condori stated that the "indigenous class" had committed crimes against the "honorable residents of Peñas." He strove both to delegitimize the Aymaras' claim to honorable status through their participation in the war and to differentiate himself—a patriot and Liberal Party supporter—from the violent and unpatriotic Aymaras he accused of rebellion.[128] The war thus provided new opportunities for claiming and shaping national identities. At first glance, the racialized reference to the "indigenous class" just quoted suggests that Condori's testimony supported the accusations of race war. Condori, however, identified himself as an indigenous person and was one of several complainants who, somewhat paradoxically, referred to the defendants' indigenous backgrounds so as to distinguish themselves as honorable Indians, unlike the accused Aymaras.

Miguel Choque, an Indian laborer and vecino of the neighboring hamlet of Urmiri, stated that "he had been a victim of the ferocious acts of the Indians of Urmiri." He claimed that the Indians had taken the title to his small farm, Colpa-Cocha, under orders from Zárate Willka. Choque claimed that "Villca got permission from Colonel Pando to confiscate all the titles to individual farms . . . and that the land was to be expropriated and given to indigenous communities."[129] This fascinating paradox, wherein complainants who self-identified as indigenous set themselves apart from the Aymara defendants by decrying the latters' savagery and alleged participation in a race war, indicates that concepts of race and ethnic identity emerged from a complex and layered process of social construction in late nineteenth- and early twentieth-century Bolivia.

Aymara complainants insisted on using a racial label in referring to the accused as the "indigenous" class. Race was not only central to the indigenous complainants' testimonies but often heightened. In testimony given on July 19, 1899, one of the men named Mariano Choque referred to the accused Aymaras as "savage 'Caribs' who victimized the most honored, established, and peaceful residents of Peñas."[130] In referencing the Caribs, Choque evoked stereotypes that tended to cast these early indigenous people of the Caribbean as the most savage, backward, and violent of Indians, and Choque equated the Aymaras with them. Degrading Indians may have been a potentially dangerous discourse for indigenous complainants, since it could potentially undermine their own credibility, but it was also a powerful way for them to debase the accused Aymaras, to disassociate themselves from the Indian majority, and to claim certain privileges as members of the select refashioned category of moral and honorable Indians. Distinctions were thus made within the category of "Indian" itself, with the notion of honor playing a major role in marking distinction among indigenous people and in explaining the use of the term *race*.

The Aymara defendants introduced new criteria in their discourse of honor. Rather than base their claims to honor on the usual categories of family, social status, race, and upbringing, both the complainants and the defendants superseded these criteria, tying their claims to honor and participation in the nation and national politics to their roles as allies of the Liberal Party. Their wartime experiences increased the Aymaras' sense of national belonging and encouraged them to claim their rights as they refuted the charges filed against them. In short, their support for the Liberal Party created a new, expanded discourse of honor and citizenship that the Aymaras wove throughout their testimonies in the Peñas trial not only to defend themselves but to transmute their status in the trial from public enemies to Bolivian citizens.[131]

To a certain degree, the Liberal Party itself capitalized on expanding the definition of honor in terms of patriotism. In attempts to explain the Indians' participation during the civil war, Creole officials argued that the Indians had no choice but to join because the abuses committed by the Conservative troops forced them to respond. "The attitude that the altiplano Indian has assumed," stated an article in the *Boletín Oficial*, "is purely the result of the murders and other atrocities that the Conservative army has been carrying out since their arrival in the highlands. . . . The massacres have produced a terrible response. The Indians felt the [Conservative army's actions] were an affront to their honor, to their property, to their very existence. . . . They had no choice but to defend themselves."[132]

Mariano Humero, a complainant who identified himself as an "indígena contribuyente" from Peñas, testified that he did not want to participate in the events he said occurred after the war: "[We] hardworking and honorable people did not want to participate in the uprising, which was not connected to the goals of the noble revolution [but rather] was characterized by theft, murder, and every kind of crime that served only to detract from the revolutionary cause."[133] Like the previously mentioned Mariano Choque, Humero used honor to set himself apart from the Aymaras against whom he was testifying.[134] Isaac Chungara, who was described as "a person of the aboriginal race and a resident of the neighboring town of Challapata," accused the Aymaras of breaking down his door and taking his things and then continuing on to his other properties to burn the houses and steal the livestock.[135] He characterized the Indian defendants as having given way to their instincts to destroy and loot after the war ended and said that they stripped him of everything he had amassed through years of hard and honorable work.[136] The contrast between the vengeful, destructive Aymara Indian who participated in the uprising and looting and the moral, hardworking, and honorable Indian who supported the Liberal Party emerged again and again in the indigenous complainants' testimonies. The Creole intellectuals and politicians were thus not the only ones to tarnish the image of the Aymara. The Aymara complainants in the Peñas trial similarly debased Aymaras, setting themselves apart from the defendants through distinctions made *within* Indian identity and in relation to the Civil War of 1899. The accused Aymaras became the "bad Indians," while the indigenous complainants refashioned themselves as "acceptable," patriotic, and honorable Indians who did not condone the Ayamara uprising that they claimed had occurred following the war's end.

The complainants were not the only ones to employ a discourse of honor. The majority of the accused Aymaras affirmed that they had fought as patriots in support of the Liberal Party. Among those who asserted this, many took advantage of the situation to expand the scope of national belonging, laying claim to a discourse of honor in their refutation of the charges. The Aymara defendant Antonio Villca employed such a discourse in his statements to the court. An indigenous man from the ayllu Callpa in the canton of Challapata, Villca stated that Polonia Limachi had falsely accused him of participating in the uprising. Much like Juan Lero in that man's refutation of the crimes imputed to him, Villca attempted to reinforce his argument by stating that he was an honorable man who had never committed a crime.[137] Apolinar Astete, an indigenous man and vecino of Chitani, in the canton of Challapata, who testified on behalf of Antonio Villca, also emphasized that defendant's honor in order to argue his innocence.[138]

In another instance, Venancio Choquerivi, whom Isaac Chungara had accused of robbery, theft, and murder, claimed he was innocent. To defend himself, he asserted that he was an honorable person and called witnesses to testify to his respectable status. Choquerivi drew clear distinctions between his actions, which he said he carried out in support of the Liberal Party effort, and random instances of looting. He expressed his support for the Liberals and explained that he had gone to Challapata only to celebrate Colonel Pando's victory. According to him, the drunken Indians from Jacagua and Angostura first cheered Pando and then commenced looting.[139] Victoriano Poquechoque, a former cacique of the ayllu Cajualli, confirmed that he had invited Choquerivi to accompany him to Challapata to celebrate the party's victory.[140] Mariano Saravia testified that he saw Choquerivi celebrating in the company of friends who had also supported the victory.[141] Nicolás Garisto testified to Choquerivi's honor, stating that the defendant had an excellent reputation and worked as a dedicated businessman. Garisto also mentioned that Choquerivi had an established home as well as additional properties and had never before faced legal problems of any kind.[142] Both Garisto in his defense of Choquerivi and Villca in his self-defense resorted to the traditional criteria of honorable behavior, yet they also used the discourse of honor and patriotism that emerged from the 1899 context and that served as a means to claim a space within the nation under Liberal Party rule in early twentieth-century Bolivia.

In his defense statement on July 18, 1899, Lero also underscored his sense of honor and morality in claiming his innocence: "Since the first moments of my life, I have always had a moral heart that cultivated within me respect for life and . . . honor. . . . I ask not for pardon, because I do not need to, [but] only for the correct application of the laws."[143] It is striking that many of the Aymaras who found themselves in desperate circumstances, stripped of all civil rights and branded as enemies of the nation, employed a discourse of defense that often both refuted the charges and expanded the discourse of national belonging by laying claim to an alternative, honorable status directly related to their support of the victorious Liberal Party.

Reconsidering the Aymaras' Participation in the Civil War of 1899

A careful rereading of primary judicial sources, focusing on the understudied testimonies from Aymara defendants, suggests that Aymara aspirations in 1899 largely concerned belonging to the nation rather than rejecting it. The evidence undermines assertions of race war as well, suggesting instead that a significant number of the Aymaras acted as supporters of the Liberal Party both before and during the civil war. During the Peñas trial, many Aymara defendants claimed a discourse of honor as supporters of the Liberal Party. In doing so, they attempted to claim a space within the nation.

The Aymaras' participation in the Civil War of 1899 in support of the Liberal effort indicates that their past is characterized by efforts to belong to the Bolivian nation as well as by instances of resistance. The Aymara defendants in the Peñas trial connected their efforts to the Liberal Party and claimed that they were falsely accused by their political opponents, both Aymara and non-Aymara, which complicates any attempt to label the Aymaras' actions in 1899 as a race war or as an autonomous Indian movement. Any investigation into the Aymara past should not suppose it to have been dominated by resistance movements. Rather, Aymara communities have elaborated a broad spectrum of political projects of both inclusion and exclusion vis-à-vis the nation at distinct historical moments. This is reflected in a letter written on February 23, 1900, by the incarcerated Aymaras charged in the Peñas trial, among them several caciques apoderados: Juan Lero, of Peñas; Diego Mamani, of Caracollo; and Rosario Mamani:

> We are in jail because of the crimes we have been accused of carrying out in the recent war and because we played an active role, even though we are Indians and therefore considered to have no political rights, as has been made clear through the "justice" being carried out against our race. Since we have been turned over to the legal system, the complaints have begun, because we, as oppressed Indians, are always accused of hating and killing the whites, and now we are in their hands, at the mercy of our oppressors.

This poignant plea makes clear the accused Aymaras' frustration as they watched their race, not their actions during the war, go on trial. Juan Lero,

Diego Mamani, and the other Aymaras on trial thus invoked their "service to the nation" and entreated the representatives of the justice system to avoid stigmatizing them racially: "We ask that you treat us as criminals, even though we have been labeled as such [as a result of] our national service [during the war], and not as public enemies, stripped of all our rights."[144] According to the accused Aymaras, it was difficult to be detained and have to prove your innocence, and it was nearly impossible to do this if you were Indian.

FROM AYMARA LIBERALS TO EXEMPLARY INCAS

Nation Building in Early Twentieth-Century Bolivia

"Would you like to know what this country is like?" The Chilean author and diplomat Abraham Konig asked his wife this rhetorical question in a letter he wrote from Bolivia in 1909, continuing:

> Here, there is no wood or coal. You have to cook your food over llama droppings. . . . As one Frenchman wrote in a very bad book about Bolivia, "damned is this country where you have to wait for animals to shit so that you can eat." . . . There are fifty Indians from Mohoza in jail, accused of murdering and then eating one hundred fifty members of President Alonso's army. . . . The Indians here are cannibals. They do not deny this. They only make the excuse that the town priest incited them. . . . The Indians of the highland region are cannibals. In a place near La Paz they ate another seven people from Sucre who were hurt and who had taken refuge inside a church. . . . I apologize for not telling you more about these Mohoza Indians, but in truth there is not much to tell, as the Indians are all alike, and the Indian servant who is entering my room in this moment is most likely just another cannibal. . . . Do you think that in Africa things worse than this happen?[1]

In 1900 much of the Bolivian public suffered from a quotidian fear of the savage, vengeful Aymara cannibal, an image promoted throughout the war by newspapers associated with the Conservative and, to a certain extent,

Liberal Parties. Indians were accused of having looted towns and murdered citizens following the Civil War of 1899, charges that were confirmed in the verdicts of the Mohoza and Peñas trials, two legal processes that resulted from the war and reverberated from the courthouse throughout Bolivian society. Konig and others unquestioningly accepted the criminalization of the Mohoza Indians and did not hesitate to regard all highland Indians as cannibals. By first branding the Aymara participation in the Liberal-led uprising as marginal and then accusing the Indians of pursuing a race war, journalists and jurists aligned with the Liberal Party separated the Indian mobilization from the Liberals' victory and deemed the indigenous inhabitants unworthy of national recognition. Yet Liberal politicians had to be careful; perceptions of the new capital set in the midst of a savage Aymara hinterland compromised their promising messages of modernization. These politicians needed to temper the image of the savage Aymara without upsetting the traditional social hierarchy that placed that population near the bottom. The Liberals needed to harness an image of the Aymaras that suggested their potential; once educated and disciplined, they might constitute a productive workforce in the highlands that would contribute to the modernization of the nation.

Paradoxically then, liberal intellectuals celebrated the Aymara past, associated with the archeological ruins of Tiahuanaco, which lie in highland Bolivia near the shores of Lake Titicaca, providing it a renaissance in the immediate aftermath of the war.[2] Attributed to the Aymara indigenous population, Tiahuanaco received attention from scholars as a national treasure that lent distinction to the new highland capital of La Paz in 1899 and legitimized the burgeoning urban center as historically important. Arthur Posnansky, Emeterio Villamil de Rada, and other scholars underscored the significance of the highlands and the Aymara past by claiming that Tiahuanaco and the Aymaras were the point of origin of the "American man." In a discussion of the turn-of-the-century Geographic Society of La Paz, Seemin Qayum states: "Emphasis on the ancient archaeological site opened the possibility for an alternative version of Andean history, one that was Tiahuanaco-centered rather than Cuzco-centered. Thus the Creole elite no longer had to have recourse to an imperial Incan past that was more closely associated with Peru as they had in the nineteenth century. For the new century they had a glorious, primordial Aymara past situated geographically within Bolivian territory."[3] The celebration of the distant Aymara past took place in an uncomfortable juxtaposition with the criminalization of the early twentieth-century Aymara population in trials that found Aymaras guilty of race war, murder, and theft. The contradictory process of recognizing historically re-

politics have tended to focus on the Aymaras' resistance to the policies and discourses that relegated them to the margins of the nation.[7] According to this perspective, indigenous issues stayed on the national agenda solely because the Aymaras insisted on it. In the early twentieth century, however, liberal intellectuals, too, were invested in defining the indigenous population, though doing so in ways that would cast the modern Bolivian nation in a favorable light. Somewhat paradoxically, the national intellectuals and the local Aymara intelligentsia unwittingly collaborated in the construction of preferred Indian identities to create a noble and progressive past for the nation and to marginalize the undesirable nonelite Aymara population. The process of narrating the native past was important both to national intellectuals and to indigenous people.

The Conservative Party was militarily defeated in 1899 but gained significant ground by destabilizing the Liberal Party. Conservatives underscored the savagery of the Aymara soldiers who mobilized for the Liberal Party throughout the highlands and thus posed a threat to liberal notions of progress and modernization. In the process of marginalizing the Aymara population in Bolivia, intellectuals spoke in terms of civilization versus barbarism, glorifying the past Inca civilization and opposing it to the present state of the Aymara population, which they viewed as lamentable. A strategy often employed in modernizing turn-of-the-century Indo-America, this selective construction, promotion, and exaltation of the past provided nations with distinctive and progressive national narratives that highlighted the historic achievements of past indigenous populations. This carefully crafted Inca image, phenotypically whiter and more "civilized," would imbue Bolivia with a promising and emblematic past that would define national identity and cast Bolivia's majority indigenous population in a progressive light. The Inca image that was taken up and refashioned in Bolivia in the early twentieth century served as a central image for nation building and as a discourse of progress. In this context, the Inca image and Inca past were tools of modernity rather than the manifestation of a collective desire to return to an Indian past.[8] Different camps of liberal intellectuals employed a stylized Inca image to deflect attention from the early twentieth-century Aymara population and to deny the central role the Aymaras had played in bringing the Liberal Party to power. In this context, however, the "Bolivian Inca" had an important ancestor: the Aymara.

Further exploration of Bolivian liberal intellectuals' national narrative reveals a more favorable Aymara image located in the pre-Incan past. The Aymaras were the primordial inhabitants and the ancestors of the Incas. In an effort to legitimize La Paz as the new highland capital and to endow it with a unique history, Creole liberals carefully constructed an image of the Incas that disparaged the contemporary Aymara population through narratives of their racial degeneration because of various environmental factors, including climate change and isolation, but they did cautiously recognize the Aymaras of the distant past as the relatives and predecessors of the Incas. In establishing this connection between the Aymaras and the Incas, these intellectuals insisted that they were of the same ethnicity. The writings of Manuel Rigoberto Paredes, Emeterio Villamil de Rada, and other early twentieth-century liberal intellectuals suggest that the narrative of the indigenous past and the role of the actual Indian population within the Bolivian nation constituted a site of negotiation that both they and indigenous actors placed at the center of national politics. The liberals' national narrative at this time marked a shift, pushing back the point of origin of national history to incorporate the distant Aymara past into the nation's historical record. Their contradictory discourse regarding both the inclusion of a specific Aymara past and the exclusion of the actual Aymara population opened up spaces for the expectant Aymaras following the war and laid the foundation of the nation that would maintain constructions of Indian identity at its core.

Bolivian Liberalism

The spread of liberalism in and modernization of Bolivia were highly racialized processes that centered on the role of the Indian within the nation. While the roots of this ideology were defined by the tenets of civilization, race, progress, individual land tenure, and citizenship common to liberalism throughout Latin American, Bolivian liberals concentrated their nation-building project in large part on remaking and remapping Indian images. Conflicts over land tenure characterized nineteenth-century Bolivia and culminated in the Disentailment Law of 1874, which privatized land held communally by indigenous inhabitants to foster a competitive land market. In the late nineteenth century, land surveys and the titling of land parcels transferred 30 percent of communal land to private, non-Indian ownership, fueling the expansion of the haciendas and leaving many Aymara community members landless.[9] Bolivian liberalism was thus shaped by the dual issues of land and the role of the indigenous population, which the urban intelligentsia often called the "Indian problem." Indigenous community leaders, or caciques apoderados, mobilized to defend their communities' lands through lawsuits, support of rival political parties, and rebellion. Social hierarchies and political control required renegotiation in the early twentieth century, when many now landless Aymara people mobilized throughout highland Bolivia, often challenging the exclusionary limits of national belonging through claims justified by their support of the Liberal Party in 1899.

Insofar as nation building was concerned, Bolivia's urban intellectuals found little value in the mixed-race, or mestizo, population.[10] Unlike Mexico or Cuba, Bolivia lacked any inclusive discourse of national belonging, such as *mestizaje* or the promotion of racelessness.[11] In addition, the highland location of La Paz, at 12,000 feet, prevented liberal officials from attracting significant European immigration to whiten the highland population. These elites thus faced an overwhelming indigenous population that was both politically active as a result of the privatization of community land and highly visible because of Aymara participation in the civil war. In addition, these liberal intellectuals needed to legitimize La Paz as the new center of the nation and to distance the Liberal Party (and the highland capital city) from its pejorative associations with the Aymara population. The liberal elite responded to these pressures by opting for a "civilizing" program that would improve Bolivia's Indian population and turn it into the laboring backbone of the modernizing nation.[12]

The liberal intelligentsia included statesmen, politicians, and writers, both Indian and Creole, from the rising intermediate sector of society. Some made personal gains in landholdings when indigenous lands were broken up, as did Manuel V. Ballivián, the director of the 1900 census.[13] Others rose more modestly in political standing, straddling the divide between indigenous and Creole society, as did the Aymara author Manuel Rigoberto Paredes, who dedicated much of his work to chronicling Aymara culture and negotiating the group's role within the nation.[14] These intellectuals were Liberal Party supporters who sought to revalorize Aymara history as part of a larger highland-based nation-building project.

According to the 1900 census, slightly more than three-fourths of the population in the Department of La Paz were indigenous; sheer demographics thus dictated that any approach to nation building had to engage the Indians' future within the modernizing nation and could therefore be considered "*indigenista.*" *Indigenismo*, which developed throughout Latin America in the first half of the twentieth century, is an ideological current focusing on the Indian population and questions of nation and of citizenship. In Bolivia, labeling certain authors and organizations as indigenista serves to distinguish them from intellectuals who sought to demote rather than to promote the Aymara past through comparisons with the Incas. These distinctions between early twentieth-century efforts to connect the Aymara past to the Inca past within the national historical narrative reflect an alternative liberal discourse on the "Indian problem."

Race and Region: Perceptions of the Highlands

The Aymara presence in La Paz merited comment in various descriptions of the city. For example, the French naturalist Alcide d'Orbigny remarked in 1830: "La Paz does not resemble in the slightest way any of the other American cities. All of the ones I had seen so far are more or less similar to our cities in Europe. In La Paz . . . not only is the mass of the population indigenous and speaks nothing but its primitive language, but national dress also dominates."[15] As this remark indicates, La Paz has historically been noted for its majority Indian population. In the wake of the civil war, Aymaras drew even more attention because they had supported the Liberal Party. Shifts of political power were negotiated through constructions of race and geography in the postwar context. While the historical development of Colombia and Brazil has often been defined through regional differences and dynamics, racialization of region played a key role in the Conservatives' attempts to destabilize the Liberal Party; it was also key to the latter's legitimation of their new capital.[16]

Highland Bolivia and its new capital city, La Paz, had historically been peripheral to Sucre, the traditional center of political power in Bolivia prior to the rise of the Liberal Party and the tin boom of the early twentieth century. The many Aymara migrants who moved to La Paz because the Disentailment Law had privatized their communal lands served as a daily reminder that the indigenous population constituted a sizable majority within Bolivia. Yet liberal intellectuals needed to legitimize La Paz as the new center of the nation and to distance the Liberal Party from pejorative associations made between region and race, which the Aymara involvement in the civil war had exacerbated.

Mariano Baptista, a leader of the Conservative Party and the president of Bolivia from 1892 to 1896, critiqued the Liberal Party and the highlands in his article "Lugentes," in which he disparaged the Aymaras within the Liberal Party's ranks by emphasizing their "hard, granite-like nature": "Everything about this Indian race appears to be made of stone: his face and his look are hard, just like the mountains of his environment. The civilized and Christian population of La Paz is deathly afraid of the Aymaras."[17] Baptista followed this unflattering description by blaming the Liberals for involving the Aymaras in national politics, remarking that hitherto no one had "dared to include the Aymaras in the political aspirations of Bolivia" or "considered the horde as a political agent."[18]

In branding the highland region as predominantly Aymara and "backward," the Conservatives found support in the verdicts, rendered by the Liberal Party government's own courts, criminalizing the Aymaras for their role in the civil war. To a certain extent, the opposing Liberal and Conservative Party politicians reconciled their differences by generating negative images of the Aymara population. For example, the liberal intellectual Pedro Aniceto Blanco, a member of the Geographic Society of La Paz, agreed with Baptista's characterization of the early twentieth-century Aymaras to a certain extent. Writing in the *Diccionario geográfico del departamento de Oruro*, published in 1904, Blanco painted the highland Indians in a negative light:

> According to their intellect, the Indian of the altiplano is the enemy of civilization. . . . The silent adversary of intellectual and material progress, he is only too happy to isolate himself in his apparent indifference, preferring the misery in which he lives to the comfort of modern societies, against which he is always ready to fight and which stirs his greatest hatred. It is for this reason that during different periods, when the country is convulsed with political activity, the Indian takes advantage of the political disorganization, committing the most savage acts against the whites . . . without a shred of humanity[,] . . . intent on spilling the whites' blood.[19]

Blanco disagreed with Baptista regarding the role of the highland environment in producing the undesirable state of the Aymaras and instead praised the "majestic peaks" of the Andes and their many bountiful mineral deposits. He also commented on the importance of the Andes as a formidable border that clearly divided the Bolivian nation from its recent military adversary, Chile. Moreover, while Blanco found the climate to be extremely cold, he also claimed it to be one of the healthiest places to live, for, he said, the cold could cure diseases and extend people's lives.[20] Given all its riches, from rare flamingo feathers to the promise of good health and mineral fortune, he regarded the highlands as a promising land; what was required, according to Blanco, was an industrious people to exploit it.

Blanco thus praised the physical geography of the highlands but reported a less sanguine opinion of its social geography. As the 1900 census had shown, highland Bolivia was a predominantly Indian region. Blanco echoed Ballivián when he stated that the early twentieth-century Quechuas (i.e., descendants of the Incas) outstripped the Aymaras in their proclivity for civilization.[21] Quantitatively, in terms of the region's large Indian population, and qualitatively, in terms of the historical significance associated with the more primitive Aymaras, *paceño* politicians faced challenges in legitimizing their rule and their region.

These pressures forced the liberal elite to address the negative image of the highland Aymara population and perceptions of their "uncivilized" and "savage" nature as representative of the altiplano. Creole liberals had to address Bolivia's fragmented national body if they were to create a viable and integrated nation. Constructions of developmental differences among indigenous groups served to cast Bolivia's Indian past in a progressive light and distanced the liberal regime from contemporary concerns regarding the Aymara population. Liberal discourse would center on marginalizing the present Aymara population while deploying the Aymara past to construct a distinguished and civilized myth of origins and thus recast the highlands as the cradle of civilization and its native inhabitants as the Incas' ancestors. The Aymaras' contributions were relegated to the distant past and seen as limited by progressively deteriorating climactic conditions.

According to some early twentieth-century intellectuals, the area's cold climate and harsh mountains limited the intellectual development of the highland Indian. The amateur scientist, explorer, and author Arthur Posnansky claimed that the highlands had once enjoyed a much more temperate climate that allowed human beings to develop both spiritually and mentally. He was convinced that such development was possible only when the struggle for existence was not arduous.[22] Climate change, he claimed, caused the region's vegetation to disappear, its fish to become scarce, and its land animals and fowl to migrate to more hospitable environs. Posnansky stated that life "became a daily battle for bread rather than for intellectual advancement" and claimed that this explained how the Aymaras had completely forgotten their past and deteriorated into the "miserable Indian that resides today on the altiplano."[23] This distinction between the productive Aymara past, which gave rise to the lauded Incas, and the lamentable Aymara present allowed Bolivian intellectuals to create a progressive history for the highlands by calling for the "regeneration" of the deteriorated Aymara.

The Inca Image

The Incas had controlled a powerful empire, taking over other indigenous groups in the Andes, including the Aymaras, to become the area's supreme rulers in the late fifteenth and early sixteenth centuries. The Inca Empire ended when the Spaniards came to the Andes in the 1530s, yet the importance of the Inca past and imagery permeated political projects for the subsequent five centuries. The Inca has served as an ambiguous symbol, appropriated by distinct sectors of Bolivian (and Peruvian) society for different social and racial constructions of identity that have resonated internationally as well as locally during both the colonial and national eras.

In the colonial Andes, the indigenous elite adopted Inca dress and an Inca identity throughout much of the eighteenth century as a sign of status during the period of Inca nationalism centering in Cuzco.[24] Influenced by the writings of Bartolomé de las Casas and Garcilaso Inca de la Vega, artists portrayed the Incas as white, Christian, and civilized.[25] Following the severance of colonial ties from Spain and the separation of Lower Peru and Upper Peru, the Peruvian nation claimed the Inca past for the development of its national narrative. Peruvian intellectuals and politicians contested any Bolivian claim to an Inca heritage, as Cecilia Méndez makes clear in her article on the political relationship between Peru and Bolivia in the early national period.[26] Yet the fact that Bolivia had been part of the Inca Empire served as a latent potential memory for Bolivia as well as Peru.

Representations of the Incas also grew in Europe in the eighteenth century. French intellectuals including Charles La Condamine and Voltaire lauded the Incas as symbolic of the ideas of the Enlightenment. These writers aired their anti-Spanish sentiments in depicting the Incas as an idyllic people who had suffered the excesses of Spanish conquest and colonialism. Jean-Philippe Rameau and Louis Fuzelier composed a ballet of the Incas entitled *Les Indes galantes*, which opened at the Royal Academy of Music in Paris in August 1735. Subsequent operas that took up the theme of the moral Incas were immensely popular; examples include *Les Indes chantantes* (1735), *Les amours des Indes* (1735), and *Les Indes dansantes* (1751).[27] Within Peru as well as internationally, then, the civilized "white Inca" came to play a key role in constructions of race and identity at various moments throughout the colonial and national periods.

The Great Rebellion of 1780–1782 dramatically halted the adoption of an Inca identity by the Cuzco indigenous elite, who had formerly cultivated the connection. José Gabriel Condorcanqui, better known as Tupac Amaru II, led the rebellion and claimed to be a direct descendant of the Inca dynasty.[28] Spanish colonial authorities repressed the movement, executed Tuapc Amaru II, and banned the circulation of Garcilaso de la Vega's *Comentarios reales*, which detailed the Inca past, including theatrical representations and the use of Inca garments. The theme of the Incas gradually disappeared from Creole political discourse, and the Cuzco elite ceased attempting to claim privilege through the appropriation of an Inca identity.[29] In the minds of the colonial officials throughout the Andes, the Inca image became associated with resistance and revolt rather than with social prestige.

It was not until the later part of the nineteenth century, when modernity and nation building began in earnest in the Andes, that the indigenous and Creole elite would again reconstruct and adopt an Inca identity as a source of privilege and national identity.[30] Such symbols and messages were often popularized through theatrical performance. These late nineteenth- and early twentieth-century attempts to consolidate political power through the Inca image drew from the earlier images of the civilized, "white," progressive Inca as established by Peruvian, Bolivian, and European writers.[31] As race became increasingly defined through the practice of scientific measurement in the early twentieth century, social, cultural, and educational factors contributed to the construction of the white, elite Indian, the Inca who escaped the Mendelian yardstick.[32]

The multiple appropriations of the Inca image reveal a highly racialized rationale. With respect to popular, indigenous sectors of society, adoption of an Inca identity was often perceived to indicate outright or latent resistance to colonial or national repression. The indigenista elite's early twentieth-century representations of the Inca, however, built on the ennobled Inca past and implied civilization, authority, and grandeur. In Bolivia, the adoption of an Inca identity served as a discursive means to shape debates on progress, race, and nation building following the Civil War of 1899.

Constructions of Race and the Civil War of 1899

Embracing the Inca past as national predecessor was not limited to academic treatises. The journalistic accounts of the civil war that appeared in the daily newspapers played a key role in forming the public's conception of the conflict and its actors. Drawing from social currents already prevalent in Bolivian society, journalists who supported the Conservative Party and wrote for Sucre-based newspapers built up the image of the backward and bloodthirsty Aymaras. These newspapers, which enjoyed significant circulation and delivered daily reports on the war's latest developments, thus constituted a crucial forum for disseminating the image of the vengeful, primitive Aymaras.

Journalists allied with the Conservative Party cast the Aymaras as barbarians who tortured and victimized their enemies rather than as war veterans who deserved public respect. Articles in the Sucre newspaper La Soberanía accused the "agitated hordes of Caribs" of killing "noble constitutionalists, . . . satisfying their thirst with the blood of their victims and devouring the human flesh that was still warm, to the cries of *Long live* Pando! Long live the federation!'"[33] Mariano Baptista, too, cast the Aymaras as barbarians who tortured and victimized their enemies. He vividly described the Aymaras' supposed brutal attack on the priest of Viacha: "The Indians scratched and cut up the priest's body with wire they had taken from the destroyed telegraph lines. Then the Indians hit him, but the priest still did not die. Finally, they ripped out his innards, causing the priest to expire at last."[34] These journalists thus sought to delegitimize the Liberal Party by characterizing the Aymaras, the party's erstwhile allies, as cannibals and by promulgating pejorative descriptions of the Indians and their highland base.

Journalists sympathetic to the Liberal Party adopted a slightly different tone; they sometimes recognized the Aymaras as an honorable, victimized people who displayed valor in their self-defensive responses to the Conservative army's gross violations of human rights and property. Indeed, the Liberal Party required these cautious attempts to improve the image of the Aymaras so as to ameliorate problems that its association with them might cause. Liberal officials and the La Paz–based press explained the Aymaras' mobilizations as an act of self-defense, however, making it a matter of self-interest instead of loyalty to the Liberal Party. In narrating the important battle of Crucero, the report in the Liberal Party organ *Boletín Oficial*, edited by Julio César Cortes, suggested that the Aymaras fought only when directly attacked: "During the battle as well as after, we did not rely on the aid of any Indian auxiliaries[;] in fact nary an Indian was to be found on the field. When we wanted them to take care of the mules, we had to go search for them."[35] Still, the explanations of the Aymaras' mobilization published in the *Official Bulletin* did at least temper the view of the Aymaras as an inherently savage people. Within this narrative, the Aymaras responded with violence only when attacked; they were not the provocateurs. Liberal journalists' reports nevertheless fell short of recognizing the Aymaras' activities as having contributed to the Liberal Party's victory.

Few dissenting voices contested the violent image of the Aymaras. In one example of this portrayal, a short story printed in the La Paz newspaper *El Comercio* played on exaggerated racist susceptibilities. Entitled "Una lugente aventura," the story satirized Baptista's infamous article "Lugentes." Quoting at times from Baptista's article, the pseudonymous author, "Tuck," plays on the supposed savagery of the Aymara. The story concerns a man who is lost on the altiplano and is forced to seek shelter among the Aymaras as night falls. Fueled by his vivid imagination and the racist attitudes prevalent in Bolivian society, the man believes that his Aymara host is preparing to kill and eat him. He overhears a conversation between the Aymara man and his wife that he supposes refers to his death:

> "He will surely leave early tomorrow. We will have to put the water on to boil at dawn."
>
> "As you wish, but I think he is too old and thin," responded the woman indifferently.

The lost traveler spends several paragraphs trembling, terrified at having come face to face with a brutal Aymara cannibal who would eat his flesh. The story takes an ironic twist, however, in the last two short paragraphs, when the agonizing man learns that his hosts were talking about killing their only chicken for the benefit of the traveler, thus revealing the profound generosity of the Aymara family rather than the rumored cannibalism. Relieved, the traveler jumps up, pays his hosts for their hospitality, and runs from the house. The Aymara man watches him go and mutters: "He is crazy, absolutely crazy."[36] Throughout the story, the author clearly shows the Aymaras to be more victims of prejudice than victimizers of the landowning class.

In another example, the author "Quillco Mamani" published a letter in the La Paz newspaper *Los Debates* on May 9, 1899, critiquing the Liberal politicians' pejorative treatment of the Aymara population. Playing on the fragile constructions of race and privilege in Bolivia, the writer claims to be a mestizo "with Aymara blood and a little Spanish blood as well, just like everyone who claims to be white in Bolivia." Identifying himself as a representative of the Aymaras (his nom de plume means "a literate Aymara"), he decries how Pando and others within the Liberal Party have treated the Aymara war veterans, who, he says, viewed Pando as "the incarnation of love and justice." He goes on to chastise the Creole liberals for their desire to rid themselves of the Aymara race once the military victory was secured. Revealing great knowledge of contemporary politics and debates on race and immigration strategies in Bolivia, Quillco Mamani underscores the Aymaras' importance to the urban elite as both high-altitude food producers and political allies: "[The Creole liberals] should not try to brand the Aymaras as subversive and rebellious when the only thing they have done is, motivated by their great love for their capital city, contribute to the liberals' military victory."[37]

Stories such as Tuck's and Quillco Mamani's, however, could not deter general perceptions of Aymara savagery. Even Colonel Pando seemed to have had serious doubts regarding the motives and reliability of his Aymara allies, as is indicated by the exchange of letters, dated March 4 and 6, 1899, between President Alonso and Pando (see chapter 1).

The defense of the Aymaras was deployed within the broader goal of defending the Liberal Party, yet Pando's misgivings regarding his military alliance with them revealed the Liberal Party leader's own fears of race war, which were most likely exacerbated by articles on Aymara savagery published in newspapers allied with the Conservative Party. Through their statements, moreover, José Mendoza, District Attorney Ballongalvarro, and other officials involved in the Peñas trial attempted to distance the Liberal Party from the Aymaras to improve the party's image. In this sense, the Aymaras could not serve as an emblematic image for the Liberal Party or the highland-based nation-building project. Paradoxically, however, La Paz intellectuals needed to improve the image of the savage highland Indian to legitimize the new capital and the Liberal Party.

Civilized Incas, Savage Aymaras

When newspapers published articles discussing Bolivia's Inca past rather than its present-day Aymaras, they treated them quite favorably; they represented Incas as the preferred Indians and the Inca Empire as the first historical marker of civilization in the Andes. These accounts did not establish connections between Aymaras and Incas. For example, the archeological remains of the Inca city in Ecuador's canton of Sigsig were worthy of public praise in the newspapers; journalists compared the wealth and greatness of the site to that of California.[38] Early twentieth-century journalists lauded the remains of other Inca cities, too, as marking great and civilized ancestors. They and others did not, however, confer the same attention or praise on Aymara artifacts and ruins. Members of the Geographic Society of La Paz, for example, treasured the highland archeological ruins of Tiahuanaco primarily because they identified the culture that produced the site as the predecessor of the great Inca civilization and, in turn, of the Bolivian nation.[39]

In underscoring the might of the Inca Empire, journalists identified it as a historical antecedent for the modernizing nation. Just as the benevolent rule of the Inca Empire had brought greatness to the region, Liberal Party tutelage could do the same for Bolivia. In addition, the Incas' great achievements stood in sharp contrast to the culture of the country's Aymara population, then widely perceived as backward. These differences allowed the promotion of Inca history to make sense of Bolivia's Indian past while affirming the nation's desire—and capacity—for progress. The explorer Charles Johnson Post, who traveled throughout the Titicaca region in 1898, emphasized the predominantly Aymara population there in subsequent articles; of the "ancient town of Achicachi" he said, "its population is still practically

FIGURE 6. Newspaper advertisement for the Inca Pharmacy, El Comercio (La Paz), March 2, 1899. Reproduced by the National Archive of Bolivia.

Aymará, with only a sprinkling of half-breed Cholos."[40] After underscoring the isolation of Achicachi, Post wrote of the dangers of living among the Aymara: "Always there is the dull hatred of the Bolivian by the Aymará which comes easily to the surface at these times. . . . If he gets dangerous when drunk; beat him; if too dangerous, kill him."[41] In a newspaper article about Lake Titicaca, however, a Bolivian journalist recounted the many marvels of the region, including Lake Titicaca's outstanding beauty and the Inca traditions that were still practiced in this Aymara region. The words *savage* and *hatred* did not appear in the narration of these charming "Inca" lands, nor did that article mention the local Aymara population.[42]

A store called "the Inca Pharmacy" regularly ran an advertisement in turn-of-the-century Bolivian newspapers that connected the Incas with civilization (fig. 6). The Inca Pharmacy advertised a series of beautifying ointments, many of them imported. Using "Inca" as the name of the store seemed to have been an effective way to attract an elite audience to the beauty products that promoted civilization and modernity, as did the Inca image.

Journalists described the Inca Empire as ushering in a civilizing epoch in the region's history and the Incas as the agents of progress in reducing the primitiveness of its otherwise barbaric "tribes." An illustrative example of this trend appeared in El Comercio in November 1898: "There arrived a point at which the barbaric state of Peru's ancient peoples was so great that Manco-Capac and Mama-Ocllo were sent [by the gods] into the midst of these backward kingdoms with the mission of civilizing them."[43] Within these accounts, the Inca Empire, not the Aymara past, was to mark the beginning of Bolivia's progressive history; the Inca had improved the Aymara. In this case, however, celebrating the Inca did not address the pejorative association between the highlands and the feared Aymara population that troubled the liberal nation-building project.

Constructing Similarity between the Aymaras and the Incas

The early twentieth-century indigenistas were a group of Indian and Creole intellectuals from the rising intermediate sector of society who supported the Liberal Party and engaged in a revalorization of Aymara history as part of a larger blueprint for the highland-based nation-building project of the early twentieth century. These authors often shifted the blame for the Indians' plight or "backwardness" to intermediate figures of local authority: priests, overseers, and local political officials such as the corregidores.[44]

This era's Bolivian indigenistas called attention to the oppression and exploitation of the indigenous race and were particularly concerned with the demotion and marginalization of the Aymara past as related to the construction of the nation. When the Liberal Party came to power after the civil war, these individuals set out to write the Aymaras into Bolivian history. They created a unique national past in which the highlands and the Aymara population became relevant to the tropes of civilization.

Former narratives of the Aymara past had underscored the Incas' role in "civilizing" the Aymaras. The indigenista narrative, however, portrayed the Aymara past as a productive force that gave rise to the Inca Empire. Not only did this connection between Aymaras and Incas incorporate the Aymaras into national history, but the Inca past was now seen to have evolved from promising Aymara beginnings. According to this account, the Incas were not the only great civilization of South America, for the Aymaras themselves deserved recognition as the root of the Incas.

Even before the early twentieth century, chroniclers and scholars often mentioned Tiahuanaco, especially for its impressive stonework and sculptures. An ancient city-state that emerged around 200 CE as the leading political and religious site near Lake Titicaca, Tiahuanaco reached its apex near the start of the sixth century and declined near the start of the twelfth.[45] Colonial chroniclers indicated that the architects of the ruins were largely unknown; only a few associated Tiahuanaco with the Aymaras.[46] During the national period, scientifically minded explorers, such as Ernest and Alfred Grandidier, who visited Tiahuanaco in 1858, attributed the archeological site to the Aymaras, but the significance of the Aymara past remained a mystery. The Grandidier brothers wrote: "The constructions [of Tiahuanaco] were built by the Aymara race, whose civilization was destroyed without any memory of it or of the cataclysmic event that abruptly ended the Aymaras' achievements." They went on to suggest a connection between the Aymaras and the

Incas by claiming that the root of Inca civilization was located in the Aymara architecture of Tiahuanaco.[47]

The Bolivian scholar Emeterio Villamil de Rada's partially completed book *La lengua de Adán* (1888) also underscored the importance of the Aymara past to theories of origins and migration. He developed a detailed outline for a book that was published in 1888 with an introduction by Nicolás Acosta. It enjoyed a second printing in 1939, sponsored by the Bolivian Ministry of Education, Art and Indigenous Affairs, with a foreword and analysis by Gustavo Adolfo Otero. In revisiting theories of migration, Villamil de Rada located the origin of humanity among the Aymaras who constructed the archeological masterpiece of Tiahuanaco. He claimed that the first *Homo sapiens* were Aymara, who crossed the Bering Strait westward and ultimately populated Egypt and India, producing the civilizations of great antiquity. If the first humans were Aymara, then Tiahuanaco was the geographical point of origin. Villamil de Rada claimed that traces of both the magnificent architecture of Tiahuanaco and the Aymara language could be found on Easter Island, in the temple to Pachacamac on the Peruvian coast, in the early astrological observatories of Guayaquil and Quito, and in the language and culture of Nicaragua and Guatemala down to Cape Horn. He referred to all these various manifestations of language and architecture as the progeny of the Aymaras of Tiahuanaco.[48] In his introduction, Acosta echoes Villamil de Rada's central claim: "The birthplace of Adam, with its perennial spring, pure sweet skies, and its pristine language, was destined to become an Aymara academy, where those who are born there or who study it identify with the Aymaras, and [dedicate] themselves to working on the grammar and on an Aymara dictionary that would serve as the source for all languages and for all ideas and conceptualizations of historical thought."[49]

Villamil de Rada's theory not only sought to identify the origins of humankind but also addressed issues of evolution, civilization, and race within the national context. In the index, Villamil de Rada framed his interest in the Aymara in relation to the Inca Empire. Prefacing his investigation, he wrote: "What kinds of people, lineage, and historical antecedents dominated the Americas before giving rise to the Incas?"[50] For Villamil de Rada, the primacy of the Aymaras, from whom the Incas evolved, validated the central questions of his research.

The early twentieth-century indigenista intellectuals fully exploited this construction of the past and characterized the Aymaras as the Incas' ancestors. They attributed Tiahuanaco to the Aymaras and incorporated Aymara history into national history. Several colonial documents that described the ruins of Tiahuanaco were reprinted in the late nineteenth and early twentieth centuries, including Father José de Acosta's *Historia natural y moral de las Indias* (1574), republished in Spain in 1898, and Father Reginaldo de Lizarraga's *Descripción de toda la tierra de Perú, Tucumán, Rio de la Plata y Chile*, republished by the Historical Institute of Peru in 1908. In addition, excerpts of many other colonial and more recent descriptions of Tiahuanaco made by scientifically motivated explorers in the nineteenth century appeared in the early twentieth century.[51] The indigenistas exploited the historical silences surrounding the Aymaras' past by capitalizing on the interest in Tiahuanaco; in doing so, they also emphasized the people of Tiahaunaco, the Aymaras. According to this perspective, the highlands had been home to a progressive people, the Aymaras, in whom humankind originated. Responding to the need to "regenerate" the majority Indian population as well as to develop a regional and national historical discourse that endowed the highlands and the new capital city of La Paz with a prominent past, the indigenista intellectuals wrote the Aymaras into national history and into world history by establishing the uniqueness of the Aymaras' distant past and thus confirming the Aymaras' link to the Incas.

The 1900 Bolivian census presented an opportunity to delineate the boundaries of national belonging and to codify definitions of race. The census's director, Manuel V. Ballivián, revealed his ambivalent feelings toward the indigenous population and its place within the Bolivian nation. Even though Indians made up the majority of Bolivia's population, Ballivián heralded the end of the Indian race due to drought, starvation, low birth rates, and alcoholism. While Ballivián welcomed the disappearance of the nation's Indian population, claiming that it would eliminate "the refractory element within [Bolivian] civilization," he also recognized the centrality of an Indian identity in the construction of Bolivia's unique national past.[52] In taking inventory of the multiple indigenous populations, he lauded some groups more than others. The Quechua and the Aymara received his highest praise. Ballivián identified the Aymaras as "the first civilized nation in South America" and the Quechuas who were in charge of the Inca Empire as the people who capitalized upon and further enhanced the Aymara civilization.[53]

Within this particular section written on the indigenous population, Ballivián was careful to establish that the Aymaras and Quechuas, or Incas, were of the same race. In writing the historical narrative for the census, however, Ballivián fell short of including the Aymaras, obliterating the history of any indigenous people other than the Incas in the development of a progressive national past. Breaking the history of Bolivia into four neat periods (the Inca Empire, 1054–1533; the Spanish Conquest, 1533–1809; independence, 1809–1825; and the Republican Era, 1825 until present), he placed the Incas at the beginning of this narrative but said nothing about the Aymara past.[54] Nevertheless, the ancestral link he established between the Aymaras and the Incas and his recognition of the Aymaras as the first "civilized people" reflected the growing tendency to include the Aymaras within the historical narrative.

Beginning in 1900, a group of indigenista intellectuals established an organization called the Aymara Academy for the purpose of addressing the question of race and modernity with respect to the Aymaras' troubled image. Its president, the La Paz historian Carlos Bravo, had been a member of a precursor organization, the Aymarista Society (Sociedad Aymarista), founded in 1882, which had lasted until the civil war broke out.[55] The historian Arturo Costa de la Torre described these Aymara associations of the late nineteenth and early twentieth centuries as "patriotic literary societies that included the most distinguished scholars of Bolivia."[56] Not much detailed information on the members of the Aymara Academy is available; the scarce documentation that does exist indicates that the academy included several members who thought deeply about societal structure and the Indian population. Antonio Garcia, for example, had worked in universities in Latin America and headed the Socialist Party in Colombia. He wrote several publications, including *La rebelión de los pueblos débiles*, which he dedicated to "the Bolivian nation, which is building the road for revolution in Indoamerica."[57] For Garcia, the indigenous population was full of potential and constituted the key leadership for any future restructuring of society, when exploited laborers would unite to throw off the neocolonial conditions of their servitude.

Another Aymara Academy member, Wenceslao Loaiza V., held, among other posts, the position of priest of Laja, a historically Aymara town located between La Paz and Lake Titicaca on the altiplano. His firsthand experience in Aymara communities nurtured his enthusiasm for the potential of the highland indigenous population. In a report that Wenceslao Loaiza prepared for the vicar of La Paz in 1911, he stated that the Indians would be an asset to society.[58] He described the Aymaras as "useful" and as a "necessary race" that had suffered extreme neglect from the affluent sectors of society. After having established the connection between the Incas and the Aymaras in his report, he referred to the Aymaras as "the children of Manco Capaj" and praised the model Inca Empire for the systematic education of its subjects.[59] Loaiza translated texts into Aymara to provide additional materials for educating the Aymara population. In 1891, while serving as the priest of San

Andrés de Machaca, he published an Aymara-language version of the *Novena de la milagrosa virgen de Copacabana*, written originally in Spanish by the priest Rafael Sans.[60] His insistence on a close connection between the Aymaras and the Incas reflected the main focus in the academy members' attempt to uplift the Aymaras.

The monthly publication of the Aymara Academy, *Academia Aymara*, portrayed this new image of the Aymara and presented concepts of race and progress being discussed at the beginning of the twentieth century. One of the few organizations to employ the term *Aymara* in its name, the academy redefined the historical role of the Aymaras as the ancestors of the Incas in order to "redeem" this indigenous group.[61] These indigenista intellectuals employed a specific discourse to uplift the Aymaras, since the historical context precluded any outright glorification of them. Within the carefully crafted indigenista discourse, the Inca was the axis. Unlike the Incas, the Aymaras had no renowned past, but the connection between the more "primitive" Aymara and the Inca Empire into which they supposedly developed illustrated a progressive evolution of Bolivian history.

If the Incas were to be lauded for their achievements and architecture, then the Aymaras, as their forebears, deserved similar praise. In his article "Los Aymaras" (1902), the Aymara Academy member P. Fernando de Sanjinés suggested that precursors to Inca architecture, such as Tiahuanaco, be studied as the work of a great nation and as an important contribution to the grandeur of Inca constructions.[62] In addition, as part of this ongoing effort to relate the Aymara to the Inca and to emphasize the Aymara contributions that helped created the great Inca Empire, an anonymous contributor to *Academia Aymara* listed all the Ayamara loan words in the Quechua language.[63]

The arguments made in defense of the Aymaras were neither bold nor radical. In forming their institution and pursuing their investigations into Ayama language and culture, the academy's members claimed, they sought to civilize the Aymaras and put an end to racial antagonism.[64] According to these scholars, racial tensions would diminish with the assimilation of the Aymaras. P. Salazar defined the academy's main goal as that of civilizing and in fact "whitening" the Aymaras so that they might insert themselves more easily into the dominant Bolivian society: "What we want is to civilize and uplift the Aymara so that he may unify with the white race, and racial antagonism will disappear. . . . The Aymara should become more like the whites, unifying with them until, if possible, they blend with the white population and become indistinguishable."[65]

In portraying the Aymaras as the ancestors of the Incas, academy members referred to the original indigenous group as the Haya-maras, which is not a name denoting a separate people but rather a descriptive title meaning "old communities" or "old nations." Indeed, academy members had to deny that the Aymaras had a separate history and development as an ethnic or racial collectivity if they were to claim them as the earlier version of the Incas and therefore directly related to the noble rulers of the Inca Empire. The differences between the Aymaras and the Incas were not great, for as one author explained, "The Inca Empire was simply an evolution of the Aymaras."[66]

Nicanor Aranzaes, another academy member, suggested that the Aymara race had fulfilled its purpose and function and needed to give way to the reign of "superior" races. As its members heralded the end of the Aymaras, the academy busied itself with documenting the group's language and culture before they disappeared.[67] In this sense, the study of the Aymara language and culture appeared to be a strictly academic affair focusing on a past or passing culture rather than an effort to address the plight facing the contemporary Aymaras. In their cautious promotion of the Aymaras, academy members never mentioned the Indians' role in the Civil War of 1899. The image the academy strove to create did not directly engage the contemporary crisis of Aymara indigenous identity but rather depicted the Aymaras as an early yet civilized people of the past, as the forebears of the Incas, and as the progenitors of the most civilized Indians.

The formation of the Aymara Academy also provides a window into urban and local actors' awareness of and responses to the negative stereotypes surrounding the Aymara population. While several of the twenty-eight founding Aymara Academy members were intellectuals and people of authority from La Paz, several others were provincial officials and local priests from rural parishes.[68] For example, Carlos Bravo, president of the Aymara Academy, had been the subprefect of Paria in the Department of Oruro during the civil war.[69] These academy members and community representatives were well versed in both national discourse and local reality; they were in a position to capitalize on the Inca discourse in order to rectify the Aymara image and to regulate local social hierarchies.

Other writers charted a different course. Unlike the Aymara Academy, which cast the Aymaras as the Incas' ancestors, Arthur Posnansky produced studies of Aymara-based "Tiahuanacology" that inserted the Aymaras into Bolivian and world history by arguing that they were the original inhabitants of the Americas. Posnansky, a Polish engineer and archeologist, was a member of the Sociedad Geográfica de La Paz, a scientific and literary organization founded in 1889 as part of a "new civilizing mission" for the Bolivian nation.[70] For Posnansky, as well as for many Bolivian intellectuals of the time, modernity involved the rectification and reelaboration of national historical narratives that would favor the highlands and that were grounded in new scientific and anthropological theories, whose importance he stressed:

> It is necessary to say a few words with regard to the old historians who are, in part, guilty of the monumental errors committed in the archaeological studies of that part of America, and whose books exercised, and still exercise, a pernicious influence on the majority of travelers. Of the chroniclers to whom we refer, the majority copied each other and the few who were original, like Felipe Guaman Poma de Ayala, drank from rather cloudy springs. . . . These observations and investigations of the author of this work, a graduate in many fields of science, who has studied in the terrain during almost a half a century, can not be compared with those of travelers who for a few days or, at the most a few weeks, take a quick turn through the altiplano and its environs. . . . For this reason it is necessary to make completely new studies and take into account what the old historians have said only when it is a question of comparing facts already proved with what they have set down. . . . Modern investigation in the so-called "Land of the Incas" must seek new routes based on anthropological, linguistic, and archaeological studies, as well as sociological studies of the present Indians who, to a certain degree, have conserved very old customs.[71]

Posnansky structured his new historical narrative with a focus on the pre-Incan past, thus highlighting the Aymaras who created the great civilization of Tiahuanaco, which he considered the most important political and religious center of the continent, especially during the Aymaras' second developmental phase. "The extraordinary progress of the Second Period of Tiahuanacu," Posnansky wrote, "is certainly due . . . to the impulse supplied by the already developed Kolla [or Aymara] race. . . . The power of the Kollas and their new language, Aymara, is extended to a great part of the continent."[72] He was convinced that the achievements of the Aymaras rivaled those of Europe; many travelers who visited Tiahuanaco and remarked on the craftsmanship of the door of the sun temple compared it to Stonehenge. Capitalizing on the comparison, Posnansky called attention to the superior Aymara craftsmanship: "Stonehenge of England consists of monoliths only crudely carved, planted in the ground in a system of circles, whose upper ends carried, in their time, horizontal blocks, like trilithons. These are the products of a very inferior period of culture, in which the most elementary ideas of art were unknown. The pillars of Tiahuanacu are of carefully worked rock, having formed in past times an integral part of the gigantic walls, and having an external ideosymbolic decoration."[73]

Rejecting facile connections between language and race, Posnansky argued that the Aymaras and the Incas constituted different developmental stages of the same race. He attributed the intelligence and leadership of the last sovereign king of the Inca Empire, Atahuallpa, to his Aymara ancestry as determined by studies of Atahuallpa's skull. In shifting the focus to the Aymaras' past and extolling their great qualities, however, Posnansky was careful to maintain their connection to the Incas. He emphasized the Aymaras' role and achievements in Bolivian history without attempting to replace the Incas with the Aymaras in national narratives. Posnansky's subsequent narrative of the decline of the Aymara population, which he attributed to climate change prior to the Inca conquest, served to limit the Aymaras' historical role to the distant past as well as to explain their present deplorable state.[74] The result was a historical narrative encompassing both groups in a symbiotic relation of development and progress; the greatness of the Incas' empire lent legitimacy to Posnansky's claims regarding their Aymara ancestors, and his favorable narrative of the Aymara past and its connection to the Incas resulted in additional praise for the Incas. The achievements of these two ancient civilizations formed, according to Posnansky, the bedrock of Bolivian nationalism as narrated from a highland perspective.

In forging their constructions of modernity, geography, and race in the early twentieth century, Bolivian liberal intellectuals represented their nation as growing from the roots of famous civilizations. The unique discourse of Inca nationalism endowed Bolivia with a progressive and noble past, and connecting the Aymaras to that past added depth to the historical importance of highland Bolivia. Posnansky emphasized the developmental aspect of this narrative: "First, one must study in the 'primary school' which is Tiahuanacu, then in the high school which is *gran* Peru, finally to enter the 'university' as represented by the study of man and his epic in Central America and especially Mexico. It is useless to carry on university studies without having had a primary education. This elementary education institution is, without the least doubt, we reiterate, in Tiahuanacu, the ancient metropolis, the cradle of civilization of man in America."[75]

The discourse of development from Aymara to Inca also responded to the dictates of eugenics and to constructions of race. According to Posnansky, the Incas were whiter than the Aymaras.[76] Such discursive whitening was characteristic of nation-building narratives in late nineteenth- and early twentieth-century Latin America. By promoting the Inca, Bolivian intellectuals suggested a whiter, more modern Bolivia; Posnansky and similar scholars fashioned the Aymara past to support the highland nation-building project then under way. Indigenista scholars writing under the Liberal Party regime sought to assign the Aymara a space within the national past to improve the image of the new national capital. Through a careful and often contradictory process, these scholars built the Aymara past into the national narrative, underscoring its connection to the lauded Incas and to the broader discourse of Bolivian Inca nationalism.

By carefully ordering historical stages and positing degeneration through climate change, the intellectuals involved in writing this new narrative attempted to relegate the Aymaras' contributions to national progress to the distant past, clearly demarcating the noteworthy Aymara past from the lamentable Aymara present. Suggestive gray spaces nevertheless emerged through the overlapping of historical epochs, as is evident in Posnansky's comparison between past and present populations: "There is no doubt that the present inhabitants of the upland of the Andes, especially those of the regions of Lupacas and those to the south and southwest of Lake Titicaca, are the descendants of those groups of races who built Tihuanacu. This opinion is proven obviously through the anthropometrical studies carried out by the author with large numbers of living aborigines and with osseous material from their pantheons, in which . . . the measurements of the present-day natives coincide with those of the crania and skeletons found in the excavations of Tihauancu and the high plateau of the Andes."[77] Connecting the progressive Aymara past to the contemporary Aymara present invited a cautious revalorization of the Aymaras and suggested their potential in the early twentieth-century context.

Whereas Posnansky's comparisons between past and present populations often suggested such ambiguous gray spaces, Manuel Rigoberto Paredes squarely inhabited them. Paredes, an early twentieth-century indigenista intellectual, identified with his Aymara heritage as a descendant of the Siñani cacique family of Carabuco. A fluent speaker of the Aymara language, he authored many books on the Bolivian highland regions and their inhabitants and held several posts in the provinces, including that of subprefect of the Inquisivi province from 1900 to 1904. Sinclair Thomson refers to Paredes as representative of an "intermediate mestizo sector of the population made up of provincial notables who constituted the rising urban professional middle class, who negotiated their relationship with the traditional elite, and who also benefited to a certain extent from the hierarchical order of society."[78]

Throughout his numerous publications, Paredes offered an aggressive critique of the Incas. In his *Tiahuanaco y la provincia de Ingavi* he claimed that the Incas never achieved anything as accomplished as Tiahuanaco, which he attributed to the Aymaras. In the light of these achievements, Paredes questioned claims that elevated the Incas over the "barbaric state of Bolivia's other tribes." Moreover, he attributed the "retardation" of the early twentieth-century Aymara population to their enslavement by the Incas. Despite his critique of the Incas, however, Paredes described the Inca Empire as "one family" that was egalitarian, mutualistic, and materially secure.[79] Ultimately, he insisted on the connection between the Aymaras and the Incas and grounded this claim in the chroniclers' texts and in the similarity of the ceramic designs in Cuzco to those in Tiahuanaco. Compiling evidence from colonial and national historians and explorers, he tried to prove that the Incas were of the same race as the Aymaras and that the Incas were the "bearers of the Aymaras' civilization."[80]

Paredes is a useful figure for exploring the limits of asserting an Aymara identity in early twentieth-century Bolivia. In defining himself, Paredes underscored his Aymara heritage. In his book *Los Siñani*, he investigated the history of his own cacique family, concluding the work with a description of his own studies at the University of San Andrés in La Paz, where he earned his law degree in 1893. "The Siñani family members," he wrote, "have always distinguished themselves through their indomitable spirit, their esteem of civil pride, and their irreproachable honor."[81] Educated, honorable, and highly active in Bolivian politics, Paredes traced his roots to the Aymara caciques, not to the Inca Empire. He was one of the few intellectuals to connect the valorized Aymara past to his own achievements as an Aymara intellectual in early twentieth-century Bolivia.

Paredes's intellectual peers also tended to describe him in terms of his Aymara heritage and his command of local customs rather than through any Inca connection. In his introductory comments to Paredes's *Tiahuanaco y la provincia de Ingavi*, José Antonio Arze y Arze described Paredes as "always proud of his indigenous heritage, which explains his great interest in Indian cultures. His appearance was one of a Creole with accentuated Aymara features, and his health was generally good, as is the health of those who are raised in the telluric highlands. He was intelligent and lively without being malicious, and he had an agreeable personality. . . . He peppered his stories with anecdotes about the people and places of Bolivia."[82]

Arze y Arze was careful to circumvent any association made between Paredes and an undesirable mestizo identity. He apparently felt the need to clarify that although Paredes was Indian, he was educated as well as "intelligent and lively." This portrait constituted a concentrated effort to describe the Aymara scholar, who did not fit easily into any category. Because Paredes was an indigenous intellectual who did not belong to the distant past and who promoted his Aymara identity over his connections to the Inca past, his very presence in political and intellectual circles presented something of a paradox for the Creole liberal politicians. The figure of Paredes thus reveals the limits of promoting a contemporary Aymara identity rather than one that resonated more directly with the veneration of the Incas.

Paredes sought to win election as the province of Muñecas's regional representative to the Liberal Party Convention of 1899. He expected to be elected easily, since he had served as district attorney of Muñecas in 1894 and had political support from several prominent politicians in the province. But when he contacted the convention's director, Dr. Manuel B. Mariaca, to discuss his nomination, he was told that Custodio Machicao had already been chosen as the sole candidate.[83] For the greater good and cohesion of the Liberal Party, Paredes decided not to run against Machicao. Just before the election Machicao abdicated, claiming he was too old to run, and passed his nomination on to Dr. Rufino Villanueva. Outraged, Paredes decided to run against Villanueva, but convention authorities denied that Villanueva was a candidate, insisting that Machicao was still a contender until eight days before the election. Paredes ran without official recognition, and according to the first count of the votes, he won by a landslide. A recount, however, showed Villanueva winning by a large margin. Paredes wrote an energetic and angry response entitled La elección de convencional en la provincia de Muñecas, published as a pamphlet in 1899. Paredes stated that the recently concluded civil war had been fought in vain if corrupt local authorities such as the electoral directorate of the town of Mocomoco, in the province of Muñecas, could commit such extreme fraud and go unpunished. Though he professed continuing allegiance to the Liberal Party, Paredes warned that any political party that did not invest the energy or possess the honor to defend electoral rights would be forever condemned to weakness.[84]

Paredes rightly located the Civil War of 1899 at the center of his argument. Yet his frustrating experience in running as the provincial representative to the Liberal Party Convention perhaps suggested the limits of asserting an Aymara identity in early twentieth-century Bolivia. Paredes never complained of ethnic discrimination in his case, however, and over the course of his career, he held several posts of authority, although these positions were mainly in the provinces rather than in the city of La Paz. The frustrated outcome of Paredes's bid to become the provincial representative to the Liberal Party Convention exemplified the exclusive nation-building project that incorporated the Aymara past but marginalized the actual Aymara population.

The Paredes case is all the more suggestive when considered in conjunction with a late nineteenth-century struggle over whether to designate Viacha or Tiahuanaco as a provincial capital. Paredes's books played an important role in underscoring the importance of the Aymaras and Tiahuanaco to the national historical narrative, as well as to Bolivia's early twentieth-century political discussions, and Paredes wrote *Tiahuanaco y la provincia de Ingavi* in response to this debate. In 1892 the town of Tiahuanaco became the provincial capital of the second section of Pacajes; in 1897 the honor was transferred to Viacha, despite extended protests from Paredes and other intellectuals. To emphasize the historical importance of Tiahuanaco and thus strengthen his case, Paredes cited the many studies of its archeological ruins generated throughout the colonial and national periods, including that of the historian Pedro Kramer, who had visited Tiahuanaco several times as part of a scholarly investigation. Kramer, too, was involved in defending Tiahuanaco's claims to become the provincial capital; he also participated in the effort to document the nation's history in his book *Historia de Bolivia*. According to Paredes, to emphasize the importance of Tiahuanaco, Kramer highlighted the Aymara architects' connections to the Incas, claiming that Manco Kapac, an early Inca leader, was an Aymara captain.[85] Posnansky had also claimed that Manco Kapac was Aymara based on measurements of the Inca leader's skull.[86]

Like Paredes's *Tiahuancu y la provincia de Ingavi*, the anonymously written publication entitled *Tiahuanaco: Datos para la defensa de la capital de la segunda sección de Pacajes* (1897) argued for designating the contemporary town of Tiahuanaco as the provincial capital. In defending Tiahuanaco, these authors listed its central location; its historical importance; its modernity, including an efficient bureaucracy; and, interestingly, according to the anonymous author, a museum of *Inca* artifacts. This author wrote: "Even if Tiahuanaco does not merit anything good from Bolivia, . . . at the very least do not commit the injustice of robbing the poor distinction which was awarded to this miserable town that was the cradle of Bolivian nationality"; "The scientific world grants more importance to Tiahuanaco than to any other city in Bolivia, and only a barbarian would, as a means of taking away its right to be the section capital, attack the *cradle of civilization in South America*, the source of our nationality, and the ark which encloses our tradition." As Seemin Qayum points out when quoting these words, the author linked the idea of Tiahuanaco as the cradle of South American civilization to the origins of Bolivian nationality.[87]

The debate regarding which town would serve as capital spoke to larger questions regarding the place of the Aymara heritage and population within the nation and the national historical narrative.

Paredes concluded the lengthy review of the literature on Tiahuanaco and the Aymaras in his *Tiahuanaco y la provincia de Ingavi* by stating that the ancient city was home to a highly advanced and unique culture from which the Incas heavily borrowed. His elevation of the Aymara past diminished the achievements of the Incas, whom Paredes labeled mere imitators of Aymara civilization. Paredes did not rupture the connection between the Aymaras and the Incas in thus critiquing the latter's glorification, but he did invert the importance attributed to each group. He recognized the Incas not as glorious forebears but rather as a vehicle in claiming a space for the Aymaras within the national narrative and in introducing and legitimizing Aymara contributions to the nation's development.

In 1897 the Bolivian Senate decreed that Viacha would be the provincial capital, citing its larger population as one of the primary reasons for the decision.[88] The historical importance of Tiahuanaco did not carry enough weight to grant it local distinction as regional capital. The Aymaras might be written into the historical narrative as the ancestors of the Incas, but the Bolivian nation was not ready to recognize contemporary Aymara achievements in the early twentieth century, whether the matter concerned electing an Aymara deputy to the Liberal Party Convention or designating a city steeped in Aymara heritage as a provincial capital.

Indigenista intellectuals' revision of the historical narrative to marginally include the Aymaras as the ancestors of the Incas—and of the nation—marked an important discursive shift following the Civil War of 1899. In Bolivia, constructions of race as well as discourses of identity and national policy were expressed through the rhetoric of civilization and modernity via adoptions of and claims to a specific "Indian" identity. The "Indian question" in Bolivian politics rests not only on centuries of Indian resistance but also on intellectuals' constructions of modernity, articulated through promotions of preferred Indian identities that created spaces for contrasting representations of Indianness.

With the Aymara participation in the recently concluded civil war and the recent prominence of La Paz ever more urgently pressing them to address the "Indian question," liberal intellectuals wrote the Aymaras into the national narrative, easing racial distinctions by establishing a connection between the lauded Incas and the Aymara past. Though this process was contested, indigenista intellectuals ultimately contributed to the promotion of an "acceptable" national Indian image, the Inca, whose ancestors were clearly identified as Aymara. Through a seemingly contradictory process, these intellectuals countered perceptions that Bolivia's "backward" Indian population limited the nation's potential through constructions of preferred Indian (Inca) images designed to marginalize the undesirable indigenous—and especially Aymara—presence in the early twentieth century. The Aymaras were marginalized within discourses of modernity and progress, but they were not excluded.

The connection between the Incas and the Aymaras gave a unique twist to Bolivian national history and played an important role in the creation of a regional history for the new highland capital of La Paz, the headquarters of the Liberal Party. With its mountain location, cold climate, and low oxygen levels, La Paz had not been a particularly compelling place to live prior to the tin boom of the early twentieth century. In large part to legitimate their reign and their region, liberal intellectuals needed to improve the image of the savage, uncivilized highland Aymara Indian that the newspapers, conservative politicians, and even many Creole liberal intellectuals had emphasized in portraying the Aymara participation in the Civil War of 1899 as a race war. The indigenista intellectuals provided La Paz with a historical narrative legitimizing it as a region that had produced great civilizations, was home to important historical leaders, and was the point of origin of humankind in the Americas.

In the early twentieth century, the Aymara past entered into the Bolivian national historical narrative with the Aymaras cast as the primitive ancestors of great civilizations and the Bolivian nation itself. While the 1880s had produced several suggestions of the Aymaras' importance to Bolivian history and national identity, the indigenista narratives that incorporated the Aymaras' historical contributions increased in number and significance under the Liberal Party regime. The recognition of the Aymaras' role within the national historical narrative reflected the liberal intellectuals' inability to write the Aymaras out of the historical register, despite initial attempts to do so.[89] The refashioned connection between Incas and the Aymaras defined liberal imaginings of nation and national belonging and connected Aymara history to the nation's origin.

The development of an Inca identity did not remain solely in the hands of indigenista intellectuals. Many Aymaras sought to claim a space within the Bolivian nation through a variety of means, including an appeal to their military service to the Liberal Party during the civil war and, subsequently, the adoption and performance of the preferred Inca identity. Issuing their own casting call, the local Aymara elite began to explore their role and their claims to lineage on the stage of national history and to exploit the possibility of connecting not only the Aymara past but also the Aymara present to the promotion of the Inca Empire through theatrical renditions of history. Capitalizing on Creole liberal intellectuals' preference for the Inca past, the provincial Aymara elite forged their own images of socially acceptable Bolivian Indians, "Incas," who were heirs of the noble indigenous tradition in Peru and who were "whitened" personages in the Bolivian context. The local Aymara elite opted to promote their Inca past via theatrical presentations and narrations of their own history *beginning with* the historical watershed of the might—and fall—of the Inca Empire. As I will show in the next chapter, the local Aymara elite in the highland town of Caracollo adopted an "Inca" identity so as to escape the unacceptable Aymara form of Indianness and to obtain a place within the nation that they could not have achieved by asserting a contemporary Aymara identity. In Bolivia, discourses of exclusion and inclusion, whether directed at or emanating from the state, historically have centered on contested images, narratives, and constructions of Indian identities.

3 INCANTATIONS OF NATION AND THE THEATRICAL PERFORMANCE OF THE INCA PAST

La Paz intellectuals were not the only group needing to redefine Aymara identity following the civil war. In the post-1899 context, Aymara communities increasingly attempted to distinguish and disassociate themselves from the infamous and stereotypical image of their people as savage. In addition, local representatives sought to differentiate segments within the Aymara population. For example, the town authority Modesto de Campo wrote in his report on the situation in Poopó that things were under control, for the indigenous people there were "more docile than those of the Choqueyapu region" in La Paz.[1]

The Civil War of 1899 and its aftermath had real consequences for Aymara communities. In the canton of Hachiri, the indigenous people were struggling with public perceptions of their identity. Writing to the subprefect of Pacajes, the mayor of Hachiri, Dionicio Mollinedo, described the problems associated with being Aymara in this era. The residents of the ayllus of Ninoca, Laura, and Collana were merchants, he explained, and thus had to travel frequently within Bolivia as well as to the neighboring countries of Chile and Peru. "However, since the revolution and the besmirching of the image of the Aymara," Mollinedo wrote, "ayllu members [comuneros] find it virtually impossible to accomplish anything on these business trips, since everywhere they go Bolivians and foreigners alike heckle them and call them . . . murderers."[2]

In response to this disparagement and discrimination, which had not only hindered their livelihoods but spilled across national borders, the Hachiri Aymaras, like those of Poopó, began to highlight ethnic distinctions and alternatives to the pejorative image of their population as savages. Along with the residents of the Ninoca, Laura, and Collana ayllus, Mollinedo recognized that some Aymaras had reacted and taken part in the war only as a result of extreme abuses carried out by the army under Conservative Party rule, but he assured the subprefect that the Aymaras of Hachiri had not taken sides in the war: "As honest and peaceful business people, we did not threaten anyone. . . . Rather, we rushed to the defense of the lives and property of the townspeople."³

In this attempt to distinguish the population of Hachiri from the popular image of the savage Aymara hordes, Mollinedo emphasized not only that the Hachiri Aymaras had not taken part in the civil war but also that they had responded as model citizens in defense of their town, regardless of considerations of race and class. Mollinedo closed the letter by requesting, on behalf of the Hachiri Aymara merchants, that the subprefect extend them a written confirmation of innocence to carry on their travels as proof that they were different from the supposedly savage Bolivian Aymaras. The requested letter was to help protect what Mollinedo called "our denigrated race." The subprefect responded favorably, extending the people of Hachiri a letter vouching for their innocence. The subprefect's letter clearly stated that the Aymaras of Hachiri were not responsible for any deaths and that they had remained peaceful and respectful during and after the war. Yet the Hachiri Aymaras deemed that the letter was not sufficiently convincing to deter the racism they faced. They returned the letter to the subprefect and asked that it be certified and signed by the prefect in addition to the subprefect.⁴ In seeking to improve their image through both the prefect's guarantee and the description of their community's inhabitants as peaceful businesspeople, the indigenous residents of Hachiri illustrate the problem of being Aymara in early twentieth-century Bolivia.

The example of the "Umala Indians" constitutes another attempt to create an identity more favorable than that of the "savage Aymara." Umala is a highland community close to Peñas whose indigenous inhabitants fought in the civil war. Through a series of weekly articles about their wartime activities published in the La Paz newspaper El Imparcial 2, the Umala Aymaras claimed a space for themselves within the nation as patriots rather than as savages. In large part they accomplished this by defining their actions as separate from those of the Aymara leader Zárate Willka and his supposed race war. According to the author of these accounts, the Umala Indians were not a threat because "they were completely aware that their race could never run a country, given their acknowledged complete ignorance, and that, if they were to attempt to run a country, science, art, writing, and commerce would die. . . . Rather, they declared that they were best suited for farming, and that they were content under 'the domain of the whites.'" According to one article in this series, Subprefect Luis F. Gémio identified the Umala Aymaras as "dedicated and honorable workers and businesspeople" and told the Aymaras that if they wanted an Indian leader, they should pick one from Umala and not listen to Zárate Willka.[5] The article reported that the Umala Indians cheered in response, "Long live Pando! Long live the subprefect! Death to the Indian Pablo Zárate!" According to the author, their "patriotic character" led Pando to use the Umala Aymaras to attack Oruro in late March after having warned them not to harm anyone and to treat the notable townspeople of Oruro as their brothers.

The article's author reported that the Umala Aymaras agreed to General Pando's orders and, underscoring their identity as businesspeople, added that since they did business in Oruro, they could never hurt their Oruro customers. After assisting Pando in his attack on Oruro, the Umala Indians returned home and resumed their work. According to the author of the newspaper articles, such was the patriotic contribution of the Umala Indians under appropriate leadership.[6] Importantly, the Umala Indians were portrayed as having contributed to the wartime effort. Their actions under Pando's leadership created new opportunities for claiming a space as "patriotic Indians" within the Bolivian nation, although ethnic descriptions played only a secondary role in their self-identification as businesspeople. The journalist responsible for these articles highlighted the Umala Indians' honor and role in commerce, as well as their steadfast opposition to Zárate Willka.

As I discussed in the previous chapter, early twentieth-century Bolivian intellectuals and journalists promoting a modernizing project sought to downplay worries about the nation's "backward" indigenous population by valorizing its Inca past. Even governmental authorities promoted anything they could relate to the Incas. In 1913, the prefect whom the Hachiri residents had petitioned suggested that the Bolivian state develop the indigenous art of weaving in the predominantly Aymara region of Oruro since, he said, the "Inca motifs and designs in the textiles were admired all over the world."[7] In another report from 1913, this prefect called attention to the Chipaya population in an attempt to generate academic interest in the Oruro region. Rather than refer to the distinctiveness of the Chipaya ethnicity, Prefect Diez de Medina claimed that the inhabitants were "worthy of study because of their 'Inca' customs, which they conserved with religious vigor."[8] Packaging all things "Indian" as "Inca" seemed to convey a favorable message that other ethnic identities could not provide.

For some of the provincial Ayamara elite, performances of the Inca past would become an effective way to distance themselves from the negative stereotypes associated with being Aymara in early twentieth-century Bolivia. Beginning in the early 1900s, the local Aymara elite of Caracollo adopted and performed a theatrical enactment of the Spanish Conquest.[9] Acting Inca during the regional celebration honoring the Virgin of the Rosary allowed Caracollo residents to project their "preferred" Indian identity to a wide audience as well as to construct a favorable narrative of the past that resonated with the liberal nation-building project. In highlighting the fall of the Inca Empire and the arrival of the Spaniards, this play figured the Incas as the most important ethnic group in this narrative. The Aymara past (as well as the Uru or Guaraní past) prior to Inca rule was rendered invisible. The decision to silence the indigenous past prior to contact with Europeans, coupled with the promotion of the Incas as the most exalted of indigenous cultures, reflects a turn-of-the-century trend that directed the nation's attention away from a non-Inca indigenous history. While the colonial legacies of performances of the Inca past did grant the early twentieth-century plays historical authority, the performance of the Inca play in Caracollo responded to liberals' promotion of the Inca past as integral to constructions of national history and identity.

This chapter focuses on the Caracollo elite's adoption of an Inca past and their performance of their Inca play in a historically Aymara region in an effort to disassociate themselves from negative perceptions of the highland Aymara Indian. After broadly surveying theatrical representations and articulations of an Inca identity in late nineteenth- and early twentieth-century Bolivia, I will look more specifically at Inca theater in post–civil war Caracollo. Through the public medium of festival and performance, the local Aymara elite attempted to claim a space for themselves within the nation as the bearers of the nation's celebrated and noble Inca past.

Acts of Modernity:
Theater and Progress in Early Twentieth-Century Bolivia

Studies of performance and specifically of Inca theater in the Andes have produced a range of interpretations that cut across the precolonial, colonial, and national eras. The genre of the Inca play has its roots in Quechua theater prior to the Spanish Conquest and corresponds most closely to the genre of the *wanka*, dramatic works designed to narrate and perform the life and death of Inca leaders or heroes.[10] In *La historia de la Villa Imperial de Potosí*, the chronicler Bartolomé Arzáns de Orsua y Vela claims that plays presenting the Inca past were performed in Potosí during the early colonial era, specifically, in 1555.[11] Some scholars argue that performances of the Inca play during the colonial and national periods symbolized acts of indigenous resistance in those eras.[12] These studies of Andean performances of the Inca past from the sixteenth to the twentieth centuries establish a connection between theater and the idea of an "Andean utopia," perhaps best understood as the desire to create a pan-Indian society under Inca leadership. These resistance-based models speak to the longevity of Inca plays that spanned both the colonial and national eras. Yet these studies rarely take into account the specific historical contexts that made the Inca past important to local and national communities during a given epoch. More than just a matter of elite imaginings of nation, Inca plays constituted one way in which indigenous people engaged *indigenista* intellectuals' appropriations and promotions of an Indian past. Through performance, Inca theater actors underscored the modernizing potential of the Indian population, turning the national discourse that favored the Inca into a reality and creating a space for the "civilized" Indian within the Bolivian nation.

Festival theater of these eras was not strictly a form of entertainment or a temporary experiment of social inversion. Nor was it a manifestation of cultural retention despite centuries of oppression or necessarily an act of resistance or a representation of fictional chaos. As Rossana Barragán points out in her study of festivals in Bolivia, there is nothing casual about festival theater and performance.[13] The theater and dance guilds assume the enormous task of organizing dozens to hundreds of dancers, hiring a suitable band, and coordinating all the outfits and dance practices, with minimal or no state support. Theatrical presentations are neither purely fiction nor fact; they serve as a venue for organizing the multiple historical narratives and protagonists that would define Bolivia's emerging national character in the late nineteenth and early twentieth centuries.

Figure 7 reproduces an illustration from the Buenos Aires magazine *Caras y Caretas* in 1901 showing the mass appeal of theater and the different theatrical genres along with the distinct socioeconomic groups they attracted. Of special interest is the illustration of "drama criollo," which, according to Sarah Townsend and Diana Taylor, dealt with "national themes."[14] It is the only drawing in this assortment that hides the theatergoer's face, save

FIGURE 7. Illustration in *Caras y Caretas*, April 27, 1901. From Diana Taylor and Sarah Townsend, eds., *Stages of Conflict: A Critical Anthology of Latin American Theater and Performance* (Ann Arbor: University of Michigan Press, 2008), 13

for a bit of protruding mustache. The man appears to be hanging his head and taking small steps; the illustration provides nothing else to create context. This individual appears to be charting an unknown route with his face hidden, representative of the ambiguities, uncertainties, and complexities of defining the national character throughout Latin America in the early twentieth century.

Bolivian theater informed negotiations over national belonging and the definition of the nation during the late nineteenth and early twentieth centuries. Progress was defined not only in terms of economic revitalization, such as the early twentieth-century highland tin boom, but also through constructions of race and social hierarchies. While the Civil War of 1899 conferred some education gains on rural highland communities, the banishment and in some cases execution of Aymaras found guilty in the Peñas trial clearly indicated that any political gains achieved through the Aymaras' wartime service would not offset ongoing abuse. Their struggle for national inclusion thus moved from the physical battlefields to the discursive grounds of constructions of ethnic identity as manifested via theatrical performance.

FIGURE 8. Official seal of the Caracollo Incas. Courtesy of the Caracollo Inca guild

The official seal of the Caracollo Inca theatrical guild locates the group's origins in 1900 (see fig. 8), a defining moment in Bolivian history, a time after the initial promise and subsequent demise of the alliance between highland Aymara communities and the Liberal Party and one when intellectuals and politicians on all sides branded the Aymara population as uncivilized. Caracollo residents used the festival setting as an alternative space to contest the marginalization of the Aymara population in the wake of the civil war. In his essay "Sinfonia aymara," the Liberal Party politician Eduardo Diez de Medina attempted to diminish the importance of festival performance, claiming that the Aymara festivals were only additional evidence of the barbaric state of the Indian population. He described the highland Indian festival participant as walking along the altiplano drunk, his eyes clouded by ignorance, producing broken sounds from his flute. "If you see one of these festival presentations," he wrote, "you will realize that these poor ignorants cling fanatically to their customs only out of habit, which seems to dictate all their actions. . . . Their music is sad and their dances are strange, . . . [representing] their profound disregard for life. [Their festivals] are a symbol of sadness and of pain. . . .

They raise their hard, dry voices [in song], which sound like wails from the tomb."[15]

Diez de Medina attempted to dismiss highland festivals as a significant social and political sphere by invoking the popular stereotype of the Aymaras as savage and primitive. He found the Aymara language to be harsh and guttural; the locutors themselves ignorant, drunk, and dangerous. Aymara festivals, in this sense, were manifestations only of the Aymaras' stubborn refusal to modernize. In serving as historians and performing the Inca past, however, highland actors in Caracollo attempted to recast themselves as Incas rather than as Aymaras, performing the play in the lyric Quechua language rather than in Aymara. The actors, that is, highlighted the Inca past in an effort to ameliorate pejorative perceptions of the highland Aymara population.

Despite critiques such as Diez de Medina's, festivals were a careful orchestration of national identity and belonging. In 1900 one La Paz newspaper commented on the many communities whose residents came to that city to take part in civic festivities with patriotic enthusiasm and to cheer for the nation's heroes, even though they were not permitted to march in the formal parades. In 1906 another La Paz newspaper recognized the patriotism of the indigenous people and observed that the Indians had learned to play the national anthem and the La Paz anthem on their *zampoñas,* or panpipes, and to enthusiastically cheer "Long live Bolivia! Long live La Paz! Long live Murillo!" While the ban on Indians formally participating in national parades was relaxed only in 1925, in 1909 some journalists suggested that the indigenous population be allowed to participate as a form of physical education. Instead of inviting them to join the parade, authorities set up a footrace pitting Indian participants from La Paz against those from Tiahuanaco.[16]

Across the Americas, performance, ritual, and theater played central roles in negotiations over the construction of the modern, progressive, unique nation and in defining national body and character.[17] According to Taylor and Townsend, "while the Church throughout the Americas became nervous about the popularity and growing secularism of theater, the municipal authorities [in Buenos Aires] defended it as 'one of the best schools for manners, language, and urbanity, and thus useful in a city that lacks other healthy diversions.'" Plays strategically looked to the past, using pre-Hispanic themes as a way of ennobling national histories. Costumbrista novels, too, focused on local settings and their typical customs and characters, thus leading readers to seek identities at home, not in European or North American sources.[18] While Diez de Medina would have reserved his praise for indoor presentations of urban theater, the local elite in Caracollo chose theater as a public forum to disseminate the town's Inca past to the audience. In addition, given the era's rather low literacy rates, which averaged 16 percent nationally and only 13 percent in the Department of Oruro, theater served as an effective means of introducing alternative narratives and exploring the boundaries of national belonging.[19]

The theater itself was a symbol of modernity and civilization that proliferated during the late nineteenth and early twentieth centuries. Theaters moved onto main plazas, standing alongside Catholic churches as an additional motor of national and moral narratives. During the tin boom, theater constituted a hallmark of modernization, rivaling the importance that the Catholic Church had enjoyed during the colonial era in its capacity to moralize, civilize, and instill patriotism in its audience. Theaters also served as essential landmarks for assessing a given region's level of progress and culture.[20] In the small highland towns that thrived during the tin boom, such as Machacamarca and Huanuni, large theaters occupied central spaces on the altiplano landscape, looming above the one-story buildings surrounding them. Photographs of the theater in the former tin-smelting center of Machacamarca, in the Department of Oruro, provide an excellent example of such theaters' centrality and importance to towns (see figs. 9 and 10). The "American," as this theater was named, was established in 1914. Its simple, geometric style represents a break with the much more ornate colonial buildings, and the inside suggests a democratization of space. Absent from this construction are the tiers of private boxes used by the elite. The theater did include three different types of seats, but the differences are not great, and no seats are dramatically partitioned off to divide audience members. Social difference and divisions are not erased, but they are minimized. The interior divisions of space suggest a more inclusive social order, while the prominence of the edifice reflects the importance of theater in the early twentieth century.

Improvements to theater buildings were regularly noted in national newspapers, which announced better seating, technological advancements in lighting, and better access via paved paths. In the La Paz municipal report of 1900, descriptions of improvements to the theater occupied nearly four pages, with the report detailing, among other things, carpeting, a new door, and an alternative entrance "to give more comfort to the upper-class theater goers and to ensure the public's safety in case of fire."[21] In his annual report from Oruro in 1898, Prefect Andrés Aramayo stated that an earlier agreement had stipulated that a certain sum from the departmental treasury be divided equally, half to extend the water service and half to improve the theater. Fol-

FIGURES 9 and 10. Cine American, Machacamarca, Bolivia. Photos by the author, 2009

FIGURE 11.
El Comercio (La Paz), March 30, 1901. Reproduced by permission from the National Archive of Bolivia

lowing appeals made by Dr. Adolfo Mier, however, all the money had been earmarked to upgrade the theater. Prefect Aramayo protested, stating that supplying water to the town was at least as important as investing in luxuries such as theater, if not more so.[22] As this disagreement over the disbursement of funds clearly shows, the modern theater had become an essential landmark of modernization, one perhaps more important than efficient water services.

Theater was important to rural and urban populations alike. Manuel de la Quintana, the director of an urban theatrical group in La Paz, the Escuela Dramática Paceña (see fig. 11), was also the editor of *Nimbas y aureolas*, an early twentieth-century journal dedicated to theater and liberalism. Through both his artistic endeavors and his literary publications, de la Quintana exemplified the connection between performance and politics in early twentieth-century La Paz. He directed one of the most successful acting companies in the city, and he provided commentary on other acting companies, such as the Serrador and the Calderón. Theater was an expression of modernity, and the Escuela Dramática Paceña put on the most shows and received the most advertising of all the troupes appearing at La Paz's municipal theater. De la Quintana believed theater to be deeply connected to the historical context. In a critique of *Mariana*, performed by the Calderón Theatrical Company in 1901, de la Quintana criticized the play for being "divorced from reality"; art was not to be produced for art's sake alone. In his exposition, de la Quintana connected theatrical performance to definitions of civilization, stating that the Calderón company's performance might have been of interest to an ignorant audience but was not acceptable to "civilized spectators."[23]

Yet urban authors were often unkind when assessing rural performances and attempted to delegitimize Indian festivals; they cited the festivals as evidence showing the limited degree of civilization of Bolivia's indigenous population. Nonetheless, indigenous populations demonstrated great interest in theater. Even in the absence of a formal theatrical edifice, performances were a mainstay of small highland towns and played an important role in the construction of local and national identities.

Theater attracted wide attention, providing one of the few places where the various strata of society might share a common recreational interest. In his study of Cuzco Inca theater in the early twentieth century, César Itier repeatedly mentions that Peruvians from all social classes were most interested in attending Inca plays. In 1913 the *cuzqueño* newspaper reported: "A human mass congregated outside the theater, filled with people who do not even read the newspaper and who never spend a cent on cultural luxuries, . . . [and] twenty policemen were unable to establish order. . . . While the struggle ensued, the wealthy families arrived for the performance and, as they entered the crowd in their attempt to reach the box office, appeared as bright patches against the dark throng of the popular masses."[24] In his study of Inca plays in Bolivia, Jesús Lara also comments on the genre's widespread appeal: "It is admirable how the Indians, isolated as they are from the cultural world, crowd around to see the rustic actors perform, and they do not leave until the play is over."[25] Indians, as I will show, not only filled the theater audience but moved onto the main stage as central protagonists in performances of the nation's past.

Inca Theater in the Andes

The most famous Andean theatrical performances are those of Inca plays. Peru and Bolivia share a common, if geopolitically unequal, Andean past centered on the might of the Inca Empire that lends certain legitimacy to performances of Inca history. Studies of Inca plays throughout the Andes privilege Peru, however, drawing on Cuzco's legitimacy as the cradle of the Inca Empire. César Itier's work on Quechua theater in Cuzco during the late nineteenth and early twentieth centuries underscores the fluidity of an Inca identity and its multiple appropriations. Itier identifies Inca theater as central to the elite's repertoire in Cuzco, performed by leading indigenista intellectuals who promoted alternative regional nation-building projects in Peru.[26] While these plays might be seen as representing the essence of indigenous culture, the actors' performances were meant to promote the importance of Cuzco within the national context and to establish difference between the Incas and undesirable manifestations of Indianness. Although his argument is limited by its regional specificity, Itier makes an important contribution in emphasizing the role of theater and the Inca in negotiating and shaping national politics and identities.

Zoila Mendoza's work on performance in Cuzco highlights the fluid constructions of identities that are negotiated in the processes of consolidating local hierarchies and articulating regional and national identities.[27] Again, however, Cuzco constitutes a privileged space, for its role as the historical center of the Inca Empire confers particular legitimacy and weight to adoptions of an Inca identity there. While some scholars have studied and written about festival and performance in Bolivia, research on performances of the Inca past focuses more on Peruvian history.[28] More recently, Cuzco's thriving tourism business, which often showcases its Inca past, has reinforced the centrality of the city's Inca heritage. But what does it mean to act Inca in a historically Aymara-populated region on the fringe of what constituted the Inca Empire? As distinct regional performances narrate their own versions of the Incas and the Spanish Conquest, they shape national history and claim a space for themselves within the nation.[29]

Bolivia cannot claim legitimacy as the heart of the Inca Empire, but Inca plays were nevertheless part of the twentieth-century landscape in the nation's highlands, even in historically Aymara-populated zones.[30] In twentieth-century Peru, communities decided whether to represent the Inca past through the dance "Inca-Capitán" or through theater;[31] in Bolivia, the Inca past has always been represented via theatrical performance. Doctor Jean-Albert Vellard, the director of Bolivia's National Museum of Archaeology in 1942, referred to a distinct "Bolivian tradition" of Inca theater and dress that was modeled on a statue of an Inca in La Paz.[32] In his analysis of twentieth-century theatrical representations of the conquest in Bolivia (which he calls the "third cycle" of Inca theater), Clemente Hernando Balmori recognizes that Inca plays of this time resonate with colonial representations of the Inca past but argues that structural features make them closer to European dramatic genres than to the early indigenous colonial theatrical representations. Balmori makes an important observation in underscoring the fact that modernization efforts in Bolivia were accompanied by the largest proliferation of Inca theater in the twentieth century.[33]

Studies of Bolivian Inca plays have focused on texts from both the highlands and the central valley region of Bolivia, working sometimes from recovered texts and sometimes from discussions in secondary sources. The majority of these plays stem from the highland region and date from the first half of the twentieth century. Two known texts come from the province of Cliza, in Cochabamba, the predominantly Quechua-speaking valley of central Bolivia. In his novel *Valle*, Mario Unzueta describes the first of these two Inca plays, this one performed in the town of Toco.[34] The second play from the valley region was staged in the town of Santa Lucia, also in the province of Cliza; Lara reports that the manuscript is entitled "El descubrimiento de la América por C. Colón." The author's name appears as "Celestino Callao B.," and the work is dated December 13, 1937.[35]

Highland Inca plays have enjoyed more attention and analysis from scholars; they come from the departments of Potosí and Oruro.[36] The earliest known text comes from San Pedro de Buenavista, in Potosí. Gerardo Tapia, who owns a manuscript of this work entitled "El relato del Inca," allowed Jesús Lara to study the text after Lara saw a Potosí troupe performing on tour in 1952. Another text from this area, *Tragedia del fin de Atahuallpa: Atau Wallpaj P'uchucacuyninpa Wankan*, also studied by Lara, comes from Chayanta, in Potosí, and dates to 1871. Lara provoked controversy by claiming that the Chayanta text is the most "authentic" Inca play in Bolivia—that is, the one closest to the genre's indigenous roots—through which the indigenous people continue to reflect on and lament the trauma of the Spanish Conquest.[37] Margot Beyersdorff reported performances of Inca plays in both Crucero de Belén and San Pedro de Challacollo, both in the Department of Oruro, during the twentieth century.[38] The Inca play performed in Oruro during Carnival has been extensively analyzed by Balmori, Wachtel, Niver Montes, and Thomas Abercrombie. The theatrical and dance group that puts on this play is one of the oldest folkloric groups performing in Oruro's Carnival festival, founded in 1910, and is believed to have originated in Caracollo; it stages the Inca play that is still performed today in Caracollo and that forms the focus of this and the next chapter.[39]

Inca theater enjoys a widespread repertoire in Bolivia, as the many theatrical representations and narrations of the Inca past throughout the highlands and valley region indicate. This corpus of plays, most of which date from the late nineteenth century and proliferated in the first half of the twentieth, indicate that theatrically performing an Inca past was important to Bolivia during its nation-building period. Specifically, the Inca image and manifestations of the Inca past were central means of expressing ideas, identities, debates, and political negotiations throughout the nation-building process for both Indian and non-Indian populations.

While the plays themselves highlight aspects of the Inca past, the historical context of their performances hints at the significance of an Inca identity. To fully understand the phenomenon of the Inca plays, then, we must explore the historical setting that fostered these performances. This methodological approach builds on yet departs from that of Nathan Wachtel, who employed contemporary folklore to understand Indian interpretations of the Spanish Conquest: "Folklore, the past living in the present, is one source for the study of permanent elements in the collective psychology of the Indians. I therefore propose to try an experiment: to proceed by a retrospective analysis from present to past, reaching back through contemporary folklore to find out what the Conquest meant to the Indian people."[40] By engaging in a comparative textual analysis of the plays and contemporary performances of the theaters of conquest, Wachtel assessed the lasting impact of the conquest and ongoing contemporary Indian nostalgia. Lack of direct access to past performances renders dramatic texts paramount to such investigations. Yet Wachtel's focus on the conquest creates an artificial frontier in Indian history; labeling the conquest as the defining act eclipses subsequent indigenous political participation in and negotiation with both the colonial and republican governments. The reason individuals "act Inca" within communities at a particular moment informs the historical significance of the play itself. Moreover, the interest in and dissemination of the Inca past in early twentieth-century discourses of nation building in Bolivia was not restricted to an Indian domain or narrative. Rather, the Inca past was negotiated between Bolivian intellectuals and indigenous communities, who both laid claim to an Inca past as a critical component in nation building and constructions of national belonging. Textual analysis thus requires historical contextualization. As I will show, one such context involved the marginalization of the Aymaras; actors and directors for the plays at issue showcased a specific narrative of the Inca past while silencing the histories of other ethnic groups indigenous to the region, many of which existed prior to and were conquered by the Incas.

Scholars and community actors have engaged in a fluid exchange regarding Inca theater and the construction and representation of the Inca past. On the academic side, Jesús Lara, a Bolivian scholar from the city of Cochabamba, made great efforts to obtain and study texts of his country's Inca plays, citing their relevance as one of the most authentic, noble, and pure forms of national expression. Many people from different classes and ethnicities shared his interest in Inca theater. In 1952, for example, when Lara was in La Paz working in the Biblioteca Andrés de Santa Cruz, he noticed a nearby man who appeared to be waiting and watching him.[41] As Lara left the building, this man stopped him and presented himself as a fan of Lara's book *La poesia quechua*.[42] Much to Lara's surprise, the man expressed his particular interest in Lara's analysis of Inca theater.[43] He identified himself as Santiago Estrada, from the province of Alonso de Ibañez, in the Department of Potosí, and to the scholar's surprise, he offered to sell Lara the script of an Inca play. Lara eventually published the script as *Tragedia del fin de Atawallpa* (1957), which he claimed had been written in 1871 in Chayanta, Potosí.

Estrada was well versed in local theatrical productions in Alonso de Ibañez and aware of the broader relevance of and interest in Inca theater.[44] His encounter with Lara seems to contradict Lara's earlier observations regarding the ignorance and lack of interest in theater among rural audiences. Estrada had read Lara's anthology of Quechua poetry, he had done his own investigation of its author, and he had made his way to the library fully aware of Lara's interest in Inca plays. As a literate person and a grassroots intellectual, he shared Lara's literary interests in the Quechua language and recognized the broader scholarly interest in local theatrical production.

In another instance showing this broad appeal, Lara sought to obtain the script for *El relato del Inca* after seeing this play performed by a troupe from Potosí in 1952. Gerardo Tapia, who owned a copy, was happy to share it with Lara on the condition that he read it and correct any historical omissions or inaccuracies.[45] Tapia sought to improve the script, to receive scholarly critique, and to exchange ideas with Lara. Rather than insist on a strictly "Indian" expression of the past, Tapia wanted the script to resonate with learned understandings of national history.

In his analysis of the Inca play performed at Oruro, the actor Luis Bredow notes exchanges between urban centers and rural areas in staging representations of the Inca past.[46] Performances do not constitute a unilateral transference from the rural to the urban sphere. Bredow recognizes a mutual interest in performing such plays and, at times, in collaborating to stage performances. Bredow attributes this shared desire between urban and rural inhabitants to a collective revindication of traditional culture.[47] Yet he does not explain why the culture to be revindicated is the Inca past, expressed in the Quechua language, a task to which I now turn. The following analysis of the Inca play performed in Caracollo will illustrate how and why the performance and dissemination of the Inca past became relevant to the inhabitants of a historically Aymara town in the early twentieth century.

The Caracollo Case: Scenes from Caracollo's Past

A canton seat, Caracollo is located in the Department of Oruro, thirty-seven kilometers north of the department's largest city, Oruro. Its name comes from the Aymara words q'ara and kollo, meaning "bald mountain," and is one of several indicators of the region's predominantly Aymara heritage.[48] The town is often described as a "ciudad intermedio" because of its elevated status, which it acquired as the provincial capital of Cercado (gaining that designation in 1980) and home to a teacher's college, the "Instituto Normal Superior Intercultural Bilingüe 'General René Barrientos Ortuño,'" named after President Barrientos (1965–1969) and founded in 1964. In Caracollo, history is constructed and delivered through theatrical representations of the past rather than through publications. The local offices of governance have few records prior to 1980, and it seems that few records were transferred to the central courthouse in Oruro. The documents of the Canchari-Guayta court case, detailing Caracollo's role in the Civil War of 1899, fell victim to a flood; the wet documents were dumped behind the cemetery in Oruro decades ago.[49] Individuals who served as town authorities may have occasionally retained documents when they left office, but if so, the documentation rarely outlived them, for descendants customarily burn a decedent's belongings.

The dearth of documentation from Caracollo's past creates a need and the space for articulations of local history. Oral and performative traditions of the Inca play have provided townspeople access to Caracollo's past and to the connections between Caracollo's past and national narratives. Indeed, the absence of historical documentation has given the performances uncanny and totalizing power and authority. The only document on Caracollo's history, which was written in 1995 by Yucra León, touches on this issue: "Our town is confronted with numerous challenges that are all the more complex because of a lack of knowledge concerning Caracollo's past. To progress efficiently, we need to know our past."[50] Great value is placed on knowledge of the past, which in turn is connected to the town's ability to progress and modernize.

The narrative of the previous generations of Caracollo is itself one of progress and civilization. Yucra León states that prior to Inca rule, Caracollo was home to Chullpas, Quechuas, and Aymaras. He describes the first indigenous group in the area, the Chullpas, as egocentric people who fought among themselves and left their enemies to die of hunger. These people were said to have lived like animals; *chullpares*, the archeological remains of this culture, were thought to be dangerous places full of powerful negative spirits. Chullpares, or funeral towers, are actually the tombs of pre-Columbian ancestors, places where community leaders and men of importance were buried. They appear in the Bolivian highlands and are in fact often associated with the Aymaras. The monuments are important sites of social memory, reminders of the ties between community authorities of past and those of the future in a given region. Chullpares are portals to the past where people made and sometimes continue to make ritual offerings to deceased leaders.[51] In the twentieth century, residents of Caracollo razed many of the local chullpares, leaving only two, to make room for a paved plaza that serves as the site for the regional market on Sundays.

Yucra argues that infighting and the resulting attrition rate meant that the original inhabitants largely vanished; he estimated their number in 1995 to be twenty-four. Yucra thus introduces a break with the non-Incan indigenous past and minimizes the role that the Chullpas played in local history. The Incas receive a brief but more favorable mention as an important point of contact for the residents of Caracollo. According to Yucra's narrative, which underscores the importance of the Incas in Caracollo's history, communication between Cuzco and Caracollo was facilitated by a series of tunnels that connected the two populations.[52]

During the colonial era, Caracollo served as a *tambo*, or place of rest on trade routes. Caracolleños participated in the wars for independence under the command of the region of Sica Sica.[53] The early twentieth-century tin boom attracted foreign merchants to Caracollo, including Turks, who brought luxury fabrics and other dry goods to the region, and Austrians, who specialized as shopkeepers. Yucra defines the town's history during the national period as one of involvement in national politics. The national census of 1900 identifies the town as falling within the province of Cercado and the canton of Paria. At that time, Caracollo had a population of 4,871, making it one of the larger small towns in the Department of Oruro, slightly smaller than Challapata (4,960) but slightly larger than Poopó (4,826). The vast majority of Caracollo's population, 88 percent, was of indigenous heritage. The white population was small, just 2 percent, and mestizos made up another 5 percent.[54] According to a report from 1905, the land in Caracollo differed from that in most other regions of Oruro in being controlled exclusively by *hacendados*. Caracollo did not have a single ayllu outside the haciendas.[55] These statistics on land tenure were reported in a study to implement the "maestro ambulante," or mobile teacher program, a Liberal Party effort to reduce illiteracy and "civilize" the Indian population. Caracollo would have been an excellent target for such a program in 1905. The illiterate population over seven years of age was 87 percent.[56] Most caracolleños made a living from agriculture (1,710 people) or weaving (1,069 people). Although Caracollo's statistics are not exceptional, aside from its dearth of ayllu communities, caracolleños have been unusual in their decision to perform dramatic representations of the past that doubled as history lessons accessible to the illiterate majority.

Located between the cities of La Paz and Oruro, Caracollo was deeply involved in the Civil War of 1899. Despite its proximity to Oruro, which was controlled by President Alonso and served as the highland headquarters for the Conservative Party army, Caracollo was a center of support for the Liberal Party and a strategic location for its forces. Newspapers make constant reference to Zárate Willka's moving his troops back to Caracollo or setting up headquarters in Caracollo.[57] In a letter to his family, a Liberal Party soldier described the warm welcome he and his comrades received on arriving in Caracollo. He recalled that the light that shone from every house was a glowing welcome to the troops. Community members displayed great enthusiasm for the Liberal cause and greeted the army with cries of "Long live the Federation!"[58]

While many of the documents connecting Caracollo to the civil war have disappeared, its residents numbered among the Aymaras detained and questioned in the Peñas trial. One of the most poignant appeals made by the jailed Aymara defendants was authored in part by the Aymaras of Caracollo, who pleaded their innocence and claimed that accusations of their wrongdoing were based on racial bias: "We are being held in this public jail for crimes pronounced against us because of our role as auxiliaries in the recent civil war and because we participated as Indians, dispossessed of all political rights, according to those who seek justice against our race. . . . We ask that you treat us as criminals, even though we have been labeled as such [as a result of] our national service [during the war], and not as public enemies."[59]

The detained Caracollo Aymaras had firsthand experience with the accusations against and racialized images of Aymaras that circulated after the civil war. Their appeal also indicates that they regarded such accusations as unjust. The Inca play performed in Caracollo following the war would address these issues; its emergence represents an initiative to refashion Aymara identities and to shore up local hierarchies under the Liberal Party regime of postwar Bolivia.

Caracollo's Inca Play

During the Virgin of the Rosary festival, held in October, "Incas" dominate the town through the annual three-hour-long theatrical representation of the Inca past. In Caracollo, local inhabitants adopted an Inca heritage. Their Inca play consists of three acts: the first is dedicated to the battle between Moors and Christians in Spain, the Reconquista; the second, to Christopher Columbus's soliloquy of discovery; and the final and longest, to the Spanish conquest of the Inca Empire. By contextualizing the Incas within other great civilizations, conquests, and world histories, the Aymara residents of Caracollo claimed a space within these world events as "Incas," or "civilized Indians," demonstrating their knowledge and authority as historians and actors.

Act 1 concerns the fate of a Christian caught by the Moors during the Reconquista. The captive refuses to convert to Islam and, under the king's orders, is tortured and eventually killed. Prior to his death, the captive prays to the Virgin of the Rosary, asking her to stay with him as he affirms his Christian faith. The captive is killed, and devils are called to take his body; the archangel Saint Michael appears, however, rescuing him and leading him bodily to heaven. The break between act 1 and act 2 is signaled by a sort of human curtain, as all the actors file across the dusty outdoor space in front of the church, encircled by spectators.

Wearing velvet knickers and boots, Christopher Columbus provides his monologue of exploration in the second act. Sounding much like someone delivering a history lesson, Columbus includes many details in his narrative: dates, attempts to secure funding, the names of his ships, the lands he explored, and a reference to the explorer Amerigo Vespucci as the inspiration for naming the new lands "America." Columbus finishes with a rousing "Por Castilla y por León, nuevo mundo halló Colón!" (for Castile and for León, Columbus discovered our new world). The human curtain again indicates a change of acts, and the Incas appear wearing long black capes studded with imitation jewels and white-skinned masks with mustaches and blue eyes.

The Incas are confronted by the Spaniards, led by Francisco Pizarro, who present the Incas with a document. The majority of the act consists of the Incas' attempts to decipher the words, which they are ultimately unable to do. They speak only Quechua, and the Spaniards only Spanish, but the central problem turns on that of literacy rather than on the ability to communicate. The Incas are aggressive in mocking the writing, which they lack even for their own language, while the Spaniards grow impatient with the "savages." Prior to going to war with the Spaniards, the Incas pray to the Virgin of the Rosary, whom they also refer to as "Mother Kollana." The name *Kollana* resonates with several points of reference in Aymara culture: Kollana is an ayllu and a place, south of the city of La Paz; Apu Kollana Awqui is a creator god in Aymara origin stories; and Kollasuyu was the portion of the Inca Empire that encompassed the Aymara kingdoms. The Incas' sudden prayer to Mother Kollana/the Virgin of the Rosary evokes the Christian captive's similar entreaty in act 1. The interchangeability of "Mother Kollana" with the Virgin of the Rosary makes a subtle reference to the Aymara past and connects it to Christianity and national history. The references to the Inca daughters of "Madre Kollana" establish the connection between the Incas and their Aymara ancestors.

The Inca king (identified most often in this play as Manco Kapac) is captured in battle and sentenced to death. He then gives away his most treasured possessions to his subjects and curses the land's silver and gold, burying them deep within the mountains to thwart the Spaniards' attempts to find them. The Spaniards kill the Inca king. Pizarro then returns to Spain to report to this own king. When he presents the Inca king's head to his ruler, the Spanish king admonishes Pizarro, telling him that his orders were not to kill such a powerful monarch. The Spanish king then launches into a historical monologue narrating Pizarro's life and explorations. Ultimately, he decides that Pizarro should suffer the same fate as the now-deceased Inca king and sentences him to death. Interestingly, the Spanish king calls for devils to take away Pizarro's body, just as the "Turkish" king had done in the case of the Christian captive in act 1. This time Saint Michael does not intervene. The finale belongs to the Incas, who lament the death of their king and reaffirm their ethnic and regional identity as Incas of the highland region, or Kollasuyu. The Caracollo Inca play sometimes ends with the resurrection of the Inca king, which I discuss in chapter 4.[60]

Scholars agree that the Caracollo Inca guild originated in the early twentieth century. Montes Camacho's study of twentieth-century Carnival festivals cites 1910 as the date that the first Caracollo Inca theatrical troupe first performed during Carnival in Oruro, thus suggesting that the group existed before then.[61] In her analysis of the contemporary Inca play in Caracollo, Margot Beyersdorff states that the play originated in 1906.[62] Alfredo Rios, a Quechua professor at the Technical University in Oruro who translated part of the Caracollo script from Quechua into Spanish, estimated the play to have originated in the late nineteenth or early twentieth century, basing his assessment on what he described as the unusual and dated style of the Quechua language employed in certain sections.[63] Balmori, in his analysis of the "cycles" of Inca theater throughout the colonial and national epochs of Bolivian history, pointed out that in the late nineteenth and early twentieth centuries, the era of modernization, historical renditions of the national Inca past were written and staged in the Quechua language rather than in Aymara.[64] The decision to perform the play in Quechua in a predominantly Aymara-speaking region is noteworthy, for municipal statistics from 1998 indicate that even at this time, late in the twentieth century, 60 percent of Caracollo's inhabitants spoke both Spanish and Aymara, while only 10 percent spoke Quechua.[65] Caracollo residents who are multilingual tend to learn Aymara before Quechua.[66] The decision to perform the Inca play in Quechua says more about social and political dynamics than about demographics.

Within local communities, obtaining a role in the Inca play is indicative of an elevated social status.[67] As does Itier in his work on Cuzco, Beyersdorff references actors' roles as "keepers of the past" whose legitimacy stems in part from their historical knowledge of the Incas.[68] The contemporary Caracollo Inca play actors confirm that the families who participated in the play during the early twentieth century were local authorities and notable residents, such as the Palaez, Ramirez, Rodriguez, Cazorla, and Bernal families. Documents show that in 1902, shortly after the civil war, the local political authority, or corregidor, was Juan Palaez, and among the other notable residents listed were Daniel Bernal (corregidor in 1905), Ramon and Francisco Rodriguez, and Lisandro Cazorla, which suggests a link between local authority and membership within the theatrical guild.[69] The festival of the Virgin of the Rosary, which Yucra León says began in 1890, emerged with the rise of liberalism. The Inca theatrical troupe was the first group founded as integral to this festival, and it has defined the population of Caracollo.[70] Its members have always led the parade, underscoring their role as the oldest established folkloric group there.

The emphasis Caracollo places on the Inca past is reflected in the broader regional setting within the Department of Oruro. Much of Bolivia's western highlands lay within the Inca Empire, and the nearby city of Oruro appeals to the Inca past as an integral part of its geography, history, and identity. For example, one well-known regional legend recorded by the Oruro scholars Josermo Murillo and Antonio Revollo ties Incan themes to local topography. According to this tale, the land now making up the Department of Oruro was populated by Urus, who worshiped Pachacamaj, or Inti.[71] The Urus were contemporaries of the Aymaras; historically, the boundaries between the two populations have been blurry, as many Urus became Aymara speakers.[72] The devout Urus celebrated Inti's luminous goodness, thus provoking the ire of the demigod Huari, who took on human form and lived among the Urus, calling attention to the poverty of the altiplano agricultural production and pointing out socioeconomic differences dividing them. Huari corrupted the simple Urus, who became selfish, jealous, cruel people, until it was said that an Uru passing by a village on the altiplano would bring bad luck.[73] A ñusta, or Inca princess, finally helped the Urus. Described as white and beautiful, the ñusta talked to the Urus in the lyric language of Quechua, reminding them of their history, their traditions, the greatness of their race, and their protector, Inti. She ordered them to abandon their evil practices, and they complied. Huari, furious, attempted to destroy the Urus. First he sent a serpent, but the ñusta appeared and chopped it in half, and its body became part of the distinctive rock formations on the edge of town. Huari then sent a toad to smash the Urus, but the ñusta again appeared and converted the toad into rock. Then he sent a lizard and a plague of ants, which the ñusta converted into rocks and sand dunes. The Inca princess is thus a highland heroine whose actions in defense of Oruro explain the region's unusual landforms. According to legend, moreover, the ñusta reappeared in 1789, during the colonial period and just before the independence wars; this time she manifested as the Virgin of the Mineshaft, who saves a repentant thief (or, depending on the version of the legend told, a lover named Nina Nina or Chiru-Chiru). Following this appearance, the cult of the Virgin of the Mineshaft crystallized around the image of the holy woman found in the repentant thief's lair, and the Inca ñusta turned Virgin of the Mineshaft became the patroness and protector of the city and surrounding area of Oruro. The immense Carnival festival in Oruro is and has been held in honor of the Virgin of the Mineshaft. This foundational story of the Oruro region, a regional claim of Inca achievement by an Inca heroine in highland Bolivia, thus emphasizes Inca contributions to the town's existence, safety, and development rather than those of the Urus or Aymaras.

The Caracollo Inca play begins with a rather singular and focused opening. Several ñustas set the scene with four stanzas that connect the Aymaras to the Incas and in turn to a positive historical narrative for the region. The opening statement of honor and greeting references "madre Kollana," a deity squarely identified with the Aymara population. This oblique reference to the Aymaras' historical presence in the region then gives way to a different invocation when the ñustas connect Mother Kollana with her beautiful Inca

daughter—"Linda niña su hija inca"—thus establishing the connection between the Aymara population and their Inca descendants and performing a
positive historical narrative of the Indian past that centers on the Incas. Later
in the play, the focus will shift from Mother Kollana and her Inca daughter to
the Virgin of the Rosary. Like the play itself, the festival celebrating la Virgen
del Rosario embodies these multiple historical references and personages. In
Bolivia, such superimposition of identities or multiple references to a festival
patroness are not unusual, but of all known Inca play texts, this is the only
one that opens with a reference to the Aymara past and connects the Aymaras
to the Incas.[74] While the early twentieth-century historical setting establishes
one context for the play, the ñustas' opening lines establish a specific rationale for the performance:

> We will tell the story of each of them
> Because in the memory of the Incas
> Everyone will be pardoned.
> Mother Inca
> We will tell the story of each of them
> To receive the Incas' blessing
> And to live in such positive memories of the past.[75]

These opening lines, meant to establish the play's context and setting, connect the Aymaras to the lauded Incas; the Aymara past, however—or any
pre-Incan past, for that matter—is only vaguely alluded to. "The memory
to be pardoned" that the ñustas mention most likely refers to the negative
perceptions of the Aymara population prevalent during and after the civil
war. In the case of the early twentieth-century theatrical performance in
Caracollo, the local Aymara elite "acted Inca," adopting and disseminating
a preferred Inca identity and past for the town. Reducing the Aymaras' role
to that of the ancestors of the Incas, they focused on the construction of a
progressive Inca narrative and identity in the postwar context.

The Historical Context and Significance of Inca Plays

The masks and uniforms used in Inca plays have generated ongoing debate
regarding the significance of the plays themselves, the identities of the actors, and the intended messages. My own research and that of other scholars
indicates that Inca actors follow a historical tradition in using masks as an
integral part of their uniform. Balmori, who found Bolivian Inca plays to
be excessively long and repetitive, states that the masks were necessary so
that several people could play the same role, for the productions lasted too

long for one actor to perform a role throughout. He also claims that the masks indicate a "primitive mentality and the lack of literary tradition."[76] Taking a different approach, Gisela Cánepa states that masks not only hide an actor's personal identity but also reveal and project another, particular identity.[77] The Incas use white-skinned masks with long mustaches and blue eyes painted on them.[78] But why is the Inca white?

Several aspects of the way in which actors assumed and projected an Inca identity in these plays resonated with early twentieth-century post–civil war liberal discourses of race and identity, shaped in large part by the prevailing eugenic theories of race, modernity, and progress. The actors wore white- or pink-skinned masks with blue eyes and mustaches, thus transforming themselves into phenotypically white Incas. The Inca image, which bore a strong historical association with civilization and progress, translated into a preferred racial difference through the performance of the play. An Aymara actor who put on his white mask at the beginning of the play, covering his brown skin and highland features, embodied the process of civilization that early twentieth-century intellectuals championed as necessary for the successful modernization of the Bolivian nation. The Aymara could evolve into the Inca; he could perform dramatic acts in elite dialects of Quechua; he could be whitened via education and "cultural improvement"; he could contribute to the progress of the nation. His performance of the preferred Inca identity earned him respect on the local level as a historian and dramaturge and resonated on the national level with discourses of progress and civilization.

The debates surrounding the various performances of the Inca plays that center on questions of historical accuracy, casting, and antiquity are conversations over what kind of Indian past would be represented as an essential component of Bolivian history. The purer the Quechua language employed, the older the text, the fewer interventions in Spanish or additions by later directors, and the greater the tendency to identify a given play as a superior and authentic Inca play in Bolivia. These ostensibly purer plays are the ones that authors such as Balmori, Lara, and Gómez-Acebo view as being an original American theater that highlights a unique and cultured performance of Bolivia's past. Having identified the old style of the Quechua language's elite performative register in the texts of Chayanta, Santa Lucia, and San Pedro de Buena Vista, Lara insists that the Chayanta play *Tragedia del fin de Atawallpa* (1871) is of the greatest literary value for its pure Quechua, which best reflects the perspective of indigenous people.[79] He discredits many Inca play scripts as "deformed" by the literary additions of later, often non-Indian authors. In reference to the Inca play from San Pedro de Buena Vista, Potosí, in which the main protagonist is not Atahuallpa but Huayna Kapac, an individual related to Tupac Amaru and Tupac Katari, Lara states: "It is obvious that parts of the play are recent additions, most likely added by some local provincial authority at a later date . . . [who,] motivated by some sort of enthusiasm, falls into representations of historical inaccuracy."[80] A play's "authenticity" is thus defined by its language and its protagonists rather than by adherence to the Spaniards' versions of conquest, as Lara himself notes.[81] An "authentic" play, however, also must resonate with its regional context and the historical setting. In Bolivia, regional debates over authenticity generally seek to define the relation between the Indian base and the history of the Bolivian nation.

Inca plays have certainly emphasized different stories. In his study of Inca theater, Balmori identifies three distinct cycles of Inca theater: one cycle highlights the protagonist Manco Kapac, another cycle features Huayna Kapac, and the twentieth-century cycle centers on the figure of Atahuallpa.[82] In the Santa Lucia script, for example, Huascar, the enemy of Atahuallpa and historical leader of the opposing faction in the Inca civil war, is cast as a supportive relative of Atahuallpa who approaches the Spaniards to find out what they want from the Inca king. Malgorzata Oleszkiewicz, in her article "El ciclo de la muerte de Atahuallpa," recognizes the variation among regional representations of the Inca past as responses to local circumstances rather than historical inaccuracies.[83] Lara, despite his pejorative description of "historically inaccurate" Inca plays, admits that the historical context in which a play was produced influenced its contents, characters, and language of expression. The Chayanta play from 1871 casts Atahuallpa as the protagonist and hero. Lara and the Peruvian Quechua specialist César Guardia Mayorga identify the language of the play as Cuzco-based Quechua but suspect that the piece might have been written first in the regional Quechua dialect of Chinchaysuyu, or Ecuador, and later transcribed into the Cuzco Quechua dialect. This hypothesis is based on the play's historical narrative, which includes a favorable representation of Atahuallpa.[84] The Cuzco region supported Huascar in his political and military struggle against his half-brother Atahuallpa, who was headquartered in Ecuador. The choice of protagonists and the historical context greatly affected the scripts' narratives. The variations are not simply inaccurate representations of history but instead reflect the regional, social, and political contexts that conditioned these portrayals of the Inca past. Both Lara and Mayorga not only comment on the transfor-

Incas and Spaniards are complex, complicating allegiances and often blurring the divide between the two groups. Francisco Pizarro, who confesses to a long-standing aversion to women but claims a great and enduring love for his country, or *patria*, falls in love with the Inca ñusta Munai-Ttica, who loves and admires him as belonging to a "superior race." Pizarro at last finds a specific object for his abstract love of patria, connecting the centrality of the Inca Empire to definitions of place and identity.[89] Pizarro's admiration of Munai-Ttica reflects the broader Spanish appreciation for and marvel at the achievements of the Inca Empire. Atahuallpa, labeled in the cast list as "Inca usurpador," is ultimately condemned to death by the Spaniards for seizing power over the Inca Empire from its rightful leader, Huascar. In this play, the Incas are articulate, attractive, and bright. Atahuallpa is condemned because of political conflict and the coup that brought him to power. Atahuallpa's political ambition, not his inability to read or communicate, causes his downfall.

In another early Inca play, the Inca is central to arguments for independence. The *Diálogo entre Atawallpa y Fernando VII en los Campos Elíseos*, a conversation between Atahuallpa and Spain's Ferdinand VII attributed to the proindependence lawyer Bernardo Monteagudo, circulated among readers and audiences in 1809. The *Diálogo* reached a broad audience, for the text was also performed as a play.[90] Atahuallpa, the last sovereign king of the Inca Empire, was selected as the spokesperson for independence. Language is not an issue; this Atahuallpa speaks eloquent Spanish, and he convinces King Ferdinand VII that his colonial subjects in Latin America have every right to fight for their independence. In his study of the *Diálogo*, Carlos Casteñon Barrientos suggests that Monteagudo chose to put on an "Inca mask" to make his arguments for independence for two main reasons. First, he argues, perceptions of the conquest in 1809, 276 years after the death of Atahuallpa, had changed from those of earlier days. Monteagudo interprets Atahuallpa as a victim of Spanish barbarism and invasion, which resonated with Ferdinand VII's own situation following Napoléon's recent takeover of Spain. Second, Casteñon Barrientos suggests, Monteagudo selected Atahuallpa to subtly remind Creole and mestizo populations of the importance of including the indigenous population in the independence movement.[91] This play also conveyed the promise of change; independence suggested and communicated a sense of the "progress and potential" of the Indian population. In the play, the Spanish king and the Indian king treat each other as equals; ultimately, Atahuallpa's logic will prevail, not that of Ferdinand VII. Could independence usher in a new social order? The Inca image was recast in the early nineteenth century as the voice, the image, and the promise of social change associated with independence.

Another Inca play, this one from the late nineteenth century, focuses on the inability to communicate verbally. In the Inca play script from Chayanta, which Lara claims to date from 1871, the Incas and the Spaniards cannot communicate at all. In a scene where the Spaniards try to talk to the Incas, the author provides only stage direction, no lines: "He only moved his lips."[92] Any communication between Incas and Spaniards in the Chayanta Inca play takes place through the efforts of Felipillo, who translates everything into Quechua; no Spanish dialogue is provided, and Felipillo never translates from Quechua into Spanish. Definitions of civilization as governed by education and literacy do not dominate this play, however; the problems center on the more basic question of language difference, not literacy.

In the early twentieth-century Caracollo Inca play the central issue is literacy. The play depicts the Incas as the astute and perceptive administrators of a great empire. They are not bewildered, intimidated, or scared by the arrival of the Spaniards. The majority of the third act focuses on the Incas' attempts to comprehend a "letter" that the Spaniards present. This letter passes through the hands of all the Incas, each of whom attempts to understand its significance. Efforts to describe the marks on the paper serve as an opportunity for the comic relief that dominates this act of the play. The Incas neither exhibit fear nor marvel, since they repeatedly ridicule the Spaniards and the document. Thus on receiving the document, the Inca king mocks his visitors: "Ay, bearded warrior with your long neck and bulging eyes, what road did you take to get lost here . . . ? What is that white thing you are carrying? Give it to me, I will receive it. . . . Oh, what is this that I cannot understand? Looking at it from this side, it looks like the footprints of my dog, from this other side it looks like the eyes of my princesses; if I look directly at it, it looks like the beards of this warrior [the Spaniard], with his beard all encrusted." Similarly, when Primo Inca takes the letter, he states: "What is this letter? I cannot understand it. From this side, it looks like a rooster's tracks, but if I look at it from this other side it does not look like a road, it does not look like a river, it does not look like a mountain." The Inca king then turns to Waylla Wisa, his advisor, and tells him to take the letter back to the Spaniards and to demand an explanation: "Tell them, and pull the ears of these bearded men, that they need to make you understand this letter, and if they will not, then hit them with the end of your honda [sling]."[93]

As the play progresses, the Spanish explorer Diego de Almagro grows impatient with the Incas' incomprehension and with the multiple attempts to make sense of the letter: "Listen, barbarous one, do you not know that this is an important document sent to you from my illustrious king of Spain . . . ? I will tell my great General Pizarro that these savage men do not want to obey me." Waylla Wisa responds to Almagro by asking, "What are you saying to me? That you want my woman? Go see if she understands you then."[94] The fluidity of insults that mark this Inca play minimizes the role of linguistic incomprehension, keeping the focus on the question of literacy.[95] Pizarro decides to use force after hearing Almagro's report: "Very well! I can be very forceful with these people, and I will let these savages know the wrong they are doing in refusing to comply with my orders."[96]

The moment when the priest Hernando de Luque extends a Bible to the Inca king does not happen until after each Inca has attempted to decipher the letter. Luque's presentation of the Bible does not involve the same concern as the letter did. Pizarro's response to the Inca king's incomprehension of the Bible mirrors his earlier response to the Indians' inability to read the letter. In short, the issue of literacy dominates this Inca play. If this historical representation justifies Spanish conquest in any way, it does so based on the Incas' illiteracy. The theme of this fatal flaw as causing the death of the Inca king resonated with and reflected early twentieth-century ideas of modernity, progress, and eugenics. It also reflects early twentieth-century Bolivia's citizenship requirements, which among other things limited voting rights to the literate.

In 1905 Alcides Arguedas published the story *Wuata Wuara*, which embodied the debate over Indians, education, and literacy that dominated liberal intellectuals' conversations. Arguedas, who had been a journalist during the Civil War of 1899 and had witnessed many of the conflicts of the time, was familiar with the landowners' treatment of the Aymaras. His vocal disapproval of liberal landowners' abusive and discriminatory practices earned him criticism from the liberal elite, and *Wuata Wuara* was quickly censored and pulled from circulation. Fifteen years later, however, the novel reemerged as the basis for Arguedas's better-known novel *Raza de bronce*.[97] The story of *Wuata Wuara* sends a critical message to the landowners and to the Liberal Party government concerning the exploitation of indigenous people, but there is another central argument concerning education and Indians. Choquehuanka, an aged Aymara cacique figure who is thought to have curative powers and who plays a father role to the lovely Aymara girl Wuata Wuara, is literate. In this sense, he stands in two worlds, for his ability to read allows him convey ideas to the hacienda workers "that the townspeople [have] never heard of, . . . things that were better dreamed but not known."[98] Yet Manuel Garcia, a young patrón who exploits the Indians, tells another landlord and the town priest that Choquehuanka helps him maintain order on his hacienda. The priest responds vehemently to Garcia: "You are tricked by Choquehuanka. He is an old hypocrite who acts submissively and respectfully in front of white people, but among his own he foments rebellion." Choquehuanka thus embodies the debate over education. Would educated Indians better serve the Creole elite? Would they become a danger to Creole privilege? Would they assimilate the ideas of dominant Creole society, or would they resist them? Would it be better to keep Indians ignorant or to educate them to serve as a skilled labor pool?[99]

As the story unfolds, it becomes clear that the patrón has recently abused some of his peons severely, ultimately causing their deaths. One of the murdered peons is the truly good, if simple, Aymara Indian female protagonist, Wuata Wuara, whom the patrón and his friends rape and kill. Choquehuanka, infuriated, assembles all the Aymaras who work on the hacienda and encourages them to seek revenge. The workers then kill the patrón and his friends. Two clear messages emerge from the story. First, the landowning elite constantly abuse the Indians who work and live on their haciendas. Arguedas dispels the Liberal Party myth that only Conservatives abused the indigenous population by depicting the other side's equally violent treatment of the hacienda workers. Choquehuanka refers to the lack of real change following the transfer of power from the Conservative Party to the Liberal Party: "Some rise, some fall. That is how things go. The wheel goes around producing these changes, but it seems that some never rise, that they are destined to always remain at the bottom."[100] Significantly, Arguedas does not use the stereotype of the savage Aymaras but rather presents the Aymaras' actions as a justified response to landowners' great abuses. In this sense, Arguedas's story is as much a critique of the Liberal Party as it is a defense of the Aymara population.

Nonetheless, Arguedas does use the figure of Choquehuanka to suggest that educated, literate Aymaras could be useful to the landowning elite. In fact, Choquehuanka's patrón says that he depends on the aged Aymara to maintain order and to see that work gets done on the estate. The patrón abuses his indigenous laborers, however, killing two of them (including Choquehuanka's protégé, Wuata Wuara) and committing scores of minor offenses, which provokes the Aymara workers to rebel. In the end, it is Choquehuanka who instigates the vengeance-fuelled rebellion. This scenario suggests that even educated Aymaras would present a constant latent threat to Bolivian society and therefore should be kept far from the nation's cities.

The story further suggests that after the civil war, the Aymaras had become more resistant to demands placed on them. In one instance, the priest is drinking with the patrón and laments the new epoch of Liberal Party rule, which for him is characterized by a lack of respect for the clergy on the part of both the Aymaras and the patrón.[101] In addition to directly referencing the Civil War of 1899, this suggests that the Aymaras were actively resisting oppression and the servile position in which the Church and landowners attempted to hold them. Arguedas's position thus resembles that of the liberal intellectual and scholar Manuel Rigoberto Paredes; both recognized the injustices the Aymaras suffered at the hands of landowners on either side of the Liberal/Conservative divide, but both feared the violence they thought the Aymaras were likely to commit in response. Arguedas, then, did not favor universal education, as did Georges Rouma, for he feared the latent danger the Aymaras presented. The directors and actors of the Caracollo Inca play, however, disagreed with Arguedas. Their reenactment of the Inca Empire's downfall depicts illiteracy as the Incas' fatal flaw in failing to negotiate with a small and outnumbered group of Spaniards and thus emphasizes the importance of literacy and education. Similar to Choquehuanka, the participants in this Inca theater production strove to define themselves through education and their roles as keepers of the past.

In the early twentieth century, national voting restrictions made literacy essential to any substantive reconsideration of the Indian as citizen.[102] The Incas may have been the leaders of a great empire and have served as an early twentieth-century ideal, but they could not manipulate the tools necessary for modernity, namely, reading and writing. Performances of the Inca past ennobled national history and connected local communities to broader national discourses. But even an "Inca" had to be literate to vote in early twentieth-century Bolivia.

The Caracollo Inca play confirms the importance of the Inca Empire in the scene where the Spanish king learns that Pizarro has killed the Inca ruler: "Oh, General Francisco Pizarro, what are you telling me? I did not tell you to kill an important king in the New World[;] . . . you have destroyed a king who was more powerful than I am."[103] The Spanish king sentences Pizarro to death for his abuses committed in the New World, thus confirming the importance and the legitimacy of the Inca Empire even in the eyes of the monarch who intended to conquer it. The king does not justify Pizarro's actions in the name of progress; rather, he laments the death of the Inca king, who was more powerful and important than the king of Spain. His negative response to Pizarro's actions mirrored the goals of liberal politicians and intellectuals who sought to "civilize" their Indian populations in the early twentieth century rather than to eradicate them. Bolivian intellectuals' designs of modernization and progress centered on the idea of "regenerating" their nation's indigenous inhabitants (and thus Bolivia itself) rather than exterminating them. The discrepancy between the monarch's orders and Pizarro's actions mirrored the problem between the central government and local representatives and actors. As suggested in the story of *Wuata Wuara*, legislation passed under Liberal Party rule sought to improve the Indians' condition and end the servitude exacted by priests and officials, as well as— at least in theory—to curb landowners' casual abuses of indigenous workers. In seeking to implement any educational reforms, the Liberal Party regime's officials had to face not only Indian illiteracy but also landlords' resistance to new programs, such as that of the maestro ambulate, in which teachers traveled to communities and haciendas to educate the indigenous workers and inhabitants.

In the early twentieth century, the Caracollo Inca play underscored the elevated status, glory, and legitimacy of the Inca Empire and actors who memorialized it, yet it also represented the limits of the Incas' status, which was conditioned by their illiteracy. In electing to represent the arrival of the Spaniards and the end of the sovereign Inca Empire, the early twentieth-century actors who created this play highlighted the intimate connection between the written word, conquest, citizenship, and the elaboration of historical narratives. Performing their learned status and garnering immediate regional recognition as literate historians and theatrical actors, the performers shored up their positions in local social hierarchies by representing an Inca past for the historically Aymara-populated region of Caracollo. Drawing from a universally recognized historical event—that of the great Inca Empire and the arrival of the Spaniards—the local elite of Caracollo presented their own version of this well-known event, one that responded to the early twentieth-century historical context.

It was hard to be Aymara in early twentieth-century Bolivia. Aymara merchants suffered insults, and the general public feared the image, popularized in the newspapers, of the savage and bloodthirsty highland Indian. Journalists further denigrated the Aymaras by contrasting their lamentable state to that of the lauded Inca Empire. Liberal intellectuals developed the idea of the progressive Inca Indian and promoted the Inca as emblematic of Bolivia's past. Cultural constructions of an Inca identity, however, did not remain solely in the hands of the press or intellectuals. Capitalizing on the intellectual current that glorified the Incas, the provincial Aymara elite forged their own images of the socially acceptable Bolivian Indians, "Incas," who were the heirs of the tradition of noble indigenous rule in Peru and "whitened" personages in the Bolivian context. Through theater, the Aymara elite constructed and performed their Inca identity, popularized through dramatic representations of the meeting between Incas and Spaniards during the early days of conquest. The performances of the Inca play in Caracollo began in the early twentieth century, and they were very much a product of the postwar nation-building process. Despite the fact that the town of Caracollo has historically had a majority Aymara population, the Aymara past prior to Inca rule is rendered marginal in the theatrical performance there. The emergence of the Inca play in Caracollo following the civil war constitutes an initiative by the local elite to recast their Aymara identity as Inca, the more acceptable "Indian" identity under Liberal Party rule, and to shore up local social hierarchies. Inca theater was not a manifestation of Indian resistance to the state but rather a vehicle through which national belonging could be negotiated.

Through their roles as local historians and actors, Inca theater performers silenced historical narratives of the "savage" Aymara population and distinguished themselves from the image of the "barbarous" Aymara popularized in the wake of the civil war. By claiming an Inca past for Caracollo, the actors separated themselves from these negative associations, representing themselves instead as "literate Incas" and as theatrical directors and actors who dominated and negotiated central historical narratives. This was especially relevant in a country in which citizenship was defined in large part via literacy. The actors in the Caracolla play highlighted the Inca population and the Spanish Conquest, which the play depicts only after an act concerning the Christian reconquest of Moorish Spain. This sets the Spanish Conquest and the history of the Andes in a canon of universal events, increasing the visibility and prestige of Andean history to a repertoire of great world events. As the actors highlight the importance of the Spanish Conquest, other conquests are silenced. The representation of the Inca past by Aymara actors subtly suggests the ability of indigenous peoples to modernize and progress. This favorable narrative of evolution, civilization, and progress took precedence over emphasizing the Incas' takeover of the Aymara population.

The Inca play underscored the end of sovereign indigenous rule while emphasizing the majority indigenous population in Bolivia. Creating difference between themselves as Inca theater actors and town historians and the rest of the "Indians," the Aymara elite highlighted both the historical and the contemporary role of illiteracy in limiting the Indians' potential. Through their performance, these actors embodied the goals of the ideal, modern Indian for the Bolivian nation: such an individual would be educated, learned, and white. Urban intellectuals and the rural Aymara elite took up the powerful Inca images in response to the actual historical context. The Inca past distinguished Bolivia's history by simultaneously marginalizing the actual Aymaras while underscoring the progressive potential of Bolivia's majority indigenous population after the Civil War of 1899.

In the early twentieth century, liberal intellectuals sought ways to distinguish what it meant to be Bolivian. They turned to the noble pre-Columbian past, even though being "Indian" designated a state of marginality within the nation.[104] Popular theatrical performances, such as those of the Inca play, offered the ideal space for the local Caracollo elite to negotiate and shape Indian identities within the liberal nation-building project. Paradoxically, preferred constructions of Indian identities marginalized the undesirable actual Indian population, but the boundaries of national belonging were established through discourses and constructions of preferential "Indian" identities.

4 NEW STAGES IN DEFINING INDIAN IDENTITY
The Ethnic Politics of Caracollo's Contemporary Inca Play

Elite residents of Caracollo acted Inca in the early twentieth century to seek resonance within the liberal nation-building project and to avoid the stigma of being Aymara; in the late twentieth and early twenty-first centuries, however, folkloric performers have created new images of highland Indian identity. The Inca theater group still performs in the Fiesta del Rosario in contemporary Caracollo, but its current actors' own memories and tradition inform the historical and contemporary significance of performing the Inca play. Where the documentary trail falters in the relatively unwritten history of Caracollo, the actors' memories and understandings help inform a historical narrative. This dialogue between written and remembered history, textual analysis and historical context, connects local performance to national history. The contemporary Caracollo Inca theater actors not only enact historical theater but are historical agents in their own rights. Given the changes this Inca group has experienced, their memories and interpretations of the past can help us understand the significance of "acting Inca."

The memories in question speak to historical images of cultural, political, and regional legitimacy now hotly contested in Bolivia. By focusing on both past and present manifestations of the Inca play, we can see the changes and challenges in this process, in which alternative and preferred symbols of Aymara identity have emerged as more "authentic" representations of highland indigenous culture and Bolivian national identity. The increasingly numerous folkloric groups in festival parades that represent aspects of high-land Aymara life reflect changes within national politics that emerged from the leadership of La Paz-based Aymara organizations in the last third of the twentieth century, entities such as CONAMAQ (El Consejo Nacional de Ayllus y Markas de Qollasuyu, or the National Council of Indigenous Communities and Towns of Kollasuyu, 1997 to present) and Taller de Historia Oral Andina (THOA, or the Andean Workshop of Oral History, 1984 to present), which seek to recover an Aymara past that has been marginalized by the Bolivian state. These organizations have sponsored research projects to document the Aymara past and popularized Aymara heroes via radio broadcasts in Aymara and Spanish that reached a broad listening audience. Political parties such as the MITKA (Movimiento Indígena Tupac Katari, 1978 to present) and MRTKA (Movimiento Revolucionario Tupac Katari, 1978 to present) named themselves after a famous Aymara leader of the 1780s and developed political platforms that reached out to the Aymara voting population.

Although the more recent "authentic" folkloric representations of Aymara life now challenge Inca theater actors' popularity, as do the previously mentioned organizations, these new groups constitute a twenty-first-century manifestation of the process of constructing and defining "preferred" Indian identities, of which the Inca play in Caracollo is an early example. Whereas Incas were important to the national narrative in 1900, today's political and cultural movements in highland Bolivia are intent on recovering and promoting the Aymaras.

The contemporary ethnographic accounts I present in this chapter also speak to questions of "authenticity" and popularity in folkloric parades during the festival of the Virgin of the Rosary in Caracollo as well as activities in nearby Oruro during that city's much larger and world-renowned Carnival celebration. The close of the early twentieth-century tin boom left the Department of Oruro, which comprises Caracollo, struggling economically. The city of Oruro is that department's main urban center. Much of contemporary Oruro is characterized by poverty, unemployment, environmental devastation resulting from mining operations, and depopulation caused by the collapse of the mining industry, which led many residents to migrate to Bolivia's larger cities. The United Nations Educational, Scientific, and Cultural Organization's (UNESCO) interest in Oruro's Carnival celebration, however, has generated renewed economic and cultural interest within the region. Carnival there includes a weeklong program of activities taking place in February or March (directly before Lent) and honoring the Virgin of the Mineshaft; the highlight of the festivities is a forty-eight-hour parade with dancers dressed mainly as Indians interspersed with devils and Afro-Bolivians. In 2001 UNESCO bestowed the prestigious title of Masterpiece of the Oral and Intangible Heritage of Humanity on Oruro's Carnival celebration. Bolivian and international tourists flock to watch or participate in the parade, filling Oruro's hotels, which stand mostly vacant the rest of the year. The physical and economic potential of Oruro's Carnival coupled with its widespread fame have led politicians to frequent the celebration and emphasize the role of Carnival in demonstrating Bolivian national unity. Former president Gonzalo Sánchez de Lozada declared himself a devout follower of the Virgin of the Mineshaft in 1994, and he attributed his presidency to her benevolence.[1] Edgar Bazán, a former mayor of Oruro, made similar statements regarding the inclusive nature of Carnival and its ability to unify Bolivia's diverse population, and in 1994 ambassadors from the United States, Japan, and Paraguay enthusiastically agreed.[2]

Oruro's departmental authorities, then, are responsible for hosting the largest parade in Bolivia, one that defines "acceptable" Indian identities in Bolivia, present and past, real or invented, so that the department negotiates its importance to the nation through the performances comprised within that event. Although few Indian communities in Bolivia are invited to participate in the main two-day Carnival parade, the middle- and upper-class participants disguise themselves as Indians.[3] Bolivian authorities use the parade to address their perennial "Indian problem" via a careful presentation of preferred Indian identities rather than through a denial of their majority indigenous population. In both the Oruro Carnival celebration and the Fiesta del Rosario in Caracollo, festival performance is central to constructions of social hierarchy and definitions of acceptable Indian identities; it serves to connect regional folkloric manifestation to broader political discourses within the Bolivian nation.

Carnival in Oruro

The composition of Oruro's Carnival parade has changed significantly over the course of the twentieth century. Beginning in the 1980s, more and more members of the upper class have participated enthusiastically in the formerly disdained plebeian street festival. Students take part in many of the new dance groups and alter, to differing degrees, the costumes, dances, and music to suit their tastes. Various universities have become nationally famous for their dance guilds.[4] While the university student population makes up the majority of these new "indigenous" folkloric dance groups, wealthy merchants constitute a significant part of the others. The Oruro-based dance guild Morenada Cocanis, which is well known and respected throughout Bolivia, has traditionally been composed of coca merchants.

Participation in Oruro's Carnival celebrations is limited by social as well as economic factors, and the culture represented in the parade is based on invented and idealized representations of indigenous peoples. While the government now subsidizes the event, other factors limit who can participate in the dance groups. For example, individuals must pay fees to join a dance group. These costs can range from a few bolivianos to more than a thousand (some two hundred dollars) for each performer, who also has to pay for an elaborate costume. These expenses make participation nearly impossible for workers and peasants, limiting membership to those of a higher socioeconomic status.

In the 1980s, new, highly popular dance groups began to perform in Oruro's Carnival festivities, seeking to present "authentic" indigenous traditions in order to more "accurately" depict highland Indian life. In part, this putative authenticity meant drawing on highland culture in the new dance groups' stylized representations of Indian customs. One ensemble, for example, comprises former town notables, or *vecinos*, from the province of Bolívar; these rural-to-urban migrants, who work as truck drivers and petty merchants, perform their own representations of Indian culture in the dance group Tinkus. The tinku dance contains a repeated accentuated "stooping lunge" movement thought to be characteristically "Indian," and the dance itself aims to represent an indigenous ritual battle from Norte Potosí. Members of the group visit the countryside to obtain information to help in fashioning the tinku dancers' costumes. The authenticity goes only so far, however; the outfits are "improved" for urban tastes.[5] The costume colors are brighter, the skirts often are shorter, and lipstick and rouge complement the fluffed bangs and braid extensions of most of the female dancers.

Victor Amoroso, the director of a group from the Universidad Privada del Altiplano that dances the tarqueada, confirmed that his particular group stylized the dance to render it "less monotonous" and more modern. The dance is accompanied by the t'arqa, a wooden musical wind instrument used in the agricultural rituals associated with Carnival.[6] He also stated that the students in his group chose to dance the tarqueada as a way of identifying with the indigenous cultures of Bolivia. Amoroso viewed this identification as necessary, since the group consists mostly of medical students who will sometimes work in the countryside and need to familiarize themselves with rural culture.[7] What Amoroso and the students presented, however, was so altered from the source and stylized that they might well have trouble recognizing the original rural dance during their medical forays into Bolivia's hinterlands.

In an effort to address the question of authenticity, some new dance groups have insisted on researching performance and culture and incorporating highland rural people into their organizations, thus relaxing the prohibitive obstacles to participation; Ayllu Sartañani, made up mainly of migrants from the Carangas region of Oruro, exemplifies this approach.[8] While such initiatives provide additional ethnographic information and heighten claims to authenticity, Ayllu Sartañani is not immune to stylizing certain elements of the performance to satisfy urban audience expectations. For example, they use neon colors in costumes rather than the more somber dark reds and browns characteristic of rural highland indigenous dress.

These developments and preferences in folkloric presentation reflect an avid interest in "improving" Oruro's Carnival celebration following UNESCO's interest in and commendation of the event. But they also respond to a growing interest in highland indigenous cultures, which reflects the increasing influence of indigenous-based political parties and the revisionist Indian historical narratives that privilege the highlands. In the late twentieth and early twenty-first centuries, dance groups have reclaimed highland identity, centering mainly on Aymara heritage. The performers moved away from the exemplary Inca Indian to Aymara highland indigenous life. This trend toward the highlands and Aymara culture permeates areas beyond Carnival in Oruro. For example, in 2001 the province of Atahuallpa, in the Department of Oruro, applied to change the name of the region to "Sabaya." The regional representative stated that this western part of the department had its "own" regional heroes, such as Don Pedro Marín Capurata Cóndor Villca, a leader of the region during the colonial era who was also known as "Mallku Sabaya." Moreover, that part of the department is home to a mountain named "Sabaya," so that renaming the province would honor it, too. The representative argued that the people living there were of Aymara origin, not Quechua, and that they did not want their province to be named for an Inca leader. In renaming the province, then, the population wished in part to highlight cultural aspects of their Aymara heritage.[9]

The importance of Oruro's Carnival celebration has affected the entire region. In the provinces, festival participants increasingly elect to join the more fashionable dance groups, such as the Llamerada (which performs the llama herder dance) and the Tinkus. With Aymara folklore becoming a viable channel through which individuals in the Department of Oruro can gain status and recognition, the more traditional dance groups, such as the Incas, have suffered. Today, national attention is directed more to the stylized folkloric presentations of Aymara life than to the Inca past.

Caracollo, only forty-five minutes from the city of Oruro, has also felt the effects of these new dance groups. One of the Caracollo Inca play actors, Juan Flores, highly aware of the growing prestige and attractiveness of the non-Inca dance groups, tries to maintain dual participation in both the Inca dance guild and the Morenada. An ambitious bar owner in Caracollo and a renowned tailor in Oruro with a store in that city, Juan has made sure that all his twelve children will receive professional training beyond the high school degree. A Caracollo native, Juan in many ways reflects the regional elites' early twentieth-century concept of a preferred Inca identity; he participates in the core decision-making group of the Inca guild, but during Carnival he is torn between dancing in the Morenada or acting with the Incas.[10] His eyes constantly open to opportunity, Juan is aware that participation in the Morenada is currently an often equally effective channel for consolidating local power. With Inca groups losing popularity in contemporary folkloric presentations, they and scholars interested in them have reached out to the Caracollo Inca guild or attempted to appropriate the Inca image for contemporary folkloric and political platforms, as I will discuss in the following two sections. The Inca image and Inca history are being reinvented, both by urban Oruro presenters of folklore who seek to make the Inca dance group more competitive in parades and by scholars who write the figure of the Inca king into a corpus of neocolonial resistance literature.

Sexy Ñustas and Winsome Inca Kings: Facing Competition in Contemporary Folkloric Presentations

The Caracollo Inca actors, with their stately but dated long black capes and muted dance steps, struggle to compete in the folkloric scene. Firm believers in the historical significance of the Incas, many Caracollo Inca guild members do not wish to dramatically alter their presentation to match current urban tastes. Their Oruro counterparts, however, the Inca dance group called Incas Hijos del Sol, are trying to compete in the Oruro Carnival celebration. Ironically, the Oruro Incas have sought to do so by including the Caracollo Incas within their ranks—but also on their terms.

Just as Caracollo lies close to but beyond the city of Oruro both physically and socially, the urban Oruro Inca dancers currently stand on the periphery of the city's Carnival parade. Unable to attract the desirable student population as members, they depend on a lower-middle-class working population, often second- or third-generation residents, to round out their ranks.

In addition, the Incas Hijos del Sol dramatically changed their costumes, re-sorting to colorful, synthetic cloth outfits with rising hemlines. Despite these changes, the Incas have lost much of their prestige in the Carnival parade. The historical significance of the Incas as one of the event's oldest dance guilds, with the privilege not only of dancing on the first day of the Oruro Carnival parade but also of being among the first groups to enter, is lost on most of the spectators, who eagerly await the larger dance troupes: the Lla-merada, Phujllay, and the Tinkus. Paralleling the Incas' decline in popularity in the parade, the Oruro Inca dancers' traditional theatrical presentation of the conquest, performed on the Monday during Carnival, is also disappear-ing. Today the Oruro Inca troupe lacks actors to fill the roles, and the play draws little attention from the audience. The Oruro Inca actors' outdoor pre-sentation, rendered nearly inaudible by spectator noise and passing bands, has been reduced from four hours to the current half-hour. The performers suffer taunts, jeers, and exploding water balloons from audience members, many of whom find the Quechua used in the production unintelligible, un-interesting, or embarrassing.

The president and other core members lament the state of the Oruro Inca group and are eager to draw new members from other areas, including Caracollo. The Oruro Inca dancers may sometimes refer to the Caracollo Incas as their poor, provincial cousins, but they also respect these actors for their representation of the conquest and desire their participation to increase the Incas' presence in Oruro's Carnival events. In a definite state of need, but also with a degree of arrogance, the Oruro Incas visited the Caracollo Incas in January 2002 to somewhat conditionally invite them to perform during Carnival in Oruro. The core representatives of the Caracollo committee faced their counterparts within the Oruro Inca dancers, and the negotiations be-gan. Untrusting from the beginning, the Caracollo Inca actors managed to slip out with the Oruro guild's documents of past performances and mem-bership lists, which they photocopied.

The Oruro Inca dancers invited the Caracollo Inca actors to dance with them and enact their play on the condition that the Caracollo Incas wear brighter, more "appealing" costumes (see fig. 12). In exchange for their participation, they would receive the prestige of having danced in Oruro's Carnival parade. In addition, the Oruro troupe offered to send a delegation to round out the Caracollo group's ranks during their town's festival hon-oring the Virgin of the Rosary, held in October. Yet the Caracollo Incas re-jected the offer. Extremely proud of their long black capes with detailed embroidery and inlaid glass stones, they made a counteroffer (see fig. 13).

▲ FIGURE 12.
Oruro Inca king's costume.
Photo by the author, 2001

◀ FIGURE 13.
Caracollo Inca costume worn
during the Fiesta del Rosario in
Caracollo. Photo by the author,
2001

They would dance, but only in their traditional costumes. The conversation deteriorated as the somewhat impatient Oruro Inca dancers flatly told the Caracollo Inca actors to burn their old clothes and adopt more contemporary fashion. Indeed, the Caracollo Inca actors were the only group still wearing black capes and skirts inlaid with glass stones and coins in their presentation. Nonetheless, despite their real interest in participating at Oruro, they hesitated to accept any invitation and retorted that the Oruro Incas looked like cross-dressers in their "contemporary" Inca outfits.

It was evident that the Caracollo Inca actors despised the superior attitude of the Oruro Inca dancers, which partly explains why they neglected all social niceties, omitting the standard offer of a soft drink. The Oruro group, however, had made and brought an alcoholic beverage to share.

Although the Caracollo Incas recognized their dwindling popularity, they refused to join the Oruro Incas if it meant giving up their distinctive style, because they still commanded more respect than did the Incas of Oruro. They were recognized for their value as popular historians. After all, the Oruro Incas had sought them out to provide a historical interpretation of the past during the largest festival in Bolivia. In Caracollo, the Inca image still constructs and regulates social dynamics and power at the local level. In the Carnival festivities of Oruro, performers gained recognition as dancers; in Caracollo, the Inca actors still gained recognition as historians who could narrate the nation's past. There have been many changes in the town's Inca play from its early twentieth-century inception to its contemporary presentations, yet casting decisions and the play's overriding theme of literacy continue to respond to its historical origins and shore up the Inca actors' social prestige as local literati.

Contemporary Caracollo Inca Actors

I worked with the Caracollo Inca actors in 2000–2002 and observed performances of the play in 2010, which acquainted me both with the play's hundred-year-old performance tradition and with more recent changes in the guild's membership. Three actors in particular represent recent transformations. Luis (Lucho) Montaño is not a Caracollo native, or *originario*. Born in the rural valley town of Tarata, Montaño and his mother left to find work after his father had abandoned the family. They settled in Caracollo when Montaño was a young adolescent. Growing up, he looked for ways to incorporate himself into the community in order to climb the ladder of social hierarchy and gain a local position of prominence. That meant waiting for an opening in the oldest and most established dance group, made up of prominent families in

Caracollo, the Inca actors. In the late 1970s, Montaño was able to become an Inca performer, beginning simply as a dancer and continuing until he gained a role as an actor in the performance of the conquest itself.[11]

When rehearsals started in 2000, Montaño held the moderately prestigious role of "Rey Turco" in the first act, which deals with conflicts between Moors and Christians in Spain. When I arranged for the Inca troupe to perform in La Paz at the Museum of Ethnography and Folklore's annual conference, however, Montaño seized the chance to promote himself to the role of Diego de Almagro.[12] Montaño included a pair of glasses as part of his attire for the role. Unlike the individuals playing Spanish soldiers, who wore sunglasses, Montaño used spectacles, meant to lend a cultured, educated, and sophisticated air to the figure of Diego de Almagro, and perhaps also to Montaño himself in his identity as president of the Inca theatrical guild in 2000. In fact, Montaño suggested as much in an exchange following the performance in La Paz. He had managed to lose the borrowed glasses during the trip to La Paz and was worrying alternately about where they were and what their owner would say about the predicament. "Why did you use the glasses anyway?" I asked him. Montaño emphatically told me that the glasses were key to his costume because they gave him an air of importance.[13]

Montaño's rise in the Inca dance group paralleled his rise in the local caracolleño social hierarchy. The owner of a small store that provided a constant backup between political appointments, Montaño had served in several political parties' terms, first as Caracollo's head of cultural affairs (oficial mayor de cultura), then as intendant, and most recently (in 2003) as subprefect.[14] After poor health compromised his political career, Montaño helped me with my research in 2010. While several Inca actors who considered themselves Caracollo natives grumbled about his ambitions and positions, Montaño had worked his way into the inner core of the local caracolleño power structure, in part by joining the Inca dance guild. The case of Lucho Montaño suggests that in the late twentieth and early twenty-first centuries, the Inca dance guild denoted and still denotes social difference and local hierarchy.

Ediberto Hinojosa, the actor who played the Inca king in 2001, is a different kind of early twenty-first century "Inca." Tall and lanky, Hinojosa always wore an old-style pilot's cap with the flaps pulled down to protect himself from Caracollo's relentless wind and cold. Employed in construction and constantly working a ball of coca in his cheek, he was rather fair-skinned, especially by Caracollo's standards. Hinojosa interpreted the role of the Inca king with more energy and aggressive humor than had many of his more composed and reserved predecessors, according to the other guild members. Although he held the prestigious role of the Inca king, he was not part of the core decision-making circle. As schisms opened up in the theatrical guild, it became clear that Hinojosa held sway over a faction of only comparatively minor actors. When the word spread around Caracollo that the group would be the featured performers at the previously mentioned folklore conference, people began to take a great interest in participating. Donato Flores, who had held several important positions of authority in Caracollo and who had played the role of Inca monarch in earlier times, expressed interest in performing as the Inca king. Mario López, who had proved reluctant to lend his support to the Inca actors in recent years—and displayed reticence toward contributing to my research—similarly stepped forth to reclaim his former role as the Inca king. Suddenly the group was inundated with Inca kings, which suggests both that people still saw the role as prestigious and that many felt Hinojosa to be a poor choice for it.[15]

Hinojosa had an extremely controlling and demanding partner who liked to accuse the actors of calling rehearsals as an excuse to take the Inca king out to drink; at one point she told the group he would no longer be acting in the play.[16] Donato Flores happily stepped up to fill the role, one of many he had held during his lengthy trajectory in the world of Inca theater. While I was grateful that Flores would accept such a late invitation to participate, other people complained. Some said he was not tall enough for the part; others, that he did not perform the role with enough energy. He certainly did not play the role with Hinojosa's vitality, which all had come to appreciate. Montaño was determined to get Hinojosa back. Visiting his house or stopping him on the street, Montaño took every opportunity to attempt to persuade Hinojosa to return as Inca king. On one occasion, a frustrated Montaño exclaimed, "Why do I have to walk behind you begging you? Why do we need you so much? Is it because you have such an Indian face [caro de indio]?"[17] I remember being struck by several things when I heard Montaño say and then repeat "Indian face." First, although Hinojosa was taller than Montaño, had lighter skin, and less stereotypically indigenous features, Montaño considered him more "Indian." Viewed from the local social constructs of race and through the discriminatory eyes of the Inca group, Hinojosa's class determined his race. Historically, only notable townspeople had acted in the Inca play. Hinojosa was grudgingly allowed to participate because he possessed physical attributes associated with the Inca king, even though his class and trade denied him the social status that would have lent real legitimacy to his holding the role.

Hinojosa represented (as did Montaño in certain ways) a new kind of Inca actor. He did not want to dominate the local hierarchy by participating in the Inca play and could not have done so in any event. In fact, one of his partner's worst fears was that Hinojosa would be made to act as a festival sponsor. An individual of humble means and background, he was content to command a small faction of marginal actors within the Inca group, and he enjoyed playing the role of the Inca king. He liked the prestige of participating in the group without taking on all the obligations associated with sponsoring festivals, as the lead actors were expected to do. When the debate about choosing an actor to play the role of the Inca king heated up again, Hinojosa returned to rehearsal to reclaim his role. On finding that he had been replaced, he threatened to take his faction of Inca actors with him, creating more gaps in the cast.[18] The dispute over the role of Inca king continued right up to the performance in La Paz. Apparently both Flores and Hinojosa boarded the bus as the Inca king. Ultimately, Hinojosa performed as the Inca king, and Flores did his best as Waylla Wisa, a role assigned to him only minutes before the curtain rose.

This anecdote concerning Hinojosa and the role of the Inca king indicates the presence of new types of actors in the early twenty-first century Caracollo Inca theatrical guild, but it also illuminates the changing significance of that role. The original construction of the Inca as white skinned and tall reflects concepts of early twentieth-century progress and evolution as applied to race. Early in the next century, however, the Inca king selected possessed the physical "Inca" traits (tall with light skin) but not the social standing that would have been required at the turn of the previous one.

Although "acting Inca" still denoted social status in Caracollo, the actors made several deprecating comments regarding the historical Incas during the extra rehearsals held to prepare for the La Paz performance. They constantly joked about the scene in which the Inca king attempts to decipher the written word. He picks up the document, tries to listen to it, smells it, and, frustrated, sends Waylla Wisa off to consult with other Incas as to what the scratches mean. There is real hilarity as the Incas describe the marks on paper as chicken scratches. More than once I heard the actors jokingly comment that this inability to read the letter showed the Inca king to be a poor, stupid Indian. People teased Hinojosa in his role as the Inca king, calling him a dumb Indian with perhaps double meaning. The Aymara support for the Liberal Party in the late nineteenth century had faded into the background. The conquest is represented as the fault of the uneducated Inca king who could not read. Perhaps this is why Montaño insisted in using glasses—a symbol of education, literacy, and status—as part of his Diego de Almagro costume. "Acting Inca" still denotes social status in Caracollo, but the comments of the contemporary actors suggest that they understand the demise of the Inca Empire to be a consequence of Indian illiteracy.

Yet the Inca king's actions and demeanor in the play, especially as performed by Hinojosa, are anything but tragic, submissive, or apologetic. Hinojosa bounces about the stage with great presence and self-assurance, aggressively mocking the Spaniards and pushing them over. In a sense, both Hinojosa and the contemporary Inca king embody overtones of the often militant, ethnic Aymara politics now at the center of political debates in Bolivia. While Hinojosa is not a member of any Aymara political organization, his role is evocative of the contemporary Indians who demand their space within the nation as Indians and not as overly civilized Incas.

The figure of Ramón Fernández and his participation within the Inca theatrical guild similarly illustrates significant changes within the group. Fernández, a former *corregidor*, or local town official, and the descendant of a line of Inca theater actors, currently holds the prestigious role of Christopher Columbus and is much sought after as a director of the play. Despite his advanced age, he continues to deliver his soliloquy of exploration and conquest with emphatic vigor and pride. Now retired, he formerly worked as a miner and later as a skilled tailor. A committed performer, he confects a new costume for the Columbus role whenever an important presentation comes up. The most recent suit was a handsome jacket and pair of knickers made of red velvet and adorned with white trim. His eminence in the Inca group as Christopher Columbus has given him the reputation of town historian. The owner of a small collection of books on Spanish exploration and conquest, he dominates the entire second act with his knowledge of Columbus's voyage and declaration claiming the land for Spain. As he moved across the dusty plaza outside Caracollo's church while performing at the Virgin of the Rosary festival in 2001, a man behind me nudged his son toward the front of the crowd and said, "Look, son, that is Christopher Columbus."

In a sense, Fernández's performance doubles as an open-air history lesson for the caracolleño youth, making him an informal teacher and historian as well as a performer. In addition, his directorial skills are highly valued. Fernández owns a complete script and possesses typing skills; each year he types up separate scripts for each role and distributes them on August 6, at the sole rehearsal for the performance at the Virgin of the Rosary festival. *Pasantes*, or festival sponsors, rely on Fernández, visiting him in his house to ask for his collaboration in directing the play. But Fernández is increasingly reluctant to type the scripts for the Inca guild members. Though the guild had experienced problems finding festival sponsors in recent years, he has demanded remuneration for his duties as scribe, arguing that his time and effort should be recognized. In some cases, his proposed fee of five bolivianos per script (approximately seventy cents) led the Inca president (when there were no festival sponsors) to look for a different director; in others, it led to chaos that lasted until the last moment, when the script ultimately appeared.

Fernández, aged and no longer holding a local post of authority, struggles to make a living in the increasingly competitive market environment Caracollo has become. He owns one of many small bars that swing into action on Sundays when the regional market dominates the town's streets. Truckloads of people arrive from the more distant canton hamlets to buy and sell livestock and produce. Local store owners use huge gunny sacks to haul out their staple goods for display in the plaza. Though the area was previously dotted with chullpares, or ancestral burial shrines, most of the monuments from and to the past were razed to make way for the market's new cement plaza. The last chullpar, impressively large, stands crumbling in the midst of the livestock section. It doubles as a trashcan on Sundays.

The market is easily accessible to both buyers and sellers, for Caracollo stands at the junction of two of Bolivia's major paved arteries. Every bus traveling between La Paz and Oruro or Cochabamba must go through Caracollo. Passengers get off to eat at the local restaurants or browse at the market while a bus tire is being repaired. With the market no longer "local," caracolleño businesses are either hurt by or take advantage of the increased competition. Key to local survival, however, is the maintenance of local friendships to ensure a constant clientele. Fernández's continued participation in the Inca play stems from this necessity as well as from personal pride in his role as Christopher Columbus.

In Caracollo, acting Inca still consolidates local social hierarchy; it reaffirms social networks among the town elites and distinguishes the Inca guild from the other dance groups as the historians of Caracollo. The Inca actors meet annually on August 6, Bolivia's independence day, to celebrate the nation by holding their single rehearsal for their performance in October. During the rehearsal in 2000, the oldest member of the Incas and honorary president, Fernández Flores, cried: "We are not old, worn-out Incas! We are the legitimate, established residents of this town. Those dancers in the Diablada and the Morenada, they are the Indians!"[19] Fernández Flores's words, spoken on Bolivia's national holiday, reaffirmed the close connection between power and historical constructions of an Inca identity, as well as the association between the Bolivian nation and the performance of the Inca play. Whereas the Carnival celebration at Oruro promotes stylized Indian identities, the Caracollo Incas have their origins in the construction of a liberal national identity in the early twentieth century. In the twenty-first century, Fernández Flores's comments reflect his view of the members of the other Indian dance guilds as inferior within Caracollo's social hierarchy. The Caracollo Inca actors desire the popularity that new highland dance groups attract, but they do not wish to join the Oruro Carnival parade as simply another Indian group precisely because the Inca guild originated to set the Caracollo elite apart from pejorative constructions of Indianness.

The Inca King and the Struggle against Neocolonialism

Like their predecessors, current Caracollo Inca actors perform the Inca play to confirm their roles as local historians and to mark their social standing within the town's population. Nonresident audiences, however, may miss much of the Inca actors' intentions and the history of the play. Observers, especially those who visit Caracollo only to see the play, witness an enactment of historical oppression and the exploitation of the Incas by the Spaniards. Students, scholars, and activists seeking to create a revisionist Indian history of Bolivia, as many have done since the 1970s, have taken a great interest in the Inca king and the Inca past as a symbol of the internal struggle against neocolonialism in Bolivia. Silvia Rivera Cusicanqui has described the emergence of the revisionist anticolonial historical narrative referred to as Katarismo: "In the late 1960s there emerged a new generation of young Aymaras, who felt they were 'foreigners in their own country,' despite their formal inclusion in the citizenry, since they experienced the daily phenomena of ethnic discrimination, political manipulation, and humiliation."[20] This generation of Aymara scholars has been forming Indian political parties and rewriting Aymara history. The Tiwanaku Manifesto of 1973, the founding statement of Katarismo, signed by members of the Tupac Katari Peasant Centre, the National Association of Peasant Teachers, and others, clearly states the common struggle of indigenous peoples in Bolivia: "We the Qhechwa and Aymara peasants, like those of other indigenous cultures in the country, say the same thing. We feel that we are economically exploited and culturally and politically oppressed."[21] This narrative downplays ethnic distinctions between Quechuas and Aymaras in an effort to forge a united front against state oppression. In the name of their fight against Creole-led neocolonialism in Bolivia, scholars such as Rivera Cusicanqui incorporate the figure of the Inca king into a pantheon of Indian leaders, such as Tupac Katari and Zárate Willka, who represent centuries of Indian resistance to colonial and neocolonial oppression in Bolivia.

The group THOA, founded by Rivera Cusicanqui, is a Katarista organization at the forefront of efforts to build oral and performative archives and to find alternative sources for studies that could revise and decolonize Indian history. This nongovernmental Aymara organization has been described as a "counterpublic sphere" functioning as an area of differential consciousness for Aymara intellectuals and activists.[22] Carlos Mamani, THOA's president, has described the organization's project of empowering the indigenous population: "It brings together Aymaraqhichwa and Uru investigators whose aim is to investigate, disseminate, and revitalize the culture, history, and identity of the indigenous peoples of the Andes. THOA seeks to promote the reconstitution of the original ayllu communities through investigation, empowerment, advice, and consultation in order to support the autonomy of the indigenous population. A broad goal is to enable indigenous people to achieve equal rights, political participation, and to be effective in negotiating with the State Government."[23]

Cristóbal Condoreno and Orlando Huanca Ticona, who are affiliated with THOA and investigate Aymara culture, took an interest in the Caracollo Inca play. Focusing solely on the third act, Condoreno made a film, *El sueño de Waylla Wisa*, in which the Incas meet the Spaniards aggressively, calling them names and insulting them. Condoreno offers his own understanding of the Caracollo Inca play, which he created by cutting and rearranging the third act. In his revisionist film, Condoreno highlights the fact that the Incas, aware and prepared, never trusted the Spaniards; they met them aggressively and attempted to defend their empire. Condoreno's film underscores the Incas' bold response to the Spaniards' arrival. The film's first four sequences depict a series of encounters between Spaniards and Incas in which the Incas repeatedly mock the Spaniards with variations of the following lines:

> Hey, bearded white man!
> What wrong paths did you take?
> Which hurricane winds brought you here?[24]

The Incas meet the Spaniards bravely and challenge them from the first moment of contact. In suggesting that the Spaniards arrived in Peru by mistake, the Incas belie the Spaniards' cartographic and navigational skills and belittle their mission of conquest. The Spaniards, a group of lost Europeans, ask each Inca if he is the king, apparently unable to distinguish between Inca commoners and the monarch. The theme of literacy and the Incas' inability to read the Spanish document appears as a secondary theme in the film, and the Incas' lack of comprehension is expressed through aggressive hilarity. The Inca actor looks at the words and exclaims: "This looks like the tassels on my ñusta's bathrobe. This looks like the belly of those bearded men!" The Inca then flings the paper at the Spaniards, yelling: "What is this, that nobody can understand it? Take it!"[25]

The Spaniards declare war, and battle ensues, but the first scenes of Condoreno's film make clear that the Incas would have fought the Spaniards even if they had been able to read the document. In the film, Waylla Wisa's dream informs the Incas of the Spaniards' goal of conquest and accumulating wealth, and they offer immediate resistance. The Incas are the heroes of the play, even if the Spaniards ultimately usurp their empire. By dropping the first and second acts of the Inca play, the scenes concerning Moors and Christians and Christopher Columbus's soliloquy, Condoreno reduces the Inca Empire's significance to world history, incorporating the Incas instead into the revisionist history of Indian leaders' resistance to colonial and neocolonial oppressors. At the end of the film, Condoreno thanks the Caracollo Inca actors for preserving the tradition of the Inca play. Yet *El sueño de Waylla Wisa* is more faithful to THOA's mission statement and ongoing negotiations between the Bolivian government and indigenous communities than it is to the play. Condoreno's retelling of the Spanish Conquest highlights Indian resistance to the colonizers, thus creating an empowering narrative of the struggle to maintain Indian autonomy in the face of great oppression. While recent folkloric trends in elements of the Carnival celebration at Oruro favor depicting rural Aymara life and thus diminish the Incas' popularity, Condoreno, Rivera Cusicanqui and other such Aymara activists and historians have offered the Inca king a place among colonial and neocolonial resistance leaders such as Tupac Katari, Zárate Willka, and Santos Marka T'ula.

Orlando Huanca Ticona is another Aymara Katarista revisionist scholar affiliated with THOA who has taken an interest in the Caracollo Inca play. In his unpublished article "Es posible un teatro andino?" he claims that Inca plays have served as an important site of anticolonial resistance since the sixteenth century. The actors, he claims, reenact the founding moment of inequality, the Spanish Conquest, which produced the hierarchical colonial and neocolonial societies.[26] Huanca Ticona does not address the use of pink-skinned masks in the Caracollo play; he refers only briefly to the masks as aesthetic props that enable actors to play with the notions of reality and fiction. Alternatively, he refers to them as "expressionless" and suggests that the masks break any emotional connection between the actors and the audience.[27]

The connection between the Incas and the Aymaras, according to Condoreno and Huanca Ticona, rests on a shared anticolonial struggle of Indian peoples.[28] Aymara intellectuals' revisionist narratives of the 1980s and 1990s reinterpret the play as a precursor of contemporary Aymara activists' neocolonial projects. This is quite a reversal from position of Bolivia's early twentieth-century local elites, who had to distance themselves from the "savage Aymara" and adopt the more acceptable Inca image. The third act of the Caracollo Inca play fits nicely within the broader themes of oppression and resistance in revisionist Indian history—if the first two acts are cut. The Caracollo Inca actors, however, still insist on presenting all three acts, which indicates that their understanding of their own play differs from that of urban Aymara Katarista scholars.

The Caracollo Inca Play

Despite facing financial challenges, the Caracollo Incas have not considered reducing the play to the third act, as Condoreno, Huanca Ticona, and the Oruro Inca group did. This insistence of locating the Inca Empire and Spanish Conquest within the context of world history informs the historical significance of their Inca play. By performing all three acts during the Fiesta del Rosario, the Caracollo Inca actors deliberately locate themselves within the broader global context. Historically, the Inca actors masqueraded as white Indians and as the bearers of a progressive past that ennobled the Bolivian nation and silenced the Aymaras' troubling participation in the Civil War of 1899; today, the actors carry on the legacy of the early twentieth-century Inca play through their performance of all three acts. Transgressing national boundaries, the Aymara elite inserted the Incas into a world history of empires; act 1, between Moors and Christians, and act 3, between Incas and Spaniards, represent transitions of power from one empire to another. These watershed moments involving Moors and Christians on one side of the Atlantic and Incas and Spaniards on the other are connected by Christopher Columbus's voyage across the ocean and his soliloquy of discovery that makes up act 2.

Condoreno's film underscores the Incas' resistance to the Spaniards as the main message of the play. Yet for the Caracollo actors, the real conflict and the fatal flaw that causes the downfall of the Inca Empire turns on the question of literacy. The majority of the third act consists of a series of brief meetings between Spaniards and Incas in which a Spaniard hands the "ch'alla," or piece of paper, to an Inca. The latter takes the paper, attempts to comprehend it, fails, and takes it to another Inca for assistance. Inca after Inca is unable to make sense of the object. The Inca king takes the letter from Almagro, stating: "What is that white thing that you are carrying? Give it to me, I will receive it. . . . Oh, what is this that I cannot understand? Looking at it from this side it looks like the footprints of my dog, from this other side it looks like the eyes of my princesses, if I look directly at it, it looks like the beards of this warrior [the Spaniard], with his beard all encrusted, ah beloved, skinny, malnutritioned one, come a little bit closer."[29] The Inca king then gives the letter to his learned assistant, Waylla Wisa, who has the power of seeing into the future, and asks him whether he can use his powers to understand its significance. Waylla Wisa is also unable to read the letter, but recognizing the urgency of understanding it, he states that he will take it to Primo Inca, who will surely be able to comprehend it. The scenario repeats itself as the paper passes from Inca to Inca without success. In each attempt to make sense of the paper, there is real hilarity and joking as the Incas make fun of the marks on it. One Inca describes the writing as "rooster tracks," while another observes that it does not look like a river or a mountain or anything else with which the Incas are familiar.

In the Caracollo Inca actors' production, two scenes from act 3 are repeated again and again. The first is the exchange between a Spaniard and an Inca on which Condoreno capitalized in *El sueño de Waylla Wisa*. This scene, which involves Incas taunting the Spaniards, shows the Incas' bravery and their knowledge that the Spaniards were not going to be a beneficial presence within the empire, both key elements in establishing the Incas as an informed people who did not hesitate to defend their land from invaders. The other central scene is the repeated attempt to make sense of the letter, which receives less attention in Condoreno's film. Yet the scenes that deal with literacy embody the crux of the conflict in the Caracollo play; reading the letter would have enabled the Incas to negotiate their future, although perhaps not to control it. It is their illiteracy that causes Almagro to label them "bárbaros" and dismiss them as stupid. The priest Hernando de Luque is similarly frustrated with the Incas' illiteracy. He tells the Incas: "This document is very important and it is from my illustrious king of Spain. I will let my general know of the insults you have heaped upon me."[30] Pizarro then takes the stage and offers a summary of his exploits. Building on Almagro and de Luque's complaints of their illiteracy, Pizarro refers to the Incas as "brutish animal savages."[31] The contemporary Inca actors' performance of the "preferred" Indian history, the Inca past, draws from the legitimacy and authority that both

Creole liberals and the Caracollo elite assigned to the Inca image in the early twentieth century; through their performances, however, the contemporary actors critique the Incas' illiteracy and consolidate their role as educated and literate town historians.

Following these insults, the Inca Huiñay Apu declares war on the Spaniards, yet before it commences, he turns toward the church and, referring to both Madre Kollana and the Virgin of the Rosary in the same sentence, asks for their blessing prior to commencing the war. The Incas may have intended to combat the Spaniards, but they did not resist Christianity. This combination of past and present permits the Incas to represent themselves as Christian and civilized; they honor the Virgin of the Rosary. The prayer to the virgin in the midst of the performance also underscores that religious conflict did not cause the downfall of the Inca Empire. The play shows the transference of religion from the Spanish to the native population even as the actors represent the historical resistance to the original bearers of Christianity, the Spaniards. The brief prayer also serves to establish a difference between the actors and the characters they play. The Incas were great, but they were illiterate and worshiped idols; the Inca actors, in contrast, are Christian and literate.

If illiteracy played a central role in the fall of the Inca Empire, literacy constituted one of the requirements for Bolivian citizenship status in the early twentieth century, effectively barring most indigenous people from obtaining their rights.[32] In the twenty-first century, literacy and knowledge continue to structure hierarchy in Caracollo. The town's Inca theater actors distinguish themselves locally as knowledgeable and literate people. For example, the Inca actor Lucho Montaño served in several capacities within the Caracollo government. Ramon Fernández participated in government as well, and he possesses a collection of books on the Spanish Conquest. Cornelio Pinaya is a professor at the Technical University in Oruro. Juan Flores is a renowned tailor in Oruro who, it is said, designs suits for visitors from Europe. Most of their children are professionals, and many of them are themselves electing to become keepers of knowledge as teachers. During an Inca reunion on August 6, 2000, one of the participants who danced in the Inca group but did not have a role in the play drank a lot of alcohol and then broke down sobbing because he had never finished high school. This individual found his truncated education both tragic and embarrassing; it also prohibited him from receiving a significant role in the Inca play.

Among the Caracollo Incas, education represents an internal conquest of knowledge; Inca actors are the keepers of the past. They garner some of their recognition through the centrality of folkloric performance in the Department of Oruro, but they receive more validation through their roles as local historians and local literati. Faced with the competition from newer, trendier folkloric groups, the Incas continue to survive and to stake their claim on their ability to narrate the Inca past. For example, the Oruro Incas do not seek out the Caracollo Incas for the latter's parading abilities, and they dislike their costumes; they include them, however, because the Caracollo troupe knows how to perform the Inca play.

There is another conquest element in the play. The Inca actors claim the noble Inca past as central to highland Bolivian history. The story the actors enact is one of brave Incas who repeatedly try to make sense of a letter so as to better defend their empire. The Inca actors themselves draw from the celebrated and world-renowned Inca past to gain social status. Through their roles, they embody the civilized "white Inca" who created a great civilization. But the play also serves as a critique. There is a line in Condoreno's film that does not fit with the other lines or with the message of Indian resistance that his film wishes to convey. In the midst of a series of funny descriptions of the written word, one Inca insults the Inca king: "Even my Inca king can't read it, although he has a head as big as a donkey."[33] This line might well be a late twentieth-century addition to the play, showing that Inca actors have learned the lessons of the past. They do not intend to succumb to the same fatal flaw that condemned the historical Incas. The Inca actors are literate; they surpass basic literacy and style themselves as local historians and experts on the past. Their authority derives in part from their acting ability but perhaps even more from their knowledge of the Inca past. Yet the actors do not simply enact a set text; they participate in its elaboration, writing the very history they perform. The Inca play directors' engagement, critique, and act of writing history confirm the Inca actors as literate members of society and town historians.

Previous analyses of Inca plays in the Andes have focused on one particular version of the play and its dutiful enactment by community members.[34] The various communities' productions of the drama were thought to represent an act of remembering the original roots of inequality, or, alternatively, a manifestation of resistance. The univocality of the plays and their textual authority are not challenged; scholars analyze the "Chayanta play" or the "Oruro play" as a set script for the actors to represent, debating the degree of authenticity each text displays. Yet my research on the Caracollo Inca play reveals that multiple versions of the script exist. While the texts share the three acts and the core set of events, directors have been more than just dramatic referees. They shape the text, adding and subtracting to it, aligning the scenes with their own interpretations of the past and in response to the sociopolitical context. The core events stay the same, as do the protagonists, but both directors and actors introduce variations, their decisions affecting how the play ends or how the protagonists are represented.

Mario López, whose father Gumercindo López directed the Caracollo play for many years, emphasized the director's responsibility in tailoring the script. Gumercindo López took a great interest in scripts in general, collecting not only Inca play scripts but also other theatrical texts. When he directed, he drew from his expanded archive and personal knowledge. Regardless of the text he selected, he always found it necessary to "correct it [corregirlo]." In fact, according to Mario López, this is one of the desirable aspects of becoming director. Directing the play involves far more than just typing out a script for each actor and providing lines and cues for the occasional forgetful or inebriated actor during performances; it is synonymous with joining the informal academy of town historians in Caracollo. López states that each director contributes something to the play and, in doing so, literally leaves his mark on the historical record. Despite his experience and his collection of scripts, he said, he would have to "correct" any script before it could be used. Scripts are passed down to family members, but they are not static documents.[35]

A brief comparison of two Caracollo Inca play scripts illustrates such variations and additions. At the end of the play, the Incas pass before the ñustas, or Inca princesses, who ask the Incas to cry with them for the death of the Inca king. Each Inca curses the Spaniards, asking the mountains to hide the mineral wealth to make it as hard as possible for the Spaniards to extract it. In an undated version of the Caracollo play as directed by Telésforo Fernández Flores, after each Inca asks that the mountains swallow up the silver and gold, the ñustas close the action with a set of short stanzas in which they confirm their identity as residents of Kollasuyu, or the highland eastern portion of the Inca Empire.[36] In a different version of the Inca play, this one performed in Caracollo in 1965, the Incas state that the Inca king's execution day was also his birthday, heightening the sense of tragedy. After each Inca has asked the earth to bury its gold, the ñustas voice a much shorter lament and the drama continues. The next stage cue reads: "Change of tone, resurrection of the Inca."[37] The script then continues with songs and prayers dedicated to the Virgin of the Holy Rosary. At certain points, it appears that the Incas give themselves over to her once the Inca king is gone, although this is complicated by the Incas' professions of Christianity earlier in the play.

The Inca king's resurrection has attracted scholars to the potentially messianic overtones of the Caracollo Inca play.[38] In the twenty-first-century performances I have seen, the Inca king does get up to dance with the Incas after his death. The ending of the play is blurred as the performance winds down; the play appears to be over, yet the band plays on, and the Incas, including the king, all dance around the Inca king's *korichambi*, or staff of authority. Huanca Ticona states that the Inca king's resurrection at the end of the play symbolizes a reaffirmation of Indian power and authority.[39] While it is tempting to read the Inca king's resurrection as reflecting the growing emphasis on Indian political mobilization in Bolivia in the twenty-first century, a more likely reading has it consolidating the Inca guild's elevated social status and importance in Caracollo. The Inca actors, "siempre de pie, nunca de rodilla" (always on their feet, never on their knees), dance proudly at the end of the play after accomplishing another successful performance of local and national history. Their value stems from their role as the town's literati. The downfall of the celebrated Inca Empire due to the illiterate Indians makes perfect sense to the actors. Performing their literacy and their knowledge of the past, the Caracollo Inca actors clearly demonstrate Caracollo's progress over time and consolidate their roles as town historians. Fernández Flores's assertion that the town's elite act Inca while "indios" fill the other dance groups emphasizes the eminence of the Inca actors as town historians, and the play underscores the Incas' place among great civilizations and illustrates global transitions of power. It also reflects distinctions between preferred "Indian" identities within Caracollo that manifest themselves through folkloric performance. The Caracollo Inca actors locate their story within the global narrative of conquest, not a narrative of Indian resistance.

Acting Inca is still a source of pride and status in Caracollo, even though the Incas' importance has dwindled in an age when folkloric dance groups increasingly depict highland indigenous life and Aymara politics predominate. The Inca image simply does not appeal to an audience the way it might have done in the early twentieth century. Still, although the Inca troupe's popularity is shrinking in the face of "authentic" Aymara dance groups, it is important to note that constructions and manifestations of "preferred" Indian ethnicities continue to dominate political and cultural life in Bolivia.

As the larger and brighter folkloric dance groups lure potential Inca players into their organizations, membership is changing, creating spaces for actors such as Ediberto Hinojosa, the construction worker. He plays the role of the Inca king more because of the physical traits he brings to the part than because of his social status. At the same time, Hinojosa is changing the role of the Inca king through his performance. He strides boisterously about the stage, crashing into Spaniards and responding to their orders with insolence. It is understandable that outside observers might interpret this as an act of neocolonial resistance. In the twenty-first century, urban La Paz–based Katarista intellectuals expect the Inca to claim his space in the nation precisely as an Indian leader of a resistance movement against neocolonial state oppression.

The Caracollo Inca actors, however, maintain their prestige through underscoring their role as local literati and historians of both the national and local past. Engaging in a critical rereading of Indian history, the director identifies the Incas' errors and shortcomings that the Caracollo elite strive to ameliorate in the twenty-first century. The process of reconsidering the fall of the Inca Empire each year in Caracollo constitutes a performative revisionist Indian narrative that insists that Indians should be literate and progressive. The director underscores his knowledge of the past by constantly "improving" the Caracollo Inca play script.

In 2009 the Caracollo government decided to construct a monument in the central plaza to honor mestizo General René Bernal Escalante (see fig. 14), a noteworthy development that counters efforts to recover Indian historical protagonists and to recognize them via monuments. In 1980 the town of Imilla-Imilla, where Zárate Willka was born, partnered with Radio San Gabriel of La Paz to build a monument to that Indian leader in the town's main plaza. The ayllu Sullcavi, in the municipality of Ayo Ayo, built a monument to honor Tupac Katari, an Indian leader who struggled against the Spaniards and who was brutally executed by his enemies in the 1780s. Communities in the surrounding region come together for three days of activities to remember Tupac Katari.[40] The memory of the Indian past is serving as a catalyst to revitalize community history and Aymara pride on the altiplano.

Caracollo's monument to Bernal does not directly refer to Indian history or identity but rather underscores his contributions to Caracollo as well as to the nation. A military man who worked closely with the populist dictator President René Barrientos during the late 1960s, René Bernal Escalante was a Caracollo native son.[41] Some caracolleños remember those years of dictatorship nostalgically, stating that if they needed something done, they simply called Bernal and the matter was dispatched.[42] In fact, caracolleños' claim to fame rests on a time when General Barrientos left the nation in Bernal's hands for three days while he was attending to other business. Perhaps not surprisingly, the Bernals were longtime Inca dancers and actors, which

Figure 14
Statue of René Bernal.
Photo by the author,
2010

reinforces the connections among citizenship, the Incas, and the Caracollo local elite. The military uniform chiseled onto the statue's stone torso reflects Bernal's service to the nation. The dedication on the plaque expresses his words to the Caracollo residents, not vice versa: "A mi pueblo querido." Bernal's success in achieving national recognition ties Caracollo to the nation in a positive way. The Inca theatrical guild historically connected the local Aymara elite to the Liberal Party's nation-building project. Today, the legacies of the guild's origins are still apparent in defining social status and prestige within Caracollo. In 1900, the town's elite founded the Inca group to resonate with liberal discourse and to set themselves apart from pejorative views of the Aymara population; today, membership in the group offers a way to create social and ethnic distinction between the Inca actors and the "Indians from other dance groups." The Inca actors do not want to be subsumed within folkloric parades or resistance movements against a neocolonial state. Annually, the Inca actors assert their authority and knowledge through their ability to narrate the past and to critique the Incas for their illiteracy; through their performance, the Inca actors display their own learned status and historical knowledge.

CONCLUSION
Inca Play, Aymara Encore

In Bolivia, the Civil War of 1899 still stands at the crossroads of fierce contemporary political and regional conflicts. The war has occupied a central space in Sucre's historical narrative for over a century; that city's historical claim as the first, and previously only, capital of Bolivia has been rekindled in the light of Evo Morales's presidency and the rewriting of the Bolivian constitution. Sucre's narrative of 1899 constitutes a constant challenge to Morales's presidency as well as to La Paz's claim as the primary capital city. The Aymara leader Zárate Willka may not have become president in 1899, but Morales did in 2005. For some, Morales's election represents the consolidation of the struggle against neocolonialism that Zárate Willka is often credited with having begun. Sucre's demands serve as the basis for virulent racism; they challenge national unity and presidential legitimacy. Narratives and counter-narratives turn on the question of Aymara participation in the civil war and actively shape current political differences. The film *La Guerra Federal*, discussed in the introduction, which ties contemporary regional conflict between La Paz and Sucre to the Civil War of 1899, is an excellent example of this ongoing style. The pejorative connotations associated with the term *Aymara* in the early twentieth century persist, only now the preferred term is *masista*, designed to insult both Morales's political party, the Movimiento Al Socialismo (MAS), and the Aymara ethnicity of the current president and many of his supporters.

146

A monument in Sucre's impressive cemetery commemorates twenty-seven students who lost their lives during the Civil War of 1899. For the city's residents, it points to a telling example of Aymara brutality. The statue is made of bronze with a cut-off pillar extending upward. The inscription reads: "A broken pillar. This column symbolizes the order established by the founding fathers[;] it was whole, but the bad Bolivians in 1899 broke it. The country is not complete[;] it is broken."[1] The column is severed but not destroyed, standing as an invitation to establish the former order and bring the capital back to Sucre. The partial column serves as a constant reminder of a situation in need of rectification.

Every year, on January 24, students from the main university in Sucre, the Universidad San Francisco Xavier, hold a vigil at the monument and narrate the killing of these martyrs of Ayo Ayo. Commemorating the soldiers as students, the orators contrast Sucre's fallen soldiers to the "savage Aymara" opponents, thus continuing to racialize and heighten differences between the two groups.[2] The Sucre youth are described as young, idealistic students who rushed to defend Sucre's title as capital. The Aymara soldiers fighting for the Liberal Party, in contrast, are cast in almost animalistic terms; according to one critic of the annual ceremony, the students conducting it depict the Aymara troops as "the Attilas of the altiplano, who ripped out their [the Sucre soldiers'] tongues, dug out their eyes, and finally killed them with axes. In the midst of a Dante-esque scene of mutilated bodies, one could hear the Indians' guttural sounds, they did not respect the sacred space [the church], and it was as if the saints themselves were crying blood."[3]

Civilized valleys, savage highlands: the regional and racial conflicts that consume the country's contemporary political debates and challenge the current shape of the sovereign Bolivian nation are rooted in the Civil War of 1899. Sucre's primary political demand has been its restoration as the only capital of Bolivia. During the commemoration of the fallen students, Sucre residents sing the popular refrain "Let's go, chuiquisaqueños, let's get the capital! No chuk'uta, damn it, should govern! Potosí is imperial, Oruro is mineral, La Paz is a garbage dump, and Sucre is the capital."[4]

The Aymara insurgents' "usurpation" of the capital has permeated Sucre's collective memory. Guides offer tours of the cemetery to guests who come to see the elegant mausoleums and final resting grounds of prominent political leaders. When they arrive at the monument to Sucre's soldiers killed in the civil war, the guides repeat the pronouncements that university students make during the annual January commemoration. The "unjust transfer" of the executive and legislative branches to La Paz, leaving only the judiciary in Sucre, is central to an unofficial yet shared civic core curriculum in Sucre, ranging from elementary school to university. The racialized language and historical understanding of 1899 has been legitimized, in part, through municipal legislation. In 2004 the city government passed a decree officially recognizing January 24 as a municipal holiday.[5] In drafting the resolution, it adhered to the aggressive narrative and racist language that holds the Aymaras responsible for the excessively brutal deaths of Sucre's martyrs of 1899.

> In the cemetery of Sucre, there is a monument to remember the fallen heroes of . . . the Civil War of 1899, who were repatriated December fifteenth of 1905, thanks to Luis de Argandoña; Chuquisaqueño martyrs who were horribly massacred by hordes of drunken Aymaras led by the cacique Pablo Zárate Willka. These soldiers belonged to the Sucre Battalion that, as they retreated toward Oruro gravely wounded, took refuge in the church of Ayo-Ayo, believing that the sanctuary would protect them; but it was to no avail. The Aymaras entered like savages thirsty for blood. They first killed the three priests responsible for the church, then they began their macabre task, cruelly killing the wounded soldiers, pulling out their eyes, ears, and tongues, and chopped off their heads with axes; they were dragged by horses, and there was no respect for the image of Christ.[6]

Given that this war made La Paz a capital city, one might expect that city to have a prominent monument marking the transfer of power to the highlands. Because of the Liberal Party's condemnation of its wartime Aymara allies and the prevailing understanding of the Aymaras' activities as a race war (or more recently, as the birth of the autonomous Aymara movement), there is no historical marker. The vast La Paz cemetery, so large that one needs a map to navigate its streets, has multiple monuments to all the other wars Bolivia fought, yet there is no monument to commemorate the Civil War of 1899. The inscription on José Manuel Pando's tomb simply reads: "Soldier and explorer" (see fig. 15).

Since the 1970s, Aymara political organizations, not the city government, have revitalized the memory of Zárate Willka and the Aymara war veterans. Recognizing Zárate Willka as an important political leader, Katarista scholars and activists have followed Condarco Morales's affirmations that the Creole-Aymara alliance deteriorated into an autonomous Aymara movement. These revisionist narratives view 1899 as the founding moment of the autonomous Aymara movement in the republican era, with Zárate Willka as its greatest protagonist in developing an "Indian," and moreover

FIGURE 15. General Pando's tomb, La Paz Cemetery. Photo by the author, 2010

Aymara, political agenda. More aggressive versions of this revisionist history also view Zárate Willka as issuing a challenge to Creole privilege and to the neocolonial nation. Pablo Mamani Ramírez, who writes for the Web site Katari.org, claims that Morales's presidency is the "revenge of Zárate Willka."[7] He understands Zárate Willka's "race war" as an effort to end the Aymaras' historical marginalization. The claim that a race war indeed took place goes unchallenged, however, thus reinforcing the Liberal Party's dismissal of the Aymara mobilization on its behalf.

The election of the Aymara president Morales and his designs to rewrite the nation's constitution rekindled political forces in Sucre. From the perspective of politicians there, Aymara forces, this time headed by Morales, were trying to usurp even more power from Sucre, the nation's traditional capital. Their demands that all sectors of the government be returned to Sucre has led to serious confrontations between Sucre residents and the national police and army. The Civil War of 1899 continues to produce casualties; three protestors died in the conflicts associated with the attempt to rewrite the constitution during "Black November," in 2007. One Sucre resident explicitly referred to the civil war in an interview about the conflicts between Sucre residents and MAS constitutional assembly members: "They want to provoke a fight between Bolivians? Do they want to repeat the war of Ayo Ayo? Well then we will do it!"[8]

Through Sucre's aggressive campaign, La Paz's official silence, revisionist Katarista history, and the intense racial and political debates that have intensified in La Paz, the events of 1899 and their Aymara protagonists are again at the heart of political struggle in contemporary Bolivia. Nonetheless, little effort has been made to review the historical sources that have contributed to understanding the Aymara participation in the Civil War of 1899 as a race war. Recent narratives of Aymara history, such as that of Mamani Ramírez, connect Tupac Katari to Zárate Willka, Santos Marka T'ula, and often Morales, highlighting a succession of great Aymara leaders and downplaying their connections to broader political coalitions and to the Bolivian nation.[9]

Urban intellectuals are not the only ones to assign significance to the Aymaras in the civil war. Indigenous people's constructions of national belonging and identity connect local understandings of 1899 with contemporary national politics, made evident in part today through the multiple views of Juan Lero. Today, over one hundred years later, narratives of the Civil War of 1899 that embody disputes over power, land, race, history, and political affiliation converge in affirming Juan Lero's role as the head of the supposed Indian government in Peñas, as discussed in chapter 1. However, these diverse contemporary narratives send different messages regarding Aymara history and the Aymaras' relationship to the nation.

In April 1991 the highland organization CONAMAQ (Consejo Nacional de Ayllus y Markas de Qollasuyu, or the National Council of Indigenous Communities and Towns of Kollasuyu) sponsored a meeting of community authorities in the Peñas region. The CONAMAQ representatives deliberately selected Peñas as the meeting site to honor the memory of the Peñas cacique apoderado Juan Lero, who was accused of establishing an Indian government in 1899 and who was characterized in the 1991 meeting as a "crusader against neo-colonialism and Indian oppression."[10] Described variously as a First Nations organization, a native rights organization, and a federation of Aymara and Quechua communities, CONAMAQ uses the ayllu model as the basic form of Indian community, emphasizing Indian identity, community, and reciprocity.[11] In large part, CONAMAQ leaders seek to recover an Aymara history that has been cannibalized by the state. The post-1970 current of revindication underscores the role of Aymara leaders such as Lero, as a pamphlet from the April 1991 meeting in Peñas suggests (see fig. 16).

The anonymous authors of the pamphlet state: "The hauq'a-tatiris [community authorities] of the ayllus and communities of Thapa-Qhari [Tapacarí,

FIGURE 16. Juan Lero as represented on the cover of a pamphlet from the Third Meeting of Indigenous Authorities, *Por los caminos de Juan Liru: Construyamos el poder communal, anti-colonialista, anti-imperialista* (Peñas, Apr. 8–9, 1991). The meeting was run by members of CONAMAQ.

the ayllu Lero was from] are committed to the revolutionary struggle to punish the colonial invaders: neo-colonialists, imperialists, and capitalists, because it is time to take vengeance for the millions of lives lost in massacres that continue today [as a result of] the politics of extermination"; they then end with the well-known revolutionary cry "Ya basta, señores!" Among the goals stated in the pamphlet is the abolition of all political parties in their community and the creation of a new, Indian-based party, one that would be representative of community experiences and that would showcase Indian leaders and heroes from various historical epochs, such as Tupac Katari and Juan Lero. At this meeting Lero was celebrated as "the first Qhisawa-Aymara president of five departments of Bolivia (Oruro, Potosí, Chuquisaca, La Paz, and Cochabamba) . . . [who] fought against injustice, against the loss of communal lands, against the priests, [and] against the exploitation and oppression by the colonial invaders."[12] The activists gathering at this meeting thus recognized Lero as a resistance leader rather than an ally of Colonel Pando and the Liberal Party. Indeed, the Aymara defendants' testimonies from the Peñas trial do not fit within these revisionist narratives of Aymara resistance to the Bolivian state.

The Caracollo Inca play constitutes an alternative narrative of the Aymara past. As a result of the Aymara indigenous group's participation in Bolivia's Civil War of 1899, which contributed to the Liberal Party's victory, intellectuals aligned with that party adopted a glorified Inca past to marginalize their former "savage" Aymara wartime allies. But constructions of an Inca identity did not remain in the hands of the elite intellectuals. Capitalizing on the intellectual current that glorified the Incas, the national elite and the provincial Aymara elite forged their own images of the socially acceptable Bolivian Indian, "Incas" who were heirs of the tradition of noble indigenous rule in Peru and who were "whitened" personages in the Bolivian context. The local Aymara elite opted to promote their Inca past via theatrical presentations and to narrate their own history beginning with the historical watershed of the might—and fall—of the Inca Empire. The pre-Incan Aymara past and actors were silenced. The local Aymara elite adopted an "Inca" identity after the war to avoid the stigma of being "Aymara"—an unacceptable form of Indianness—and to mobilize for national inclusion. Appropriating and promoting their Inca past allowed the local Aymara elite to consolidate power on the local level as well as to claim a space for themselves as "progressive Indians" within the nation in ways that an assertion of an Aymara identity would have prohibited.

The Inca play that emerged in Caracollo during the early twentieth century, shortly after the civil war, constituted the local Aymaras' attempt to find resonance with the ruling Liberal Party as "acceptable Indians," not an act of resistance to the nation. The Aymaras demonstrated their support for José Manuel Pando, for the Liberal Party, and for federalism through demonstrations of support during the 1896 elections, through military support in 1899, and in the postwar era through performances of the Inca past. Rather than connect the Inca king to other great Indian leaders, the Inca theatrical guilds and the numerous directors who have shaped the scripts have opted instead to underscore the Incas' place among great world civilizations of the past, such as the Moorish kingdom and Spanish colonialism. The Aymara past is carefully folded into the margins of this historical narrative, with the Aymaras serving as the ancestral people who evolved into the great Incas. In performing their Inca play, Caracollo's Inca theater actors negotiate their places within the nation and connect their region's past to the broader themes of empire, conquest, and world history. The play's directors serve as the town historians and "correct" the script for each performance, showcasing Indian leaders with the goal of connecting these protagonists and the Indian history they represent to broader national and global political processes, parties, and institutions.

In Peñas, diverse narratives of the Civil War of 1899 indicate that the significance of the Aymara participation does not univocally follow Katarista interpretations. In interviews with me or others, several people supported the Aymaras' testimonies from the Peñas trial and my interpretation of the purpose of the Inca play, conveying an alternative significance to the Aymaras' past and their involvement in national politics. When I interviewed Felipe Lero, Juan Lero's great-grandnephew, he refused to talk about his fore-bear and the war.[13] His face twisted into an expression of great sadness as I tried to ask him questions about it. He would say only that Juan Lero had worked with the Liberal Party and that he had helped round up defeated Conservative soldiers after victory had been pronounced. He did not wish to elaborate, and the very act of thinking about it seemed to cause him pain. Nevertheless, Felipe Lero connected Juan Lero, Feliciano Mamani, and other Peñas residents to the Liberal Party, thus indicating Juan Lero's support of it.

Felipe Lero certainly did not proudly point to Juan Lero as a symbol of neocolonial resistance. As Felipe's younger relative Toribia Lero suggested, the aged gentleman, very much a product of past generations whose members recalled the fear the Leros felt in the wake of the civil war, was more embarrassed than proud of the stories that construct Juan Lero as a threat to the nation. Toribia Lero stated that the repression against the Leros was so severe that some family members changed their last name to Ledo so as to avoid punishment.[14] While Felipe Lero did not address the topic of Juan Lero as president of the region or the nation, his reaction suggests that the image put forth by the Kataristas, who portray the events of 1899 as a manifestation of an agenda of Aymara autonomy, is not met with unanimous approval.

As I walked back and forth through the outlaying communities of Peñas, I was especially struck by Añahuayani, the community that had been Juan Lero's home, located about three to four kilometers from Peñas. Scattered throughout the sparsely populated community were attractive, well-built outhouses that included exterior sinks with running water. As I stood there admiring the outhouses, I talked with local residents about Juan Lero, 1899, and the Liberal Party. Francisco Flores, a senior resident of Añahuayani, was unsure exactly how Juan Lero had been affiliated with the Liberal Party, but he knew that there had been a connection. Flores was sure of Lero's political importance as a national leader: "Lero was the president, with the poncho and the ch'ullu and everything!"[15] The possibility of an Indian as president dressed in traditional attire did not seem to be a far stretch for Flores. As I walked away, he called after me, "Make sure you look where those cows are grazing. That was the Liberal camp, right there. When it rains hard, sometimes bullets still turn up." I did take a good look at the area. Without the help of local residents such as Francisco Flores, who preserve the geographic record of 1899, I would have walked across that historical site without even knowing it.

Later, I met a man passing through with his sheep; I would later come to know him as Vicente Pacheco, a local authority of Añahuayani. To Pacheco, a man who appeared to be in his thirties, Juan Lero bore a different, contemporary significance. He spoke easily and proudly of Juan Lero and in fact connected the latrines that I had been admiring to Lero as a symbol of progress. "This was Juan Lero's home," he said, "and Juan Lero was an important man[;] he was president—I'm not sure if he was president of the region or the country, but he was important. If this is the home of that important man, how could we stay behind and not progress too? Of course we have good latrines. How could we have anything less?"[16]

Pacheco then took me to see the remains of Lero's house, abandoned and crumbling. He expressed his interest in restoring it as a historic monument, as a testament to the region's importance and the achievements of the local population. Añahuayani is filled with sites that keep the memory of 1899 and Juan Lero alive in the Peñas region; they generate multiple oral histories within local communities that in turn reveal how the residents understand local events and realities as shaping the broader national context. "Look over there, to the left. That is where the Liberal soldiers would march," said Pacheco. Talking with both Pacheco and Flores made it clear that the history of Liberal Party support in Peñas had been passed down in detail from generation to generation. Pacheco stopped and turned to look at me with a serious expression on his face. "Juan Lero is an excellent example for us all of what we can become," he stated. "Many times I talk to the youth of our community about Juan Lero, and I tell them, look, if Lero, an Indian, could become president, then you too can do great things. Don't sell yourself short."[17] Pacheco stated that the example of Juan Lero as president had motivated him to run for political office in his province. He failed to win (he blamed his defeat on racism and corruption), but he has not abandoned his goal of participating in national politics. So far he has run for office three times.

Pacheco's understanding of Juan Lero constructs this historical figure as a symbol of citizenship for indigenous people within the nation. His reference to Lero as president suggests the possibility for indigenous people to lead the nation. If Lero was president in 1899, he had set the precedent for indigenous people to rise in power and to be successful in national politics. Pacheco's recognition of him as president establishes the national importance of both Lero and the events that occurred in Peñas during 1899, and it resonates with Pacheco's own desire to gain a position in regional government and to actively participate within national politics.

In Bolivia's early twentieth-century sociopolitical discourses, which were highly influenced by the tenets of modernity, eugenics, and a highly politicized and politically active indigenous population whose presence could not be denied, we can see the roots of ethnic politics in the nation-building process that define the county's past as well as its present. Images and constructions of an Indian identity have remained at the core of nation building in Bolivia. While liberal discourses certainly included ethnocidal elements, they nevertheless employed the promise of the glorified Inca past to express Bolivian modernity. Constructions of identity as well as discourses on identity, redress, and national policy were expressed through the rhetoric of civilization and modernity by adopting a "preferred Indian" identity. The Aymaras' participation in the Civil War of 1899 sought to expand the ambit of national belonging under the Liberal Party regime through an Aymara-Creole alliance to bring that party to power. The Aymara population was marginalized (but not excluded) in the discourses of modernity, and yet the image of the Indian was not and could not be absent from the party's blueprints of nation. The refashioned trope of the Inca defined liberal imaginings of nation and national belonging; it also served as a visual and discursive means for the local Aymara elite to maintain local hierarchies and to participate in the construction of "preferred" Indian identities.

The complicated process of nation building in Bolivia has led Brooke Larson to observe that "the Andes entered the twentieth century without having built a hegemonic 'language of contention' to replace the shattered colonial heritage of 'dual republics' or to contain the resurgence of ethnic politics."[18] No state-recognized Indian hero emerged from the Civil War of 1899. Whereas Cuba came to laud the late nineteenth-century Afro-Cuban independence leader Antonio Maceo, and Mexico, the early twentieth-century revolutionary leader Emiliano Zapata, the Bolivian government did not recognize any Indian hero from the Civil War of 1899. The Aymara war veterans who did not die in jail awaiting the verdict in the Peñas trial were sentenced to death, jail, or exile. Historical sources that would shed more light on the Aymaras' political involvement have quietly disappeared. The pantheon of the massive La Paz cemetery includes no tomb or monument dedicated to the soldiers who fought on behalf of the Liberal Party in 1899.

Yet liberal intellectuals, pressed to address the "Indian question" even more urgently after the civil war precisely because of the Aymaras' participation in it, opted to employ a preferred Inca image to marginalize the less desirable Aymara Indian population. Both Creole intellectuals and the Caracollo elite negotiated definitions of national belonging; this process took place through a discourse on preferred Indian identities. Any promotion of the Aymaras depended on establishing links with the Inca image. Nonindigenista intellectuals strove to maintain racial difference between the Aymaras and the Incas, while indigenista intellectuals sought to erase racial distinctions and to establish a connection between the lauded Incas and the Aymara past. Though this process of racial differentiation was contested, indigenista intellectuals and the Caracollo elite ultimately contributed to the promotion of an acceptable Indian image, the Inca. The local Aymara elite of Caracollo developed and performed an alternative Indian identity as Incas through which they attempted to claim a space within the Bolivian nation as civilized, progressive Indians.

The contemporary political arena reflects the centrality of an Indian identity in ambivalent historical discourses that have kept the Indian question at the center of the national agenda. Evo Morales's presidency is not only the result of over a century of Aymara resistance to the nation; rather, Evo Morales is in significant ways the greatest legacy of the efforts of Pablo Zárate Willka, Juan Lero, and other early twentieth-century caciques apoderados, who forged alliances among themselves and with national political parties. These Aymara leaders proved their valor on the battlefields and petitioned the government for land rights and education, expanding the scope of the Bolivian nation-building project in the late nineteenth and early twentieth centuries. "Acting Inca" reveals the shared script between liberal intellectuals and the Caracollo Aymara elite in early twentieth-century Bolivia, which underscores the close connection between constructions of indigenous identities and the nation's future that would come to dominate national politics throughout the twentieth and, so far, twenty-first centuries.

NOTES

Introduction: Indian Problems, Indian Solutions

1. "Al Sr. Gobernador de Tapacarí en Peñas, de José Maria Galligo, Guayllani," Peñas trial records, Mar. 29, 1899, vol. 6, 1119, Archivo Judicial de Oruro (AJO).

2. "Al Sr. Don Juan Liro [sic], de Cesiliano Gallego, Merque Aimaya," Peñas trial records, Apr. 7, 1899, vol. 6, 1072, AJO.

3. "Al Sr. Juez Instructor, de Esteban Ari," Peñas trial records, Nov. 25, 1899, vol. 5, 922, AJO.

4. See Laura Gotkowitz, *A Revolution for Our Rights: Indigenous Struggles for Land and Justice in Bolivia, 1880–1952* (Durham, N.C.: Duke University Press, 2007), 43–68.

5. See correspondence between José M. Pando and Pablo Zárate Willka, June 27, 1896, repr. in Ramiro Condarco Morales, *Zárate, el "temible" Willka: Historia de la rebelión indígena de 1899 en la república de Boliva*, 2d ed. (La Paz: Imprenta Renovación, 1983), 96.

6. See Forrest Hylton, Adolfo Gilly, and Sinclair Thomson, *Revolutionary Horizons: Past and Present in Bolivian Politics* (London: Verso, 2007), 54.

7. See, for example, Bautista Saavedra, *El ayllu* (La Paz: Imprenta Artística Velarde, Aldazosa, 1903).

8. Pablo Zárate Willka, "Proclama de Caracollo," in *De la revolución al Pachakuti: El aprendizaje del respeto recíproco entre blancos e indianos*, by Filemón Escóbar (La Paz: Garz Azul, 2008), 310.

9. Hylton and Thomson, *Revolutionary Horizons*, 57; Pablo Zárate Willka, "Proclama de Caracollo," 309–18; Brooke Larson, *Trials of Nation Making: Liberalism, Race, and Ethnicity in the Andes, 1810–1910* (Cambridge: Cambridge University Press, 2004); "Indagatoria de Juan Lero," Peñas trial records, Apr. 21, 1899, vol. 1, 8, AJO.

10. See Silvia Rivera Cusicanqui, *Oppressed but Not Defeated: Peasant Struggles among the Aymara and the Qhechwa in Bolivia, 1900–1980* (Geneva: United Nations Research Institute for Social Development, 1987); Larson, *Trials of Nation Making*.

11. Condarco Morales pioneered this theory in *Zárate*. Also see Pilar Mendieta Parada, "De la alianza a la confrontación: Pablo Zárate Willka y la rebelión indígena de 1899 en Bolivia" (PhD diss., Universidad Nacional de San Marcos, Lima, Facultad de Ciencias Sociales, 2006).

12. See Condarco Morales, *Zárate*. Mendieta Parada ("De la alianza), Larson (*Trials of Nation Making*), and Hylton and Thomson (*Revolutionary Horizons*) all stress Aymara ethnic autonomy rather than a "race war" as the key factor in the deterioration of the initial alliance between Aymaras and the Liberal Party. Larson states: "It was a pact of political convenience—inevitably precarious and dangerous" (233).

13. Rivera Cusicanqui, *Oppressed but Not Defeated*; Roberto Choque Canqui et al., eds. *Educación indígena: Ciudadanía o colonización?* (La Paz: Ediciones Aruwiyiri/Taller de Historia Oral Andina, 1992).

14. Condarco Morales, *Zárate*; Mendieta Parada, "De la alianza"; Saavedra, *El ayllu*.

15. Brooke Larson, "Redeemed Indians, 'Barbarized Cholos': Crafting Neocolonial Modernity in Liberal Bolivia, 1900–1910," in *Political Cultures in the Andes, 1750–1950*, ed. Nils Jacobsen and Cristóbal Aljovín de Losada (Durham, N.C.: Duke University Press, 2005), 230–52.

16. Larson, "Redeemed Indians"; Seemin Qayum, "Nationalism, Internal Colonialism, and the Spatial Imagination: The Geographic Society of La Paz in Turn-of-the-Century Bolivia," in *Studies in the Formation of the Nation State in Latin America*, ed. James Dunkerley (London: Institute of Latin American Studies, 202), 279–98.

17. Rebecca Earle, *The Return of the Native: Indians and Myth-Making in Spanish America, 1810–1930* (Durham, N.C.: Duke University Press, 2007); David Brading, *The First America: The Spanish Monarchy, Creole Patriots, and the Liberal State, 1492–1867* (Cambridge: Cambridge University Press, 1991); Alexander Dawson, "From Models for the Nation to Model Citizens: Indigenismo and the 'Revindication' of the Mexican Nation, 1920–1940," *Journal of Latin American Studies* 30, no. 2 (1998): 279–308.

18. Mariano Baptista, "Lugentes," *La Soberanía* (Oruro), Feb. 18, 1899, Archivo Nacional de Bolivia (ANB).

19. For Mexico, see José Vasconcelos, *The Cosmic Race = La raza cósmica*, trans. Didier Tisdel Jaén (Los Angeles: Centro de Publicaciones, Dept. of Chicano Studies, California State University, 1979). For Cuba, see Ada Ferrer, *Insurgent Cuba: Race, Nation, and Revolution, 1868–1898* (Chapel Hill: University of North Carolina Press, 1999); Aline Helg, *Our Rightful Share: The Afro-Cuban Struggle for Equality, 1886–1912* (Chapel Hill: University of North Carolina Press, 1995).

20. For studies that link manifestations of Inca theater and imagery to indigenous resistance efforts or to a desire to return to an Indian past, see Nathan Wachtel, *The Vision of the Vanquished: The Spanish Conquest of Peru through Indian Eyes, 1530–1570*, trans. Ben Reynolds and Siân Reynolds (New York: Barnes and Noble, 1977); Manuel Burga, *Nacimiento de una utopia: Muerte y resurrección de los Incas* (Lima: Instituto de Apoyo Agrario, 1988); Raquel Chang-Rodríguez, "Cultural Resistance in the Andes and Its Depiction in *Atau Wallpaj P'uchukakuyninpa Wankan or Tragedy of Atahualpa's Death*," in *Coded Encounters: Writing, Gender, and Ethnicity in Colonial Latin America*, ed. Francisco Javier Cevallos-Candau et al. (Amherst: University of Massachusetts Press, 1994), 115–32; Jesús Lara, *Tragedia del fin de Atahuallpa: Atau Wallpaj p'uchukakuyninpa wankan* (Cochabamba, Bolivia: Los Amigos del Libro; Buenos Aires: Ediciones del Sol, 1989).

21. In Challacollo, a town south of the city of Oruro, the Inca play has been performed by the local elite throughout much of the twentieth century. According to interviews carried out by Margot Beyersdorff, the residents continue to perform an Inca identity and to claim an Inca past via the public venue of festival performances.

The town's residents, however, recognize the Uru roots of Challacollo, stating that Challacollo was an Uru town under Aymara rule prior to the arrival of the Spaniards. The decision to promote an Inca identity and past resonates with the case of Caracollo in suggestive ways, although further investigation is needed to determine when and in what historical context this happened. See Beyersdorff, *Historia y drama ritual en los Andes bolivianos: Siglos XV–XX* (La Paz: Plural Editores, 1998), 260–62.

22. Manuel Ballivián and Luis Crespo, *Censo nacional de la población de Bolivia* (1ero de *septiembre de* 1900), vol. 2, *Parte histórica* (La Paz: Tipo-Litográfico de José M. Gamarra, 1904), 32, ANB.

23. Ibid., 26.

24. Carlos Mesa Gisbert and Mario Espinoza Osorio, *La Guerra Federal*, DVD (La Paz: Plano Medio, 2009).

25. Ibid (my transcription and translation).

26. Kjell Nilsson-Maki, "Indian Attack," www.cartoonstock.com, catalog reference, knin147 (accessed Jan. 2010).

Chapter 1. The Aymara in the Civil War of 1899: Enemy or Ally of the Liberal Party?

1. Pablo Zárate Willka's "Proclama de Caracollo" is reprinted in Filemón Escóbar, *De la revolución al Pachakuti: El aprendizaje del respeto recíproco entre blancos e indianos* (La Paz: Garza Azul, 2008), 310.

2. José M. Mendoza, Peñas trial records, Jan. 14, 1901, vol. 8, 1487, Archivo Judicial de Oruro (AJO).

3. Peñas trial records, July 20, 1900, vol. 6, 1177, AJO, document incomplete. C'aras is a derogatory term used to refer to non-Indian people.

4. "Confesión de Pablo Zárate Willka," Peñas trial records, July 20, 1900, vol. 6, 1177, AJO.

5. "Al Señores de José M. Mendoza," Peñas trial records, Jan. 14, 1901, vol. 8, 1487, AJO.

6. "Al Sr. Juez de Partido del Fiscal Ballongalvarro," Peñas trial records, ca. Mar. 1900, vol. 6, 1062, AJO, document incomplete.

7. "Sentencia," Peñas trial records, Jan. 25, 1901, vol. 8, 1519–24, AJO.

8. "Sentencia," Peñas trial records, Feb. 27, 1902, vol. 9, 1622–27, AJO.

9. My analysis of the Aymaras' participation in the Civil War of 1899 builds on Gilbert Joseph's critique of Eric Hobsbawm's book *Bandits*, in which Hobsbawm understands banditry as a primitive form of popular protest that was void of political ideology or broader social program. See Eric Hobsbawm, *Bandits*, 2d ed. (New York: Pantheon, 1981). Several studies have made key contributions in moving the field of peasant studies in new directions by insisting that peasant resistance must be understood not in essentialist terms but rather in its specific historical context; these include Steve Stern, ed., *Resistance, Rebellion, and Consciousness in the Andean Peasant World, 18th to 20th Centuries* (Madison: University of Wisconsin Press, 1987); Gilbert Joseph, "On the Trail of Latin American Bandits: A Reexamination of Peasant Resistance," *Latin American Research Review* 25, no. 3 (1990): 7–53; Ranajit Guha, *Elementary Aspects of Peasant Insurgency in Colonial India* (Delhi: Oxford University Press, 1983); and James Scott, *Weapons of the Weak: Everyday Forms of Peasant Resistance* (New Haven, Conn.: Yale University Press, 1985).

10. Silvia Rivera Cusicanqui, *Oppressed but Not Defeated: Peasant Struggles among the Aymara and Qhechwa in Bolivia, 1900–1980* (Geneva: United Nations Research Institute for Social Development, 1987).

11. Nils Jacobsen, "The Long and the Short of It," in *Political Cultures in the Andes, 1750–1950*, ed. Nils Jacobsen and Cristóbal Aljovín de Losada (Durham, N.C.: Duke University Press, 2005), 1–25.

12. Esteban Ticona Alejo, *Los Andes desde los Andes: Aymaranakana, Qhichwanakana, Yatxatawipa, Lup'iwipa* (La Paz: Ediciones Yachaywasi, 2003).

13. Zárate Willka, "Proclama."

14. See, e.g., Ticona Alejo, *Los Andes desde los Andes*; Roberto Choque Canqui et al., eds., *Educación indígena: Cuidadanía o colonización?* (La Paz: Ediciones Aruwiyiri/Taller de Historia Oral Andina, 1992).

15. Rossana Barragán, *Indios, mujeres, y ciudadanos: Legislación y ejercicio de la ciudadanía en Bolivia, siglo XIX* (La Paz: Fundación Diálogo, 1999).

16. Herbert Klein, *Bolivia: Evolution of a Multi-Ethnic Society* (New York: Oxford University Press, 1992), 142–43.

17. Herbert Klein, *Peasant Response to the Market and the Land Question in Eighteenth- and Nineteenth-Century Bolivia* (Washington, D.C.: Wilson Center, 1982), 5.

18. Condarco Morales, *Zárate*, 44.

19. Ibid., 43.

20. Ibid., 95. The term *Willka* is a title meaning "first" and denoting a person of importance within the native hierarchy; see ibid., 81.

21. The taxes were higher as they were to be paid in the devalued currency of the boliviano; see Brooke Larson, *Trials of Nation Making: Liberalism, Race and Ethnicity in the Andes, 1810–1910* (Cambridge: Cambridge University Press, 2004).

22. José de Mesa, Teresa Gisbert, and Carlos Mesa Gisbert, eds., *Historia de Bolivia* (La Paz: Editorial Gisbert, 2001), 486.

23. In 1881, Augstín Aspiazu, the director of the land surveys, emphasized the profitability of the altiplano haciendas. Aspiazu claimed not only that the value of the haciendas had doubled between 1860 and 1880 but also that they represented a safe and sure investment. Haciendas required little investment, for the peasants supplied much of the labor, and the nearby market of La Paz promised to grow. See Klein, *Peasant Response*, 8.

24. Ibid.

25. Erwin Grieshaber, "Survival of Indian Communities in Nineteenth-Century Bolivia: A Regional Comparison," *Journal of Latin American Studies* 12, no. 2 (1980): 223–69.

26. Brooke Larson, "Andean Highland Peasants and the Trials of Nation Making during the Nineteenth Century," in *Cambridge History of the Native Peoples of the Americas*, ed. Stuart Schwartz and Frank Salomon, vol. 3 (Cambridge: Cambridge University Press, 1999), 668.

27. Ibid., 667.

28. Ibid.

29. Pilar Mendieta Parada, "De la alianza a la confrontación: Pablo Zárate Willka y la rebelión indígena de 1899 en Bolivia" (PhD diss., Universidad Nacional de San Marcos, Facultad de Ciencias Sociales, 2006). Mendieta Parada cites Archivo de La Paz (ALP)/PR, vol. 46 (1894), 148.

30. Ibid.

31. Condarco Morales, Zárate, 96–97.

32. Ibid..

33. Ibid.

34. Ibid.

35. Diego Caricari et al., "Carta al Presidente de la República, dirigida por los representantes de las comunidades de 24 cantones y provincias (19 de noviembre de 1889)," expedientes, prefectura 1890, ALP, uncataloged series.

36. Ibid.

37. Ibid.

38. In 1885 the Colquechaca population exceeded 10,000 people. See Tristan Platt, Estado boliviano y ayllu andino: Tierra y tributo en el Norte de Potosí (Lima: Instituto de Estudios Peruanos, 1982), 298. With 2,000 miners working in the cavernous tunnels of the silver-rich mountains, Colquechaca constituted a rising center of trade and commerce in Norte Potosí that affected the whole region.

39. Ibid., 309–10.

40. Mendieta Parada, "De la alianza," 224, citing La Capital (Sucre), Dec. 28, 1891.

41. Ibid., 226.

42. Platt, Estado boliviano, 311.

43. Mendieta Parada, "De la alianza," 226.

44. Ibid., citing "Un peligro social," El Comercio (La Paz), May 7, 1896.

45. "La representación paceña," El Comercio (La Paz), Nov. 30, 1898, 3, Archivo Nacional de Bolivia (ANB).

46. Isaac Campero, Historia del parlamento boliviano de 1898 y la revolución de La Paz (La Paz: Imprenta y Litografía Boliviana, 1899).

47. "Del boletín oficial," El Comercio (La Paz), Feb. 28, 1899, 3, ANB.

48. Soria Choque also recognizes that the rise of the Liberal Party regime offered a space of opportunity for indigenous peoples in that the Liberals proclaimed equality for all Bolivians. Legal equality was an important gain for the caciques apoderados in their constant efforts to obtain legal protection for indigenous communities. See Vitaliano Soria Choque, "Los caciques-apoderados y la lucha por la escuela," in Educación indígena, ed. Choque Canqui et al., 60.

Tristan Platt also notes that the disliked Conservative revisita surveys made liberalism an attractive alternative for indigenous peoples but interprets the comuneros' experience with liberalism within what he refers to as an "Andean framework." In this sense, Platt suggests that the Liberal Party represented the dawn of a new age of justice. "Between 1890 and 1897," Platt states, "Indians and mestizos in both provinces were finally driven into each other's arms, in part through Liberal Party agitation, but more decisively by the Constitutionalist insistence on renewing the land commissions. . . . The Party offered a Catholic mirage, a reflection of existing society with the Constitutionalist 'taint' removed, a mirror in which all who looked might hope to see themselves whole. To this extent, it could be seen as the latest in a long line of Andean movements that aimed to restore a 'just order' that had been betrayed, to realign a social project that had become distorted" (Platt, "The Andean Experience of Bolivian Liberalism: Roots of Rebellion in 19th-Century Chayanta [Bolivia]," in Resistance, Rebellion, and Consciousness in the

Andean Peasant World, 18th–20th Centuries, ed. Steve Stern [Madison: University of Wisconsin Press, 1987], 311, 315.).

Whereas other studies (e.g., Luis Antezana Ergueta, *La guerra entre La Paz y Chuquisaca* [La Paz: H. Municipalidad de La Paz, 1999]) have focused on the elites' interpretation of the Aymaras' participation in the revolution, Platt's study strives to illustrate how highland Indian communities in Potosí interpreted national politics. Neither perspective is successful in breaking down the polarized representation of Bolivian society and politics as divided into rural/urban or Indian/white; these studies do not sufficiently explore the Aymaras' efforts to claim a space within the nation. Platt's study, however, is suggestive regarding the Inca image's centrality to liberalism in Bolivia.

49. Forrest Hylton and Sinclair Thomson, *Revolutionary Horizons: Past and Present in Bolivian Politics* (London: Verso, 2007), 54.

50. *Boletín Oficial,* no. 37, 168. Letter dated Feb. 5, 1899.

51. Zárate Willka, "Proclama," 310.

52. Pilar Mendieta Parada, "Entre el caudillismo y la modernidad: Poder local y política en la provincia de Inquisivi, el caso de Mohoza (1880–1899) (master's thesis, ciencias políticas, Centro de Estudios Superiores del Centro Boliviano de Estudios Multidisciplinarios, 1999), 279.

53. "Letter from José Manuel Pando to Cesareo Zalles," May 6, 1896, Fondo José Manuel Pando, ANB. I would like to thank Pilar Mendieta for calling this letter to my attention.

54. "Para la historia," *Los Debates* (La Paz), Mar. 14, 1899, Archivo de la Casa de la Libertad (CdL), Sucre; the letters also appeared in *El Comercio* (La Paz), Mar. 15, 1899, ANB.

55. The story of this incident appears in "Alrededor de la mission Monasterios; Datos interesantes," *La Soberanía* (Oruro), Mar. 11, 1899, ANB.

56. "Para la historia."

57. Al Señor Pando," Peñas trial records, April 20, 1899, vol. 1, 27, AJO.

58. See, for example, "Un capítulo de la historia de la revolución," *El Comercio* (La Paz), Jan. 26, 1900, 2, ANB.

59. "Interogatoria de Mariano Condori," Peñas trial records, Feb. 10, 1900, vol. 4, 654, AJO. There is significant variation among the names of those thought to have made up the indigenous government of Peñas. Most testimonies agree that Lero was president, but they differ as to the names of the intendant, judge, and the ministers.

60. "Al Sr. Fiscal del Distrito, de J. Miranda, por los presentantes," Peñas trial records, Aug. 19, 1900, vol. 6, 1197, AJO.

61. Condarco Morales, *Zárate,* 377, quoting "Testimonio de Manuel Rivera," Peñas trial records, vol. 1, 4 (c. 1, f. 4), AJO.

62. Ibid., 378, quoting "Del corregidor de Huancané Mariano Sánchez, al corregidor de Urmiri," Peñas trial records, Apr. 13, 1899, c. 7, f. 65, AJO.

63. "Al Sr. Prefecto i Comandante General del departamento de Oruro, de la Sub-prefectura de Paria," Peñas trial records, April 24, 1899, vol. 1, 29, AJO.

64. "Al Sr. Juez Instructor," Peñas trial records, May 26, 1899, vol. 1, 186, AJO.

65. "Al Sr. Juez Instructor," Peñas trial records, Feb. 29, 1900, vol. 6, 1034, AJO.

66. "Al Sr. Juez de Partido," Peñas trial records, estimated date May 1900, vol. 6, 1042, AJO, document incomplete.

67. "Al Sr. Juez de Partido del Fiscal Ballongalvarro," Peñas trial records, estimated date Mar. 1900, vol. 6, 1042, AJO, document incomplete.

68. Chervin ctd. in Larson, *Trials of Nation Making*, 240–41. For the original, see Arthur Chervin, *Anthropologie bolivienne*, 3 vols. (Paris: Imprimerie Nationale/Librairie H. Le Soudier, 1907–8).

69. "Del Agente Fiscal Ballongalvarro," Peñas trial records, estimated date Mar. 1900, vol. 6, 1062, AJO, document incomplete.

70. See, for example, the following testimonies taken in April and May 1899, all in Peñas trial records, vol. 1, AJO: José Manuel Sequera, 11; Mariano Achacollo, 6; Mariano Ururi, 10; Teodoro Muruchi, 49; and Mariano Mamani, 56.

71. "Debates del dia," Peñas trial records, Dec. 27, 1900, vol. 8, 1472, AJO.

72. Ibid.

73. Two facts suggest that the individual responsible for the tally worked in the early twentieth century. First, the handwriting is similar to that used in the trial records; second, the additions were written boldly, as if by someone who felt entitled to mark up the trial records.

74. "Al Presidente & V. V. de la Corte Suprema, de Gabino Jereira," Peñas trial records, Aug. 29, 1901, vol. 4, 1588, AJO.

75. "A los Senores, de José M. Mendoza," Peñas trial records, Jan. 14, 1901, vol. 8, 1487, AJO.

76. "Sentencia," Jan. 25, 1901, Peñas trial records, vol. 8, 1519–24, AJO.

77. "Sentencia," Peñas trial records, Feb. 27, 1902, vol. 9, 1622–27, AJO.

78. In 1901 the following eleven individuals were sentenced to die: Asencio Fuentes, Feliciano Mamani, Lazaro Condori, Gregorio Chaparro, Gabriel Gutierrez, Manuel Flores, José Manuel Apasa, Evaristo Guaricollo, Mariano Muruchi, Eusebio Colque, and Casimiro Choque. Sixteen others were sentenced to ten years in jail and to witness the executions of those facing capital punishment: Lorenzo Fuentes, Mariano Choque no. 2, Nicanor Quispe, Francisco Sequera, Teodoro Muruchi, Calisto Ramos, Bernardino Capurata, Miguel Victoria, Rojano Choque, Agustin Condori, Casimiro Ortiz, Cruz Choque, Santiago Ayala, Mariano Choque no. 1, Hilarion Fuentes, and Miguel Sequera. In addition, the men in the second group were forced to participate in a lottery to select two of them for execution. Matias Hurtado and Pablo Zárate Willca were absolved, and Juan Lero died in jail awaiting the verdict. See "Sentencia," Peñas trial records, Jan. 25, 1901, vol. 8, 1522–23, AJO.

In 1902 only Asencio Fuentes, Gregorio Chaparro, and Mariano Choque no. 1 were sentenced to death. Feliciano Mamani, Lazaro Condori, Gabriel Gutierrez, José Manuel Apasa, Manuel Flores, Evaristo Guaricollo, Mariano Muruchi, Eusebio Colque, Casimiro Choque, Nicanor Quispe, Francisco Sequera, Teodoro Muruchi, Calisto Ramos, Bernardino Capurata, Miguel Victoria, Rojano Choque, Agustin Condori, Casimiro Ortiz, Cruz Choque, Lorenzo Fuente, and Miguel Sequera received ten years in jail plus additional confinement in the distant hamlet of Salinas de Garci Mendoza. See "Sentencia," Peñas trial records, Feb. 27, 1902, vol. 9, 1625, AJO.

The second sentence seems to have arisen from a battle between legal authorities rather than a thorough reconsideration of the evidence. The accused said they were not part of the debates that took place to determine the second sentence. Others said they found out that the debates had occurred only after they were over. The court received appeal after appeal from the accused indigenous men decrying the extralegal proceedings in arriving at the new sentence. Frustrated, the defendant Gabriel Gutierres wrote: "I would one thousand times prefer death over this cruel suffering and great injustice that they make us go through, which is worse than ten death sentences. I ask you, judge, to repeal the new sentence as we did not participate in any debates and do not even know if these debates actually took place. This new sentence violates the legal codes 223 and 224, as none of the accused participated in or even witnessed these debates" ("Al Sr. Presidente de la corte de Manuel Rios por Gabriel Gutierres," Peñas trial records, June 7, 1902, vol. 9, 1656, AJO).

79. "Al Sr. Fiscal del Partido, de Mariano Urori, Juan Lero, et al.," Peñas trial records, June 7, 1899, vol. 2, 271, AJO.

80. "Interogatoria de Francisco Sequera," Peñas trial records, May 8, 1899, vol. 1, 94, AJO.

81. "Indagatoria de Casimiro Ortiz," Peñas trial records, Feb. 21, 1900, vol. 4, 720, AJO.

82. "Indagatoria de Francisco Chaca," Peñas trial records, June 13, 1899, vol. 2, 286, AJO.

83. "Sr. Juez Instructor," Peñas trial records, May 17, 1899, vol. 1, 167, AJO.

84. "Indagatoria de Elias Atanacio," Peñas trial records, Feb. 20, 1900, vol. 4, 718, AJO.

85. "Indagatoria de Mariano Muruchi," Peñas trial records, Feb. 21, 1900, vol. 4, 722, AJO.

86. "Testimonio de Manuel Hachacollo," Peñas trial records, Apr. 27, 1899, vol. 2, 386, AJO.

87. "Indagatorio de Juan Lero," Peñas trial records, Apr. 25, 1899, vol. 1, 8, AJO.

88. "Al Sr. Cacique Gobemador de la parcialidad de Tapacarí en el Vice Canton Provicia de Poopó, de Villca," Peñas trial records, March 20, 1899, vol. 1, 28, AJO.

89. "Indagatoria de Juan Lero," Peñas trial records, Feb. 19, 1901, vol. 4, 713, AJO.

90. "Al Sr. Juez Instructor de turno en lo criminal de la ciudad de Challapata," Peñas trial records, Sept. 30, 1899, vol. 5, 924, AJO.

91. "A Juan Lero, de la Comunidad de Chayanta," Peñas trial records, Mar. 28, 1899, vol. 6, 1119, AJO.

92. "A Juan Lero de José Maria Galligo," Peñas trial records, Mar. 29, 1899, vol. 6, 1119, AJO.

93. "A los señores hilacatas del anejo Machacamarca de Juan Lero," Peñas trial records, Mar. 28, 1899, vol. 6, 1119, AJO.

94. "De Pastor Salazar de Quillacas a Martín Codori," Peñas trial records, Apr. 5, 1899, vol. 6, 1117, AJO.

95. "Indagatoria de Juan Lero," Peñas trial records, Apr. 21, 1899, vol. 1, 8, AJO.

96. "Al Sr. Juez Instructor, de Juan Lero," Peñas trial records, July 26, 1899, vol. 3, 379, AJO.

97. "Al Sr. Juez, del Medico del hospital, Ricardo Guzman," Peñas trial records, Jan., 1901, vol. 8, 1481, AJO.

98. "Indagatoria de Pablo Zárate Willka," Peñas trial records, June 7, 1899, vol. 2, 257, AJO.

99. I limit examples of indigenous people testifying against indigenous people to cases where the former identified themselves as indigenous or were identified as such by the lawyer filing the complaint.

100. "Al Sr. Agente Fiscal, de Manuel Garnica, por Felisa Choque," Peñas trial records, Nov. 21, 1899, vol. 4, 785, AJO. See also Maria Escobar's testimony, Peñas trial records, Oct. 18, 1899, vol. 4, 758, AJO.

101. "Al Sr. Agente Fiscal, de José Mendoza, por Leonarda Sequeda," Peñas trial records, Oct. 18, 1899, vol. 4, 733, AJO.

102. "Al Sr. Agente Fiscal, de José Mendoza, por Escobar," Peñas trial records, Nov. 27, 1899, vol. 4, 790, AJO.

103. "Al Sr. Agente Fiscal, de Camilo Graviel y Francisca Humire," Peñas trial records, Feb. 10, 1899, vol. 4, 700, AJO. Regarding economic hardship, see also the testimony of Paula Fernández, "Al Sr. Agente Fiscal, de Demetrio Vaca Gusman, por Fernández," Peñas trial records, Nov. 29, 1900, vol. 8, 1410, AJO.

104. "Al Sr. Agente Fiscal de Distrito, de Florencio Medina, por Nazario Choque, Pedro Sequera, y Aquilina Davalos," Peñas trial records, Jan. 2, 1900, vol. 3, 589, AJO.

105. "Al Sr. Juez Instructor, de Manuel Garcia, por Nazario Choque," Peñas trial records, approximate date Jan. 1900, vol. 3, 586, AJO.

106. "De Monteso, Sierra, y Quinteros," Peñas trial records, Dec. 16, 1901, vol. 9, 1606, AJO.

107. "Al Sr. Juez de Partido, de Asencio Fuentes," Peñas trial records, Jan. 7, 1902, vol. 9, 1614, AJO.

108. "Sentencia," Peñas trial records, Feb. 27, 1902, vol. 9, 1622–27, AJO.

109. See "Al Srs. Presidente & V. V. de la Corte Superior, de Prudencio de Alarcon," Peñas trial records, June 3, 1902, vol. 9, 1657, AJO; "Al Presidente & V. V. de la Corte Superior, de Mariano Choque," Peñas trial records, July 11, 1902, vol. 9, 1668, AJO; "Al Sres. Presidente y V. V. de la Corte Suprema, de Victor Torrico, por Mariano Choque," Peñas trial records, Aug. 18, 1902, vol. 9, 1676, AJO; "Al Sr. Juez de Partido, de Federico Pizarro, por Mariano Choque," Peñas trial records, Nov. 6, 1902, vol. 9, 1683, AJO.

110. "Al Sr. corregidor de Huancani, de Modesto Reque, por Isaac Chungara," Peñas trial records, Aug. 1899, vol. 4, 888, AJO.

111. "Al Sr. Fiscal del Distrito," Peñas trial records, June 10, 1899, vol. 2, 279, AJO.

112. "Al Sr. Juez Instructor," Peñas trial records, June 19, 1899, vol. 2, 300, AJO.

113. "Instructiva de Felipa Atahuchi," Peñas trial records, July 26, 1899, vol. 2, 374, AJO.

114. "Sr. Fiscal de Partido," Peñas trial records, June 7, 1899, vol. 2, 271, AJO.

115. Ibid.

116. Ibid.

117. "Del Boletín official," El Comercio (La Paz), Feb. 4, 1899, 3, ANB.

118. "Sublevación," El Comercio (La Paz), Jan. 26, 1899, 2, ANB.

119. See also "Ecos de la revolución boliviana: Reportaje al subteniente Anabolon, fuerza aloncista," Los Debates (La Paz), May 6, 1899, 1, 23. In this report, one of the Conservative military authorities, Lieutenant Anabalon, admitted that discipline within the ranks broke down following defeat. He stated that one by one, the Conservative soldiers broke off from the group to make their own ways home. As the chaos mounted, Lieutenant Anabalon thought it prudent to hide until he could make his way south at

a later date. See also "La raza indígena," *Los Debates* (La Paz), Oct. 27, 1899, 2, CdL, for more on abuses by the Conservative army.

120. "Transcripciones: El proceso del ejercito unitario," *La Libertad* (Oruro), Aug. 15, 1899, 3, ANB.

121. "Sr. Fiscal de Partido," Peñas trial records, June 7, 1899, vol. 2, 271, AJO.

122. "Al Sr. Juez Instructor 2ndo," Peñas trial records, Sept. 27, 1899, vol. 3, 475–76, AJO.

123. While the colonial legislation was far from a favorable arrangement for Bolivia's indigenous population, it accorded them a special status as "miserables," which equated them with imbeciles who were unable to fully understand the concepts and laws that defined their status. While both the title of this status as well as the definition reflect the Indians' undesirable position in society, the designation entitled them to small potential benefits. The colonial administrators viewed the indigenous inhabitants as needing protection and tutelage and therefore extended a certain leniency in legal disputes. Additionally, indigenous communities throughout much of the Andes paid tribute to the Spanish crown in exchange for recognition of their communal landholdings. While indigenous communities continued to pay a similar "contribution" to the republican government throughout much of the nineteenth century, the Liberals' promotion of private ownership of land threatened the communities, especially in the late nineteenth century. For a more radical and contemporary interpretation of the significance of independence for indigenous people in Bolivia, see Carlos Mamani and Maria Eugenia Choque, "Reconstitución del ayllu y derechos de los pueblos indígenas: El movimiento indio en los Andes de Bolivia," *Journal of American Anthropology* 6, no. 1 (2001): 202–23. The pro-Aymara Mamani and Choque assert that while the colonial state relied on indigenous communities for labor and tribute, the republican authorities wished to eliminate the indigenous population by breaking up their communities and transforming them into landless peasant laborers.

124. Barragán, *Indios, mujeres*, 43.

125. Ibid, 45.

126. Ibid.

127. "Al Sr. Juez Instructor," Peñas trial records, May 26, 1899, vol. 1, 186, AJO. See also "Al Sr. Juez Instructor," Peñas trial records, June 5, 1899, vol. 2, 250, AJO.

128. "Al Sr. Juez Instructor," Peñas trial records, May 26, 1899, vol. 1, 186, AJO.

129. "Al Sr. Fiscal de Partido," Peñas trial records, May 7, 1899, vol. 1, 155, AJO.

130. "Al Juez Instructor," Peñas trial records, July 19, 1899, Peñas trial records, vol. 2, 364, AJO.

131. Sarah Chambers discusses how nonelite groups appropriated the notion of honor in Peruvian legal procedures during the independence era, using it to claim citizenship status within the new republic based on constitutional rights. Her argument regarding the plebeians' appropriation of honor to broaden the scope of citizenship is similar to the argument I make for the Aymaras regarding their participation in the civil war and citizenship status. See Sarah Chambers, *From Subjects to Citizens: Honor, Gender, and Politics in Arequipa, Peru, 1780–1854* (University Park: Pennsylvania State University Press, 1999).

132. *Boletín Oficial* no. 32, Feb. 6, 1899, 148, ANB.

133. "Al Sr. de la Exelentísima Junta de Gobierno," Peñas trial records, Apr. 29, 1899, vol. 2, 233–34, AJO.

134. See "Al Sr. Fiscal de Partido," Peñas trial records, May 7, 1899, vol. 2, AJO; "Instructiva de Mariano Condori," Peñas trial records, July 5, 1899, vol. 2, 340, AJO.

135. "Al Sr. Fiscal, de Isaac Chugara," Peñas trial records, Apr. 21, 1899, vol. 5, 864, AJO.

136. "Al Sr. Fiscal de Partido, de Isaac Chungara," Peñas trial records, July 11, 1899, vol. 5, 875, AJO.

137. "Al Sr. Juez Instructor, del abogado Rengel, por Antonio Villca," Peñas trial records, June 22, 1899, vol. 5, 846, AJO.

138. "Testimonio de Apolinar Astete," Peñas trial records, Nov. 18, 1899, vol. 5, 850, AJO.

139. "Al Sr. Alcalde de Parroquial 1er de Challapata, de Eduardo Pecho, por Choquerivi," Peñas trial records, Dec. 13, 1899, vol. 5, 958, AJO.

140. "Testimonio de Victoriano Poquechoque," Peñas trial records, Dec. 15, 1899, vol. 5, 962, AJO.

141. "Testimonio de Mariano Saravia," Peñas trial records, Dec. 15, 1899, vol. 5, 961, AJO.

142. "Testimonio de Nicolas Garisto," Peñas trial records, Dec. 15, 1899, vol. 5, 961, AJO.

143. "Al Sr. Juez Instructor, de Juan Lero," written by the lawyer M. Herrera, Peñas trial records, July 18, 1899, vol. 2, 352–53, AJO.

144. "Al Sr. Presidente de la visita del carcel," written by Juan Lero, Diego Mamani, et al., Peñas trial records, Feb. 23, 1900, vol. 6, 1140, AJO.

Chapter 2. From Aymara Liberals to Exemplary Incas: Nation Building in Early Twentieth-Century Bolivia

1. Abraham Konig, "Indios de Mohoza," in *La Paz vista por extranjeros y autores nacionales, siglos XVI al XX*, ed. Mariano Baptista Gumucio (La Paz: Anthropos, 1997), 103. Mohoza is a small town on the altiplano, located between La Paz and Oruro. The Aymaras of Mohoza were accused of killing soldiers fighting for the Liberal Party; the event served as a central piece of evidence supporting the prosecution's charges of an Aymara-led race war. See Ramiro Condarco Morales, *Zárate, el "temible" Willka: Historia de la rebelión indígena de 1899* (La Paz: Imprenta Renovación, 1983); and Pilar Mendieta Parada, "Entre el caudillismo y la modernidad: Poder local y política en la provincia de Inquisivi, el caso de Mohoza (1880–1899)," (master's thesis, Centro de Estudios Superiores del Centro Boliviano de Estudios Multidisciplinarios, La Paz, 1999).

2. Although the site's name has been spelled several ways (as cited titles and quoted material indicate), I use *Tiahuanaco* in my own text.

3. Seemin Qayum, "Creole Imaginings: Space, Race, and Gender in the Making of Republican Bolivia" (PhD diss., University of London, Goldsmiths College, 2002), 219–20.

4. Condarco Morales, *Zárate*; Marie-Danielle Demelás, "Darwinismo a la criolla: El darwinismo social en Bolivia, 1809–1910," *Historia Boliviana* 1, no. 2 (1981): 55–82; Tristan Platt, "Liberalism and Ethnocide in the Southern Andes," *History Workshop* 17 (1984): 3–18.

5. Brooke Larson, "Redeemed Indians, Barbarized Cholos: Crafting Neocolonial Modernity in Neocolonial Bolivia, 1900–1910," in *Political Cultures in the Andes, 1750–1950*, ed. Nils Jacobsen and Cristóbal Aljovín de Losada (Durham, N.C.: Duke University Press, 2005), 230–52; Qayum, "Creole Imaginings."

6. For the ethnocidal perspective, see Tristan Platt, "Liberalism and Ethnocide"; for Creole-styled Darwinism, see Demelás, "Darwinismo a la criolla"; for reference to the neocolonial quality of the nation-building project, see Larson, "Redeemed Indians"; for "internal colonialism," see Seemin Qayum, "Nationalism, Internal Colonialism, and the Spatial Imagination: The Geographic Society of La Paz in Turn-of-the-Century Bolivia," in *Studies in the Formation of the Nation-State in Latin America*, ed. James Dunkerley (London: Institute of Latin American Studies, 2002), 279–98.

7. Thus, beginning in the 1970s, Aymara scholars took up the task of writing Bolivian history from an indigenous perspective. Silvia Rivera Cusicanqui, Roberto Choque Canqui, and others wrote indigenous history, and especially Aymara history, into the national narrative. See, for example, Silvia Rivera Cusicanqui, *Oppressed but Not Defeated: Peasant Struggles among the Aymara and Qhechwa in Bolivia, 1900–1980* (Geneva: United National Research Institute for Social Development, 1987); Roberto Choque Canqui et al., eds., *Educación indígena: Ciudadanía o colonización?* (La Paz: Ediciones Aruwiyiri/Taller de Historia Oral Andina, 1992). In doing so, these scholars strove to combat the representation of indigenous movements as spontaneous, irrational uprisings by tracing instead the historical trajectories and political processes that led indigenous people to mobilize. At the same time, these new narratives responded to a national history that marginalized and belittled the Aymaras' role within the nation. This "new" history was a parallel history written against a state that threatened to cannibalize the Aymara past. According to Marcia Stephenson, leaders of this initiative, such as the Workshop for Oral Andean History, or THOA (Taller de Historia Oral Andina), founded in 1983, were instrumental in forging "counter-discourses" where oppositional cultural and political issues could be discussed. See Marcia Stephenson, "Forging an Indigenous Counterpublic Sphere: The Taller de Historia Oral Andina in Bolivia," *Latin American Research Review* 37, no. 2 (2002): 99–118.

In addition, the recent ascendency of Evo Morales, who was elected as Bolivia's first Indian president in 2005, has generated unprecedented interest in that nation, which has led scholars elsewhere to investigate Aymara politics and their responses to globalization. For example, Benjamin Dangl, in *The Price of Fire: Resource Wars and Social Movements in Bolivia* (Edinburgh: AK Press, 2007), proposed to tell "the larger story of a region in revolt, beginning with indigenous uprisings against Spanish rule, focusing in on social movements in the last six years and ending with reports from the first year of the administration of indigenous president Evo Morales" (7). In lieu of historical depth, the book comprises a chapter on the Water War of 2003 as well as ones on the coca leaf eradication program and Evo Morales's presidency to emphasize resistance to globalization and indigenous oppression. As a result, Bolivia, according to Dangl, has one of the more dynamic historiographies that tends to underscore the role of indigenous resistance to national and global processes.

8. For studies that link manifestations of Inca theater and imagery to indigenous resistance efforts or to a desire to return to an Indian past, see Nathan Wachtel, *The Vision of the Vanquished: The Spanish Conquest of Peru through Indian Eyes, 1530–1570*, trans. Ben Reynolds

and Siân Reynolds (New York: Barnes and Noble, 1977); Manuel Burga, *Nacimiento de una utopia: Muerte y resurrección de los Incas* (Lima: Instituto de Apoyo Agrario, 1988); Raquel Chang-Rodríguez, "Cultural Resistance in the Andes and Its Depiction in *Atau Wallpaj P'uchukakuyninpa Wankan or Tragedy of Atahualpa's Death*," in *Coded Encounters: Writing, Gender, and Ethnicity in Colonial Latin America,* ed. Francisco Javier Cevallos-Candau et al. (Amherst: University of Massachusetts Press, 1994), 115–32; Jesús Lara, *Tragedia del fin de Atahuallpa: Atau Wallpaj p'uchukakuyninpa wankan* (Cochabamba, Bolivia: Los Amigos del Libro; Buenos Aires: Ediciones del Sol, 1989).

9. See Seemin Qayum, "Nationalism, Internal Colonialism."

10. See Brooke Larson, "Redeemed Indians."

11. See Ada Ferrer, *Insurgent Cuba: Race, Nation, and Revolution, 1868–1898* (Chapel Hill: University of North Carolina Press, 1999); José Vasconcelos, *The Cosmic Race = La raza cósmica,* trans. Didier Tisdel Jaén (Los Angeles: Centro de Publicaciones, Dept. of Chicano Studies, California State University, 1979); José Martí, *Obras completas,* 28 vols. (Havana: Editorial Nacional de Cuba, 1963–73).

12. Larson, "Redeemed Indians."

13. Qayum, "Nationalism, Internal Colonialism"; Larson, "Redeemed Indians."

14. See the following works by Manuel Rigoberto Paredes: *Provincia de Inquisivi: Estudios geográficos y sociales* (La Paz: Taller Tipo-Litográfico, 1906), *La Altiplanicie* (La Paz: Ediciones Isla, 1965), *Tiahuanacu y la provincia de Ingavi* (La Paz: Ediciones Isla, 1955), and *Los Siñani: Tradiciones y crónicas del pueblo de Carabuco* (La Paz: Ediciones Isla, 1968).

15. D'Orbigny qtd. in Qayum, "Nationalism, Internal Colonialism," 276; for the original, see Alcide d'Orbigny, *Viaje a la América meridional* (Buenos Aires: Editorial Futuro, 1945), 982.

16. See Peter Wade, *Blackness and Race Mixture: The Dynamics of Racial Identity in Columbia* (Baltimore, Md.: Johns Hopkins University Press, 1993); Peter Wade, *Race and Ethnicity in Latin America* (London: Pluto, 1997); Nancy Appelbaum, *Muddied Waters: Race, Region, and Local History in Columbia, 1846–1948* (Durham, N.C.: Duke University Press, 2003); Barbara Weinstein, "Racializing Regional Difference: Sao Paulo versus Brazil, 1932," in *Race and Nation in Modern Latin America,* ed. Nancy Appelbaum, Anne Macpherson, and Karin Rosemblatt (Chapel Hill: University of North Carolina Press, 2003), 237–62.

17. Mariano Baptista, "Lugentes," *La Soberania* (Oruro), Feb. 18, 1899, 2, Archivo Nacional de Bolivia (ANB).

18. Ibid.

19. Pedro Ancieto Blanco, *Diccionario geográfico del departamento de Oruro* (Oruro, Bolivia: Instituto de Estudios Bolivianos/Instituto Francés de Estudios Andinos/ASDI-SAREC/Alcaldia Municipal de Oruro: 2004 [1904]).

20. Ibid., 64.

21. Ibid., 69.

22. Arthur Posnansky, *Tihuanacu: La cuna del hombre Americano/Tihuanacu: The Cradle of American Man,* vol. 1 (New York: Augustin, 1945), 10–11. Posnansky first published the ideas in *Tihuanacu* in a work titled *Una metrópoli prehistórica en la América del sud* (Berlin: Reimer, 1914).

23. Arthur Posnansky, "Tiahuanacu y la civilización prehistórica en el altiplano," *Boletin de la Sociedad Geográfica de La Paz* (1911): 31, 32.

24. See John Rowe, "El movimiento nacional Inca del siglo XVIII," in *Tupac Amaru*

II—1780: *Sociedad colonial y sublevaciones populares*, ed. Alberto Flores Galindo (Lima: Retablo de Papel Ediciones, 1976), 11–66.

25. See Carolyn Dean, *Inca Bodies and the Body of Christ: Corpus Christi in Colonial Cuzco, Peru* (Durham, N.C.: Duke University Press, 1999); Deborah Poole, *Vision, Race, and Modernity: A Visual Economy of the Andean Image World* (Princeton, N.J.: Princeton University Press, 1997).

26. Cecilia Méndez, "Incas Sí, Indios No: Notes on Peruvian Creole Nationalism and Its Contemporary Crisis," *Journal of Latin American Studies* 28, no. 1 (1996): 197–225.

27. Poole, *Vision, Race and Modernity*, 29–32, 42.

28. David Garrett analyzes Tupac Amaru's problematic claims to Inca lineage in "His Majesty's Most Loyal Vassals: The Indian Nobility and Tupac Amaru," *Hispanic American Historical Review* 84, no. 4 (2004): 575–617.

29. See Alberto Flores Galindo, "In Search of an Inca," in *Resistance, Rebellion, and Consciousness in the Andean Peasant World, 18th to 20th Centuries*, ed. Steve Stern (Madison: University of Wisconsin Press, 1987), 193–212.

30. For Cuzco, see César Itier, ed., *El teatro quechua en el Cuzco*, 2 vols. (Lima: Institut Français d'Etudes Andines; Cuzco: Centro de Estudios Regionales Andinos "Bartolomé de las Casas," 1995, 2000). For Bolivia, see Emeterio Villamil de Rada and Nicolás Acosta, *La lengua de Adán y el hombre de Tiahuanaco: Resumen de estas obras* (La Paz: La Razón, 1888); Pedro Kramer, *Historia de Bolivia* (La Paz: Taller Tipo-Litográfico, 1899); Posnansky, *Tihuanacu*; Margot Beyersdorff, *Historia y drama ritual en los Andes bolivianos: Siglos XV–XX* (La Paz: Plural Editores, 1998); and the analysis of the Caracollo Inca play provided in chapter 3 of this book.

31. Interestingly, the idea of the Inca entered into important discussions of race in Cuba in the late nineteenth century. When General Antonio Maceo's remains were exhumed in Cuba in September 1899 to determine the race to which the famous Afro-Cuban independence warrior belonged, the Inca served as an image of racial whitening. Experts claimed that his skull possessed the "bone of the Inca" and eventually proclaimed Maceo more white than black. See Alejandro de la Fuente, *A Nation for All: Race, Inequality, and Politics in Twentieth-Century Cuba* (Chapel Hill: University of North Carolina Press, 2001), 39.

32. See Nancy Leys Stepan, *The Hour of Eugenics: Race, Gender, and Nation in Latin America* (Ithaca, N.Y.: Cornell University Press, 1991).

33. *La Soberania* (Oruro), Jan. 31, 1899, ANB. In using the word *Carib*, the author implied the savagery and cannibalism pejoratively associated with the "Carib" Indian group, which resided in the Lesser Antilles.

34. Baptista, "Lugentes."

35. *El Boletín Oficial* (La Paz), no. 38, Feb. 16, 1899, ANB.

36. Tuck, "Una lugente aventura," *El Comercio* (La Paz) Mar. 23, 1899, ANB.

37. Quillco Mamani, "Carta de un semi-indio," *Los Debates* (La Paz), May 9, 1899, ANB.

38. "Objetos arqueológicos," *Los Debates* (La Paz), Sept. 6, 1899, ANB.

39. The celebration of Tiahuanaco did promote highland indigenous cultures—and specifically the Aymara—as suggestive symbols of a distinct Bolivian nationalism, as Qayum suggests in her dissertation "Creole Imaginings" (219–20). However, the promotion of archeological ruins such as Tiahuanaco resulted less in an acceptance of

contemporary highland indigenous populations than in an underscoring of the early highland people's connections to civilizations such as that of the Incas.

40. Charles Johnson Post, *Across the Andes: A Tale of Wandering Days among the Mountains of Bolivia and the Jungles of the Upper Amazon* (New York: Outing, 1912), 266.

41. Ibid., 257.

42. "La isla Titicaca," *El Comercio* (La Paz), June 24, 1899, 2, ANB.

43. "Fundación del imperio de los incas," *El Comercio* (La Paz), Nov. 25, 1898, ANB.

44. See Qayum, "Creole Imaginings," 220–22; Josefa Salmon, *El espejo indígena: El discurso indigenista en Bolivia, 1900–1956* (La Paz: Plural, 1997); Sinclair Thomson, "Bolivia's Turn-of the-Century Indian Problem: The Case of Manuel Rigoberto Paredes" (master's thesis, University of Wisconsin, 1987), 65–67.

45. Qayum, "Creole Imaginings," 220.

46. Cieza de León and Fray Antonio de Calancha qtd. in Paredes, *Tiahuanacu*, 49, 66; Paredes cites as his sources Pedro Cieza de León, *Segunda parte de la crónica del Perú: Que se trata del señorio de los Incas yupanquis y de sus grandes hechos y gobernación* (Madrid: Imprenta M. Ginés Hernández, 1880 [1553]); and Fray Antonio de Calancha, *Crónica Moralizada del Orden de San Agustín en el Perú* (Barcelona: P. Lavacalleria, 1651 [1638]).

47. Grandidier qtd. in Paredes, *Tiahuanacu*, 79; the original source is Ernest Grandidier, *Voyage dans l'Amérique du Sud: Pérou et Bolivie* (Paris: Michel Lévy Frères, 1861).

48. Villamil de Rada and Acosta, *La lengua de Adán*, 8–9.

49. Ibid., xvii.

50. Ibid., 7.

51. For a thorough compilation of books and articles written on Tiahuanaco during the colonial and national periods, see Manuel Rigoberto Paredes, *Tiahuanacu*.

52. Manuel Ballivián and Luis Crespo, *Censo nacional de la población de la República (1ero de septiembre de 1900)* (La Paz: Tipo-Litográfico de José M. Gamarra, 1904), 28.

53. Ibid., 26.

54. Ibid., xxvii.

55. See Arturo Costa de la Torre, "Las academias aymaras bolivianas del pasado y presente siglo," *Pumapunku* 6 (1972): 41–53.

56. Ibid.

57. Antonio Garcia, *La rebelión de los pueblos débiles* (La Paz: Imprenta E. Burillo, 1955).

58. Wenceslao Loaiza V., *Instrucción y educación de la raza indígena: Informe presentado al ilustrísimo señor Vicario Capitular por el señor cura propio de Laja* (La Paz: La Union, 1911).

59. Ibid., 2.

60. Rafael Sans, *Novena de la milagrosa virgen de Copacabana*, trans. into Aymara by Wenceslao Loaiza V. (La Paz: Imprenta Yungas, 1891).

61. I borrow the term *redeem* from Brooke Larson's article "Redeemed Indians."

62. P. Fernando de Sanjinés, "Los Aymaras," *Academia Aymara* 1, no. 2 (July 20, 1902): 26, ANB.

63. "Aymaras," *Academia Aymara* 1, no. 2 (July 20, 1902): 37, ANB.

64. "Sesión ordinaria 27 de julio de 1902," *Academia Aymara* 1, no. 2 (July 20, 1902): 39–40, ANB.

65. Nicanor Aranzaes, "Sesión ordinaria 27 de Julio de 1902," *Academia Aymara* 1, no. 2 (July 20, 1902): 39–40, ANB. This article records a conversation at an Aymara Academy meeting.

66. "Aymaras," *Academia Aymara* 1, no. 1 (Oct. 20, 1901): 21, ANB.

67. Aranzaes, "Sesión ordinaria," 40.

68. *Academia Aymara* 1, no. 1 (Oct. 20, 1901), ANB.

69. "Al Sr. Prefecto y Comandante General del Departamento de Oruro de la Subprefectura de Paria," Peñas trial records, Apr. 24, 1899, vol. 1, 29, Archivo Judicial de Oruro (AJO).

70. Qayum, "Creole Imaginings," 193.

71. Posnansky, *Tihuanacu*, 50.

72. Ibid, 53–54; these pages also contain Posnansky's explanation of the five stages of cultural development in the Americas. (Posnansky used the terms *Kolla* and *Aymara* interchangeably, though often employing the former to avoid connections between language and race.)

73. Ibid., 84.

74. Ibid., 31.

75. Ibid., 11.

76. Ibid., 32.

77. Ibid., 89.

78. Sinclair Thomson, "Bolivia's Turn-of-the-Century Indian Problem," 87–90, 27.

79. Paredes, *Tiahuanacu*, 41.

80. Ibid., 40.

81. Paredes, *Los Siñani*, 77.

82. Paredes, *Tiahuanacu*, x–xi.

83. Manuel Rigoberto Paredes, *La elección de convencional en la provincia de Muñecas: Fraudes de la mesa escrutadora de Mocomoco* (La Paz: Imprenta Richter, 1899).

84. Ibid., 23.

85. Kramer qtd. in Paredes, *Tiahuanacu*, 101.

86. Posnansky, *Tihuanacu*, pl. 65.

87. Qayum, "Creole Imaginings," 235; Qayum quotes the source (*Tiahuanaco: Datos para la defensa de la segunda sección de Pacajes* [La Paz, 1897], 53–54) on 235, 224.

88. *Sesiones del senado nacional en la legislatura de 1898* (Sucre, Bolivia: Imprenta Bolívar, 1897), ANB.

89. Manuel Vicente de Ballivián, the director of the 1900 census, initially heralded the end of Indians before recognizing the achievements of certain Indian groups, namely, the Incas and their predecessors, the Aymaras. See Ballivián and Crespo, *Censo nacional*, 28.

Chapter 3. Incantations of Nation and the Theatrical Performance of the Inca Past

1. "Corresponsales de Poopó; mantenimiento del orden," *La Soberania* (Oruro), Mar. 7, 1899, ANB.

2. "Remitidos—Sr. Subprefecto," *Los Debates* (La Paz), May 2, 1899, ANB. The letter was written Apr. 11, 1899.

3. Ibid.

4. Ibid.

5. "Los indios de Umala," *El Imparcial* 2 (La Paz) Sept. 14, 1899, ANB. "Los indios de

Umala" ran as a weekly contribution in the newspaper. The author of this series might very well have been Manuel Rigoberto Paredes.

6. Ibid.

7. "Memorial anual, 1926, al Sr. Ministro de Estado," *Informes prefecturales*, vol. 184 (1913), Archivo de la Prefectura de Oruro (APO).

8. *Ministerio de Industria y agricultura*, vol. 191 (1913), 139, APO.

9. Margot Beyersdorff cites 1906 as the origin of the Caracollo Inca play in her book *Historia y drama ritual en los Andes bolivianos: Siglos XVI–XX* (La Paz: Plural Editores, 1998). See also Niver Montes Camacho, *Proceso íntimo del carnival de Oruro* (Oruro, Bolivia: Editorial Universitaria, 1986).

10. See Jesús Lara, *Tragedia del fin de Atawallpa: Atau Wallpaj p'uchukakuyninpa wankan* (Cochabamba, Bolivia: Los Amigos del Libro; Buenos Aires: Ediciones del Sol, 1989), and Daniel González Gómez-Acebo, *Teatro originario boliviano: Estudio histórico del teatro y la teatralidad de las culturas quechua, aymará, y guaraní* (La Paz: Sagitario, 2009), 40.

11. Bartolomé Arzáns de Orsua y Vela, with Hanke Lewis and Gunnar Mendoza, *Historia de la villa imperial de Potosí* (Providence, R.I.: Brown University Press, 1965).

12. For Bolivia, see Lara, *Tragedia*; Raquel Chang-Rodríguez, "Cultural Resistance in the Andes and Its Depiction in *Atau Wallpaj P'uchukakuyninpa Wankan* or *Tragedy of Atahualpa's Death*," in *Coded Encounters: Writing, Gender, and Ethnicity in Colonial Latin America*, ed. Francisco Javier Cevallos-Candau et al. (Amherst: University of Massachusetts Press, 1994), 115–34; Roger Neil Rasnake, *Domination and Cultural Resistance: Authority and Power among an Andean People* (Durham, N.C.: Duke University Press, 1988); Nathan Wachtel, *The Vision of the Vanquished: The Spanish Conquest of Peru through Indian Eyes, 1530–1570*, trans. Ben Reynolds and Siân Reynolds (New York: Barnes and Noble, 1977); Montes Camacho, *Proceso íntimo*; Beyersdorff, *Historia y drama*. For Peru, see Manuel Burga, *Nacimiento de una utopia: Muerte y resurrección de los Incas* (Lima: Instituto de Apoyo Agrario, 1988); Marisol de la Cadena, *Indigenous Mestizos: The Politics of Race and Culture in Cuzco, Peru, 1919–1991* (Durham, N.C.: Duke University Press, 2000); Alberto Flores Galindo, *Buscando un Inca: Identidad y utopia en los Andes* (Lima: Instituto de Apoyo Agrario, 1987); Cecilia Méndez, "Incas Sí, Indios No: Notes on Peruvian Creole Nationalism and Its Contemporary Crisis," *Journal of Latin American Studies* 28, no. 1 (1996): 197–225; Zoila Mendoza, *Creating Our Own: Folklore, Performance, and Identity in Cuzco, Peru* (Durham, N.C.: Duke University Press, 2008); Luis Millones, *Actores de altura: Ensayos sobre el teatro popular andino* (Lima: Editorial Horizonte, 1992); Deborah Poole, *Vision, Race, and Modernity: A Visual Economy of the Andean Image World* (Princeton, N.J.: Princeton University Press, 1997).

13. Rossana Barragán and Cleverth Cárdenas, *Gran Poder: La Morenada* (La Paz: Instituto de Estudios Bolivianos, 2009), 29.

14. Diana Taylor and Sarah Townsend, eds., *Stages of Conflict: A Critical Anthology of Latin American Theater and Performance* (Ann Arbor: University of Michigan Press, 2008), 13.

15. Eduardo Diez de Medina, "Sinfonia aymara," *La musa americana: Revista de arte de La Paz* (Nov. 20, 1904): n.p., Archivo Costa de la Torre (CdT).

16. Eugenia Bridikhina, "La inclusion de las indígenas," in *Fiesta cívica: Construcción de lo cívico y políticas festivas*, ed. Eugenia Bridikhina (La Paz: Instituto de Estudios Bolivianos, 2009), 108, 109.

17. Diana Taylor and Sarah Townsend, in their anthology of Latin American theater,

as well as César Itier, Gisela Cánepa Koch, and Jill Lane, underscore the growing importance of theater during the nineteenth century as a forum for national debate and the formation of an orderly civic character. See César Itier, ed., *El teatro quechua en el Cuzco*, 2 vols. (Lima: Institut Français d'Etudes Andines; Cuzco: Centro "Bartolomé de las Casas," 1995, 2000); Jill Lane, *Blackface Cuba, 1840–1895* (Philadelphia: University of Pennsylvania Press, 2005); Taylor and Townsend, *Stages of Conflict*; Gisela Cánepa Koch, *Máscara, transformación, e identidad en los Andes: La fiesta de la Virgen del Carmen, Paucartambo-Cuzco* (Lima: Pontificia Universidad Católica del Peru, 1998); Gisela Cánepa Koch, "Redefining Andean Sacred Landscapes and Identities: Authenticity, Migration, and Visual Reproduction in Andean Religious Rituals," in *Performing Religion in the Americas: Media, Politics, and Devotional Practices of the Twenty-First Century*, ed. Alyshia Galvez (London: Seagull, 2007), 35–46.

18. Taylor and Townsend, *Stages of Conflict*, 10, 11, 12.

19. Manuel Ballivián and Luis Crespo, *Censo nacional de la población de la República (1ero de septiembre)* (La Paz: Tipo-Litográfico de Gamarra, 1904), vol. 2, table following p. 34. The literacy percents are estimated excluding children under seven years of age.

20. César Itier, "La tragedia de la muerte de Atahuallpa de Jesús Lara, historia de una supercheria literaria," in *Anuario del Archivo Nacional Boliviano* 15 (2009): 220.

21. "Memoria Municipal de 1899," *Publicaciones Oficiales, Municipalidad de La Paz*, anexos (La Paz: Imprenta y Litogáfico de el Nacional de Isaac W. Willa, 1900), 43, ANB.

22. Ibid.

23. "Arte y artistas," *Nimbas y aureolas* (July 1, 1901), 6, CdT.

24. *El Sol* (Cuzco), Aug. 9, 1913, cited in Itier, *Teatro quechua*, 2:37.

25. Lara, *Tragedia*, 17.

26. Itier, *Teatro quechua*, 1:25–42.

27. See, e.g., Mendoza, *Creating Our Own*.

28. For Bolivia, see, for example, Thomas Abercrombie, *Pathways of Memory and Power: Ethnography and History among an Andean People* (Madison: University of Wisconsin Press, 1998); Clemente Hernando Balmori, *La conquista de los españoles y el teatro indígena americano: Drama indígena bilingüe quechua-castellano* (Tucumán, Argentina: Universidad Nacional de Tucumán, 1955); Daniel M. Goldstein, *The Spectacular City: Violence and Performance in Urban Bolivia* (Durham, N.C.: Duke University Press, 2004); Lara, *Tragedia*; Wachtel, *Vision of the Vanquished*; Rasnake, *Domination and Cultural Resistance*. For Peru, see Poole, *Vision, Race, and Modernity*; De la Cadena, *Indigenous Mestizos*; Millones, *Actores de altura*; Burga, *Nacimiento de una utopia*.

29. See Cánepa, *Máscara, transformación e identidad*, 15.

30. Previous studies on Inca play performance in highland Bolivia have tied the plays' Inca imagery and constructions of the Inca past to political projects such as the Great Rebellion of the 1780s, the independence era, and nation building in the late nineteenth and early twentieth centuries. See Balmori, *La conquista*; Beyersdorff, *Historia y drama ritual*; Lara, *Tragedia*; Montes Camacho, *Proceso íntimo*; Tristan Platt, "Simón Bolívar, the Sun of Justice, and the Amerindian Virgin: Andean Conceptions of the Patria in Nineteenth-Century Potosi," *Journal of Latin American Studies* 25, no. 1 (1993): 159–85.

31. Burga, *Nacimiento de una utopia*.

32. See Balmori, *La conquista*, 47.

33. Ibid.

34. Mario Unzueta qtd. in Lara, *Tragedia* (original source, Mario Unzueta, *Valle*

[Cochabamba, Bolivia: La Epoca, 1945]); John F. Goins, "The Death of Atahuallpa," *Journal of American Folklore* 74, no. 293 (1961): 252–57. No text for the Cliza play remains, leaving the description in Unzueta's novel as the only direct report of it.

35. Lara, *Tragedia*.

36. Inca plays were performed in the Department of La Paz as well, although texts are not currently available for analysis. See Balmori, *La conquista*, 46–50.

37. See Lara, *Tragedia*. Beyersdorff (*Historia y drama ritual*, 190) suggests that the manuscript Lara studied was written or refurbished by the priest Carlos Felipe Beltrán. César Itier questions Lara's "authenticity" claims regarding the Chayanta text in *La tragedia*.

38. Beyersdorff, *Historia y drama ritual*, 192.

39. Niver Montes, *Proceso íntimo*, 51.

40. Wachtel, *Vision of the Vanquished*, 34.

41. Lara, *Tragedia*, 22.

42. Jesús Lara, *La poesia quechua: Ensayo y antologia* (Cochabamba, Bolivia: Universidad Mayor de San Simón, 1947).

43. Lara, *Tragedia*, 22.

44. Ibid., 17.

45. Ibid., 19.

46. Luis Bredow, "La escena de la muerte de Atahuallpa," *Hipótesis* 23–24 (1987): 319–29.

47. Ibid., 324.

48. Oscar Villca Yapari, "Caracollo celebra CDLXI años de fundacion," *La Patria* (Oruro), Nov. 25, 2000, personal papers of Luis Montaño.

49. Personal communication, don Emilio, archivist at the courthouse in Oruro, 2001.

50. Victor Yucra León, "Trabajo de investigación: Caracollo como un pueblo plurinacional dentro la sociedad boliviana," unpublished manuscript, Nov. 14, 1995, personal papers of Luis Montaño.

51. Abercrombie, *Pathways of Memory*, 181–84.

52. Yucra León, "Trabajo de investigación."

53. Ibid.

54. Ballivián and Crespo, *Censo nacional*, 29, 30, 31.

55. "Al Sr. Ministro de E. en D. de Justicia e Instrucción," Ministerio de Justicia y Industria (Instrucción), Aug. 26, 1905, to Feb. 2, 1909, 789, APO.

56. Ballivián and Crespo, *Censo nacional*, 31.

57. "Los indios de Umala," *El Imparcial* 2 (La Paz) Sept. 14, 1899, ANB; "Los indios de Umala," *El Imparcial* 2 (La Paz) Sept. 19, 1899, ANB.

58. "Del boletín official," *El Comercio* (La Paz), Feb. 28, 1899, 3 ANB.

59. "Al Sr. Presidente de la visita de cárcel," Peñas trial records, Feb. 23, 1900, vol. 6, 1140, AJO.

60. "Relación de la gran comparsa de los Incas," unpublished manuscript. This script is used for the Caracollo Inca play, recently directed by Telésforo Fernández Flores. I worked with the translated version Alfredo Rios provided. The description of the play is also based on my own observations of the Inca play, which I attended in 2001, 2002, and 2009.

61. Montes Camacho, *Proceso íntimo*.

62. Beyersdorff, *Historia y drama ritual*, 227.

63. Alfredo Rios, personal communication, Mar. 2001.

64. Balmori, *La conquista*.

65. These statistics are based on the annual report of 1998 for Caracollo. See Asociación Civil Kramer, *Plan participativo de desarrollo municipal de Caracollo* (Caracollo: USAID/ Honorable Alcaldía Municipal de Caracollo, 1998). Beyersdorff suggests that during the colonial era, the parish churches and the tambos, or rest stops, spread the Quechua language. The plays proliferated especially in the second half of the nineteenth century, which Beyersdorff attributes to the migration of people from the valleys who sought work in the mines of Oruro. This does not explain, however, why representations of an Inca past were performed by and relevant to an altiplano audience in the early twentieth century, nor does it explain the differences among the Inca plays. See Beyersdorff, *Historia y drama ritual*, 220.

66. Yucra León, "Trabajo de investigación."

67. See Beyersdorff, *Historia y drama ritual*; de la Cadena, *Indigenous Mestizos*; Itier, *Teatro quechua*; Millones, *Actores de altura*.

68. Beyersdorff, *Historia y drama ritual*, 242.

69. "Caracollo," October 1902, in bundle marked "Caracollo," Monseñor Taborga Archive, Sucre, Bolivia. Significantly, no Bullaín figures on the list of vecinos, or notable residents, suggesting a certain reconfiguration of the local elite. Carlos Bullaín had been a large property owner who was killed during the Civil War of 1899.

70. Yucra León, "Tabajo de investigación." The Virgin of the Rosary festival in Bolivia is certainly older than the 1890s, but perhaps Yucra León means that the festival was revitalized in Caracollo in the 1890s, although this is unclear.

71. Josermo Murillo and Antonio Revollo, *La Virgen del Socavón y su carnival* (Oruro, Bolivia: Centro Diocesano de Pastoral Social, 1992).

72. For the historical relationship between Urus and Aymaras, see Catherine Julien, "The Uru Tribute Category: Ethnic Boundaries and Empire in the Andes," *Proceedings of the American Philosophical Society* 131, no. 1 (1987): 53–91; Nathan Wachtel and Laura Ciezar, *El regreso de los antepasados: Los indios urus de Bolivia del siglo XX al XVI* (Mexico City: El Colegio de México, Fondo de Cultura Económica, 2001).

73. Murillo and Revollo, *Virgen del Socavón*.

74. The Virgin of the Mineshaft, for example, is associated with la Virgen de la Candelaria (i.e., the Virgin of Candlemas), whose festival is celebrated on February 2; this day commemorates the presentation of Jesus at the temple and the ritual purification of Mary after she gave birth. In Oruro Mary is also referred to as the Virgin of the Mineshaft because she is said to have appeared to a repentant thief hiding in a mine in 1789. In Oruro the Carnival festival, which often falls near Candlemas, is dedicated to her. For more on images of the Virgin Mary in Bolivia, see Murillo and Revollo, *La Virgen del Socavón*; Thomas Abercrombie, "Mothers and Mistresses of the Urban Bolivian Public Sphere: Postcolonial Predicament and National Imaginary in Oruro's Carnival," in *After Spanish Rule: Postcolonial Predicaments of the Americas*, ed. Mark Thurner and Andrés Guerrero (Durham, N.C.: Duke University Press, 2003), 184.

75. "Relación de la gran comparsa."

76. Balmori, *La conquista*, 41.

77. Cánepa, *Máscara, transformación e identidad*.

78. Balmori's photographs from the 1942 Oruro Inca play depict the Inca king wearing a mask with these European features, suggesting the historical use of the mask. See Balmori, *La conquista*, 6.

79. Lara, *Tragedia*, 57.

80. Ibid., 58, 27.

81. Ibid., 45. Lara states: "The contents of the play reveal that the authors have no interest in approximating the historical truth written down by the Spaniards" (ibid.). But see Patricia Seed, "Failing to Marvel: Atahuallpa's Encounter with the Word," *Latin American Research Review* 26, no. 1 (1991): 7–32. Seed analyzes the many different ways the Spaniards narrated the conquest, thus complicating the idea of one homogeneous Spanish version of conquest.

82. Balmori, *La conquista*, 47–53.

83. Malgorzata Oleszkiewicz, "El ciclo de la muerte de Atahuallpa: De la fiesta popular a la representación teatral," *Allpanchis* (Cuzco) 39 (1992): 185–220.

84. Lara, *Tragedia*, 61.

85. Ibid., 29.

86. The script simply refers to the "Inca king," creating ambiguity as to which "Inca king" is meant. The Inca king defines himself as Manco Kapac several times throughout the play (and as Huayna Manco Kapac); however, the Spaniards refer to the Inca king as "Atahuallpa."

87. Seed, "Failing to Marvel," 30.

88. See *Catálogo de la bibliografía boliviana*, vol. 1 (La Paz: 1966), 341, CdT. The plays have been published as David Berrios, *Huascar y Atahuallpa*, verse drama in three acts (Potosí: Tipo-Litográfico del Progreso, 1879); and David Berrios, *Atahuallpa y Pizarro* (pt. 2 of *Huscar y Atahuallpa*), verse drama in five acts (Potosí: Tipo-Litográfico del Progreso, 1878). Both scripts can be found at the CdT.

89. Berrios, *Atahuallpa y Pizarro*, 60–61, 32–33.

90. See Carlos Castañón Barrientos, *El "Diálogo" de Bernardo Monteagudo: Estudio literario seguido del texto de dicho Diálogo* (La Paz: Editora Universo, 1974).

91. Ibid., 32.

92. Lara, *Tragedia*, 132.

93. "Relación de la gran comparsa," 4, 5.

94. Ibid., 5.

95. Beyersdorff (*Historia y drama ritual*, 210–12) states that two of the main challenges in the Inca play are the Incas' inability of understand the written word and the incomprehension between Spaniards and Incas. In the Caracollo play, the factor of linguistic difference and incomprehension plays a much smaller role; the central issue is that of literacy.

96. "Relación de la gran comparsa," 8.

97. Juan Albarracín, "Alcides Arguedas, iniciador del indigenismo boliviano," in *Raza de bronce/Wuata Wuara*, by Alcides Arguedas, critical ed., ed. Antonio Lorente Medina (Nanterre, France: ALLCA XX, 1988), 487–96.

98. Alcides Arguedas, *Wuata Wara*, in *Raza de bronce/Wuata Wuara*, critical ed., ed. Antonio Lorente Medina (Nanterre, France: ALLCA XX, 1988), 359–417 (quotation on 368).

99. Ibid., 368, 379.

100. Ibid., 366.

101. Ibid., 381.

102. See Rossana Barragán, *Indios, mujeres, y ciudadanos: Legislación y ejercicio de la ciudadanía en Bolivia, siglo XIX* (La Paz: Fundación Diálogo, 1999); Abercrombie, "Mothers and Mistresses."

103. "Relación de la gran comparsa," 12.

104. Abercrombie, "Mothers and Mistresses."

Chapter 4. New Stages in Defining Indian Identity: The Ethnic Politics of Caracollo's Contemporary Inca Play

1. See "La Virgen del Socavón me hizo presidente y por eso estoy aquí," *Presencia* (La Paz), Feb. 13, 1994, Archivo National de Bolivia (ANB).

2. See "Es auténtica expresión de nuestro folklore andino," *Presencia* (La Paz), Feb. 13, 1994, ANB.

3. E. Gabrielle Kuenzli, "At the Interstices of Identity on Exhibit: The Politics of Ethnicity and Citizenship in the Festival Rituals of Bolivia" (master's thesis, University of Wisconsin, 1998).

4. Ascanio J. Nava Rodríguez, *Referencias sobre el carnaval de Oruro* (Oruro, Bolivia: Editoriales Latinas, 2004), 36.

5. Thomas Abercrombie, "Mothers and Mistresses of the Urban Bolivian Public Sphere: Postcolonial Predicament and National Imaginary in Oruro's Carnival," in *After Spanish Rule: Postcolonial Predicaments of the Americas*, ed. Mark Thurner and Andrés Guerrero (Durham, N.C.: Duke University Press, 2003), 205.

6. Nava Rodríguez, *Referencias*, 32.

7. Victor Amoroso, interview with author, Oruro, Jan. 1995.

8. Abercrombie, "Mothers and Mistresses," 204.

9. "Propuesta de pobladores de las tres secciones: La provincia Atahuallpa quiere llamarse Sabaya," *La Patria*, Nov. 13, 2001.

10. Juan Flores, interview with author, Caracollo, Apr. 2001.

11. Luis Montaño, interview with author, Caracollo, Nov. 8, 2000, and other informal conversations between March 2000 and May 2002.

12. The self-promotion occurred in October 2001, just before the conference.

13. Luis Montaño, conversation with author, Caracollo, Dec. 2001.

14. Luis Montaño, interviews with author, Caracollo, Nov. 8, 2001, and Oct. 2003.

15. Conversations between Inca actors and author in Caracollo, Oct. 2001, during rehearsals for a performance in La Paz. These were often informal conversations rather than organized interviews.

16. Information relayed indirectly through several Inca guild members who had talked to both Ediberto and his wife, Oct. 2001.

17. Luis Montaño, conversation with Ediberto Hinojosa, Caracollo, Oct. 2001, overheard by author.

18. These developments occurred in October 2001 shortly before a presentation of the Inca play in La Paz.

19. Telésforo Fernández Flores, annual Inca troupe meeting, Caracollo, Aug. 6, 2000.

20. Silvia Rivera Cusicanqui, *Oppressed but Not Defeated: Peasant Struggles among the Aymara and the Qhechwa in Bolivia, 1900–1980* (Geneva: United Nations Research Institute for Social Development, 1987), 149.

21. Qtd. in ibid., 117–18.

22. Marcia Stephenson, "Forging an Indigenous Counterpublic Sphere: The Taller de Historia Oral Andina in Bolivia," *Latin American Research Review* 37, no. 2 (2002): 99–118.

23. The manifesto can be found on the Communication Initiative Web site, http://comminit.com/en/node/122345/348 (accessed Jan. 2010).

24. Cristóbal Condoreno, dir., *El sueño de Waylla Wisa: Profecia de la conquista,* film (La Paz: THOA, 1992).

25. Ibid.

26. Orlando Huanca Ticona, "Es posible un teatro andino?" unpublished manuscript, ca. early 1990s.

27. Ibid, 4. Huanca Ticona's statement regarding the significance of the masks echoes the findings of Luis Bredow in "La escena de la muerte de Atahuallpa," *Hipótesis* 23–24 (1987): 319–29.

28. Ibid., 35–36.

29. "Relación de la gran comparsa de los Incas," unpublished script for a production directed by Telésforo Fernández Flores, Caracollo, Bolivia, n.d., 4.

30. Ibid., 9.

31. Ibid., 8–9.

32. Rossana Barragán, *Indios, mujeres, y ciudadanos: Legislación y ejercicio de la ciudadanía en Bolivia, siglo XX* (La Paz: Fundación Diálogo, 1999).

33. Condoreno, *El sueño.*

34. See Teodoro Meneses, *La muerte de Atahualpa: Drama quechua* (Lima: Universidad Mayor Nacional de San Marcos, 1987); Jesús Lara, *Tragedia del fin de Atawallpa: Atau Wallpaj p'uchukakuyninpa wankan* (Cochabamba, Bolivia: Los Amigos del Libro; Buenos Aires: Ediciones del Sol, 1989); Clemente Hernando Balmori, *La conquista de los españoles y el teatro indígena americano: Drama indígena bilingüe quechua-castellano* (Tucumán, Argentina: Universidad Nacional de Tucumán, 1955).

35. Interview with Mario López, Caracollo, May 29, 2010.

36. "Relación de la gran comparsa de los Incas."

37. "Relación de la gran comparsa de los Incas," unpublished script for a production directed by Telésforo Fernández Flores, Caracollo, Bolivia, perfomance dated 1965, 34.

38. Huanca Ticona, "Es posible?"

39. Ibid., 9.

40. "Bolivia: 229 Years since the Sacrifice of Tupac Katari," http:// http://global-voicesonline.org/2010/11/23/bolivia-229-years-since-the-sacrifice-of-tupac-katari/ (accessed Vo. 7, 2012).

41. See Xavier Albó, "From MNRistas to Kataristas to Katari," in *Resistance, Rebellion, and Consciousness in the Andean Peasant World, 18th to 20th Centuries,* ed. Steve Stern (Madison: University of Wisconsin Press, 1987), 397–98.

42. Hermogenes Flores, interview with author, Caracollo, Apr. 2001; Juan Flores, interview with author, Caracollo, Apr. 2001; Cornelio Pinaya, interview with author, Oruro, Apr. 2001; Luis Montaño, interview with author, Caracollo, Sept. 2001;

additional references made by these individuals, other Inca players, and other actors in informal conversations, 2000 to 2002.

Conclusion: Inca Play, Aymara Encore

1. Luis Bredow and Defensor del Pueblo, eds., *Observando el racismo: Racismo y regionalismo en el proceso constituyente* (La Paz: Universidad de la Cordillera, 2008), 80.

2. For an example of Sucre residents' mourning of the "fine students" who lost their lives on the altiplano to the "savage" Aymaras, see "El sacrificio de la juventud sucrense," *La Nación* (Sucre), Jan. 26, 1899.

3. Martin Gabriel Torrico Zas, "El mito que reactualizó el racismo y reavivó una guerra heredada," in *Observando el racismo*, ed. Bredow and Defensor del Pueblo, 77.

4. Ibid.

5. Ibid., 78.

6. Qtd. in ibid., 79.

7. Pablo Mamani Ramírez, "Venganza de Zárate Willka," July 3, 2007, http://www.katari.org/archives/venganza-de-zarate-willka (accessed Nov. 7, 2012).

8. Qtd. in Isadora Corla Nina, "Los días de violencia," in *Observando el racismo*, 21.

9. Mamani Ramírez, "Venganza de Zárate Willka."

10. *Por los caminos de Juan Liru: Construyamos el poder communal, anti-colonialista, anti-imperialista,* Third Meeting of Community Authorities, pamphlet, Apr. 8–9, 1991, Peñas, Bolivia.

11. Robert Albro, "Bolivia Rising: The Culture of Democracy and Bolivia's Indigenous Movements (Part II)," http://boliviarising.blogspot.com/2007/06/culture-of-democracy-and-bolivias_13.html (accessed Jan. 2010).

12. "Por los caminos de Juan Liru."

13. Felipe Lero, interview by author, Añahuayani, Aug. 15, 2003.

14. Toribia Lero, interviewed by Idon Churi, Oruro, exact date unknown (ca. 1990s), tape from Pilar Mendieta.

15. Francisco Flores, interview by author, Añahuayani, Aug. 15, 2003.

16. Vicente Pacheco, interview by author, Añahuayani, Aug. 15, 2003.

17. Ibid.

18. Brooke Larson, *Trials of Nation Making: Liberalism, Race, and Ethnicity in the Andes, 1810–1910* (Cambridge: Cambridge University Press, 2004), 13.

BIBLIOGRAPHY

Abercrombie, Thomas. "Mothers and Mistresses of the Urban Bolivian Public Sphere: Postcolonial Predicament and National Imaginary in Oruro's Carnival." In *After Spanish Rule: Postcolonial Predicaments of the Americas*, edited by Mark Thurner and Andrés Guerrero, 173–220. Durham, N.C.: Duke University Press, 2003.

———. *Pathways of Memory and Power: Ethnography and History among an Andean People*. Madison: University of Wisconsin Press, 1998.

Albarracín, Juan. "Alcides Arguedas, iniciador del indigenismo boliviano." In *Raza de bronce/Wuata Wuara*, by Alcides Arguedas, critical edition, edited by Antonio Lorente Medina, 417–86. Nanterre, France: ALLCA XX, 1988.

Albó, Xavier. "From MNRistas to Kataristas to Katari." In *Resistance, Rebellion, and Consciousness in the Andean Peasant World, 18th to 20th Centuries*, edited by Steve Stern, 379–419. Madison: University of Wisconsin Press, 1987.

Antezana Ergueta, Luis. *La guerra entre La Paz y Chuquisaca*. La Paz: H. Municipalidad de La Paz, 1999.

Appelbaum, Nancy. *Muddied Waters: Race, Region, and Local History in Columbia, 1846–1948*. Durham, N.C.: Duke University Press, 2003.

Arguedas, Alcides. *Wuata Wara*. In *Raza de bronce/Wuata Wuara*, by Arguedas, critical edition, edited by Antonio Lorente Medina, 359–417. Nanterre, France: ALLCA XX, 1988.

Arzáns de Orsua y Vela, Bartolomé, with Hank Lewis and Gunnar Mendoza. *Historia de la villa imperial de Potosí*. Providence, R.I.: Brown University Press, 1965.

Asociación Civil Kramer. *Plan participativo de desarollo municipal de Caracollo*. Caracollo, Bolivia: USAID/Honorable Alcaldía Municipal de Caracollo, 1998.

Ballivián, Manuel, and Luis Crespo. *Censo nacional de la población de República (1ero de septiembre de 1900)*. La Paz: Tipo-Litográfico de José M. Gamarra, 1904.

Balmori, Clemente Hernando. *La conquista de los españoles y el teatro indígena americano: Drama indígena bilingüe quechua-castellano*. Tucumán, Argentina: Universidad Nacional de Tucumán, 1955.

Barragán, Rossana. *Indios, mujeres, y ciudadanos: Legislación y ejercicio de la ciudadanía en Bolivia, siglo XIX*. La Paz: Fundación Diálogo, 1999.

Barragán, Rossana, and Cleverth Cárdenas. *Gran Poder: La Morenada*. La Paz: Instituto de Estudios Bolivianos, 2009.

Berrios, David. *Atahuallpa y Pizarro: Segunda parta de "Huáscar I Atahuallpa": Drama histórico en cinco actos I en verso original*. Potosí: Tipo-Litográfico del Progreso, 1879.

———. *Huáscar y Atahuallpa: Drama en tres actos i en verso*. Potosí: Tipo-Litográfico del Progreso, 1879.

Beyersdorff, Margot. *Historia y drama ritual en los Andes bolivianos: Siglos XV–XX*. La Paz: Plural Editores, 1998.

Blanco, Pedro Ancieto. *Diccionario geográfico del departamento de Oruro*. 1904. Reprint, Oruro, Bolivia: Instituto de Estudios Bolivianos/Instituto Francés de Estudios Andinos/ ASDI-SAREC/Alcaldía Municipal de Oruro, 2009.

Brading, David. *The First America: The Spanish Monarchy, Creole Patriots, and the Liberal State, 1492–1867*. Cambridge: Cambridge University Press, 1991.

Bredow, Luis. "La escena de la muerte de Atahuallapa." *Hipótesis* 23–24 (1987): 319–29.

Bredow, Luis, and Defensor del Pueblo, eds. *Observando el racismo: Racismo y regionalismo en el proceso constituyente*. La Paz: Defensor del Pueblo, Universidad de la Cordillera, 2008.

Bridikhina, Eugenia. "La inclusión de los indígenas." In *Fiesta cívica: Construcción de lo cívico y políticas festivas*, edited by Eugenia Bridikhina, 108–22. La Paz: Instituto de Estudios Bolivianos, 2009.

Burga, Manuel. *Nacimiento de una utopia: Muerte y resurrección de los Incas*. Lima: Instituto de Apoyo Agrario, 1988.

Campero, Isaac. *Historia del parlamento boliviano de 1898 y la revolución de La Paz*. La Paz: Imprenta y Litografía Boliviana, 1899.

Cánepa Koch, Gisela. *Máscara, transformación, e identidad en los Andes: La fiesta de la Virgen del Carmen, Paucartambo-Cuzco*. Lima: Pontífica Universidad Católica del Peru, 1998.

———. "Redefining Andean Sacred Landscapes and Identities: Authenticity, Migration, and Visual Reproduction in Andean Religious Rituals." In *Performing Religion in the Americas: Media, Politics, and Devotional Practices of the Twenty-First Century*, edited by Alyshia Galvez, 35–46. London: Seagull, 2007.

Castañón Barrientos, Carlos. *El "Diálogo" de Bernardo Monteagudo: Estudio literario seguido del texto de dicho Diálogo*. La Paz: Editora Universo, 1974.

Chambers, Sarah. *From Subjects to Citizens: Honor, Gender, and Politics in Arequipa, Peru, 1780–1854*. University Park: Pennsylvania State University Press, 1999.

Chang-Rodríguez, Raquel. "Cultural Resistance in the Andes and Its Depiction in *Atau Wallpaj P'uchukakuyninpa Wankan or Tragedy of Atahualpa's Death*." In *Coded Encounters: Writing, Gender, and Ethnicity in Colonial Latin America*, edited by Francisco Javier Cevallos-Candau, Jeffrey A. Cole, Nina M. Scott, and Nicomedes Suárez-Araúz, 115–34. Amherst: University of Massachusetts Press, 1994.

Chervin, Arthur. *Anthropologie bolivienne*. 3 vols. Paris: Imprimerie Nationale/Librairie H. Le Soudier, 1907–8.

Choque Canqui, Roberto, Vitalino Soria, Humberto Mamani, Esteban Ticona, and Ramón Conde, eds. *Educación indígena: Ciudadanía o colonización?* La Paz: Ediciones Aruwiyiri/Taller de Historia Oral Andina, 1992.

Condarco Morales, Ramiro. *Zárate, El "temible" Willka: Historia de la rebelión indígena de 1899*. 1965. Reprint, La Paz: Imprenta Renovación, 1983.

Condoreno, Cristóbal, dir. *El sueño de Waylla Wisa: Profecia de la conquista*. Film. La Paz: Taller de Historia Oral Andina, 2002.

Corla Nina, Isadora. "Los días de violencia." In *Observando el racismo: Racismo y regionalismo en el proceso constituyente*, edited by Luis Bredow and Defensor del Pueblo, 16–37. La Paz: Defensor del Pueblo, 2008.

Costa de la Torre, Arturo. "Las academias aymaras bolivianas del pasado y presente siglo." *Pumapunku* 6 (1972): 41–53.

Dangl, Benjamin. *The Price of Fire: Resource Wars and Social Movements in Bolivia*. Edinburgh: AK Press, 2007.

Dawson, Alexander. "From Models for the Nation to Model Citizens: Indigenismo and the 'Revindication' of the Mexican Nation, 1920–1940." *Journal of Latin American Studies* 30, no. 2 (1998): 279–308.

Dean, Carolyn. *Inca Bodies and the Body of Christ: Corpus Christi in Colonial Cuzco, Peru*. Chapel Hill: University of North Carolina Press, 1999.

De Calancha, Fray Antonio. *Crónica moralizada del Orden de San Agustín en el Perú*. 1638. Reprint, Barcelona: P. Lacavalleria, 1651.

De Cieza de León, Pedro. *Segunda parte de la crónica de Perú: Que se trata del señorio de los Incas yupanquis y de sus grandes hechos y gobernación*. 1553. Reprint, Madrid: Imprenta M. Ginés Hernández, 1880.

De la Cadena, Marisol. *Indigenous Mestizos: The Politics of Race and Culture in Cuzco, Peru, 1919–1991*. Durham, N.C.: Duke University Press, 2000.

De la Fuente, Alejandro. *A Nation for All: Race, Inequality, and Politics in Twentieth-Century Cuba*. Chapel Hill: University of North Carolina Press, 2001.

Demelás, Marie-Danielle. "Darwinismo a la criolla: El darwinismo social en Bolivia, 1809–1910." *Historia Boliviana* 1, no. 20 (1981): 55–82.

Diez de Medina, Eduardo. "Sinfonia aymara." *La musa americana: Revista de arte de La Paz* (Nov. 20, 1904): n.p.

D'Orbigny, Alcide. *Viaje a la América meridional*. Buenos Aires: Editorial Futuro, 1945.

Earle, Rebecca. *The Return of the Native: Indians and Myth-Making in Spanish America, 1810–1930*. Durham, N.C.: Duke University Press, 2007.

Escobar, Filemón. *De la revolución al Pachakuti: El aprendizaje del respeto recíproco entre blancos e indianos*. La Paz: Garza Azul, 2008.

Ferrer, Ada. *Insurgent Cuba: Race, Nation, and Revolution, 1868–1898*. Chapel Hill: University of North Carolina Press, 1999.

Flores Galindo, Alberto. *Buscando un Inca: Identidad y utopia en los Andes*. Lima: Instituto de Apoyo Agrario, 1987.

———. "In Search of an Inca." In *Resistance, Rebellion, and Consciousness in the Andean Peasant World, 18th to 20th Centuries*, edited by Steve Stern, 193–212. Madison: University of Wisconsin Press, 1987.

Garcia, Antonio. *La rebelión de los pueblos débiles*. La Paz: Imprenta E. Burillo, 1955.

Garrett, David. "His Majesty's Most Loyal Vassals: The Indian Nobility and Tupac Amaru." *Hispanic American Historical Review* 84, no. 4 (2004): 575–617.

Goins, John. "The Death of Atahuallpa." *Journal of American Folklore* 74, no. 293 (1961): 252–57.

Goldstein, Daniel. *The Spectacular City: Violence and Performance in Urban Bolivia*. Durham, N.C.: Duke University Press, 2004.

Gómez-Acebo, Daniel González. *Teatro originario boliviano: Estudio histórico del teatro y la teatralidad de las culturas quechua, aymará, y guaraní.* La Paz: Sagitario, 2009.

Gotkowitz, Laura. *A Revolution for Our Rights: Indigenous Struggles for Land and Justice in Bolivia.* Durham, N.C.: Duke University Press, 2007.

Grandidier, Ernest. *Voyage dan l'Amérique du Sud: Pérou et Bolivie.* Paris: Michel Lévy Frères, 1861.

Grieshaber, Erwin. "Survival of Indian Communities in Nineteenth-Century Bolivia: A Regional Comparison." *Journal of Latin American Studies* 12, no. 2 (1980): 223–69.

Guha, Ranajit. *Elementary Aspects of Peasant Insurgency in Colonial India.* Delhi: Oxford University Press, 1983.

Gustafson, Bret. *New Languages of the State: Indigenous Resurgence and the Politics of Knowledge in Bolivia.* Durham, N.C.: Duke University Press, 2009.

Helg, Aline. *Our Rightful Share: The Afro-Cuban Struggle for Equality, 1886–1912.* Chapel Hill: University of North Carolina Press, 1995.

Hobsbawm, Eric. *Bandits.* 2d ed. New York: Pantheon, 1981.

Huanca Ticona, Orlando. "Es possible un teatro andino?" Unpublished manuscript, n.d.

Hylton, Forrest, and Sinclair Thomson. *Revolutionary Horizons: Past and Present in Bolivian Politics.* London: Verso, 2007.

Irurozqui, Marta. *La armonía de las desigualdades: Elites y conflictos de poder en Bolivia, 1880–1920.* Madrid: Consejo Superior de Investigaciones Científicas; Cuzco, Peru: Centro de Estudios Regioanles Andinos Bartolomé de las Casas, 1994.

Itier, César, ed. *El teatro quechua en el Cuzco.* 2 vols. Lima: Institut Français d'Etudes Andines; Cuzco: Centro de Estudios Regioanles Andinos Bartolomé de las Casas, 1995, 2000.

———. "La tragedia de la muerte de Atahuallpa de Jesús Lara, historia de una supercheria literaria." In *Anuario del Archivo Nacional Boliviano,* 215–29. Sucre: ANB, 2009.

Jacobsen, Nils. "The Long and the Short of It." In *Political Cultures in the Andes, 1750–1950,* edited by Nils Jacobsen and Cristóbal Aljovín de Losada, 1–25. Durham, N.C.: Duke University Press, 2005.

Joseph, Gilbert. "On the Trail of Latin American Bandits: A Reexamination of Peasant Resistance." *Latin American Research Review* 25, no. 3 (1990): 7–53.

Julien, Catherine. "The Uru Tribute Category: Ethnic Boundaries and Empire in the Andes." *Proceedings of the American Philosophical Society* 131, no. 1 (1987): 53–91.

Klein, Herbert. *Bolivia: Evolution of a Multi-Ethnic Society.* New York: Oxford University Press, 1992.

———. *Peasant Response to the Market and the Land Question in Eighteenth- and Nineteenth-Century Bolivia.* Washington, D.C.: Wilson Center, 1982.

Konig, Abraham. "Indios de Mohoza." In *La Paz visto por extranjeros y autores nacionales, siglos XVI al XX,* edited by Mariano Baptista Gumucio, 95. La Paz: Anthropos, 1997.

Kramer, Pedro. *Historia de Bolivia.* La Paz: Tipo-Litográfico, 1899.

Kuenzli, E. Gabrielle. "Acting Inca: The Parameters of National Belonging in Early Twentieth-Century Bolivia." *Hispanic American Historical Review* 90, no. 22 (2010): 247–81.

———. "At the Interstices of Identity on Exhibit: The Politics of Ethnicity and Citizenship in the Festival Rituals of Bolivia." Master's thesis, University of Wisconsin, 1998.

Lane, Jill. *Blackface Cuba, 1840–1895.* Philadelphia: University of Pennsylvania Press, 2005.

Lara, Jesús. *La poesia quechua: Ensayo y antologia.* Cochabamba, Bolivia: Universidad Mayor de San Simón, 1947.

———. *Tragedia del fin de Atawallpa: Atau Wallpaj p'uchukakuyninpa wankan.* Cochabamba, Bolivia: Los Amigos del Libro; Buenos Aires: Ediciones del Sol, 1989.

Larson, Brooke. "Andean Highland Peasants and the Trials of Nation Making during the Nineteenth Century." In *Cambridge History of the Native Peoples of the Americas,* edited by Stuart Schwartz and Frank Salomon, vol. 3, 558–703. Cambridge: Cambridge University Press, 1999.

———. "Redeemed Indians, 'Barbarized Cholos': Crafting Neocolonial Modernity in Liberal Bolivia, 1900–1910." In *Political Cultures in the Andes, 1750–1950,* edited by Nils Jacobsen and Cristóbal Aljovín de Losada, 230–52. Durham, N.C.: Duke University Press, 2005.

———. *Trials of Nation Making: Liberalism, Race, and Ethnicity in the Andes, 1810–1910.* Cambridge: Cambridge University Press, 2004.

Loaiza, Wenceslao. *Instrucción y educación de la raza indígena: Informe presentado al ilustrísimo señor Vicario Capitular por el señor cura propio de Laja.* La Paz: La Union, 1911.

Mamani, Carlos, and Maria Eugenia Choque. "Reconstitución del ayllu y derechos de los pueblos indígenas: El movimiento indio en los Andes de Bolivia." *Journal of American Anthropology* 6, no. 1 (2001): 202–23.

Martí, José. *Obras completas.* 28 vols. Havana: Ediciones Nacional de Cuba, 1963–73.

"Memoria Municipal de 1899." Publicaciones Oficiales, Municipalidad de La Paz, anexos, 43. La Paz: Imprenta y Litográfico de el Nacional de Isac W. Willa, 1900.

Méndez, Cecilia. "Incas Sí, Indios No: Notes on Peruvian Creole Nationalism and Its Contemporary Crisis." *Journal of Latin American Studies* 28, no. 1 (1996): 197–225.

Mendieta Parada, Pilar. "De la alianza a la confrontación: Pablo Zárate Willka y la rebelión indígena de 1899 en Bolivia." PhD diss., Universidad Nacional de San Marcos, Facultad de Ciencias Sociales, 2006.

———. "Entre el caudillismo y la modernidad: Poder local y política en la provincia de Inquisivi, el caso de Mohoza (1880–1899). Master's thesis, ciencias políticas, Centro de Estudios Superiores del Centro Boliviano de Estudios Multidisciplinarios, 1999.

Mendoza, Zoila. *Creating Our Own: Folklore, Performance, and Identity in Cuzco, Peru.* Durham, N.C.: Duke University Press, 2008.

Meneses, Teodoro. *La muerte de Atahualpa: Drama quechua.* Lima: Universidad Mayor Nacional de San Marcos, 1987.

Mesa Gisbert, Carlos, and Mario Espinoza Osorio, dirs. *La Guerra Federal.* DVD. La Paz: Plano Medio, 2009.

Mesa, José de, Teresa Gisbert, and Carlos Mesa Gisbert. *Historia de Bolivia.* La Paz: Editorial Gisbert, 2001.

Millones, Luis. *Actores de altura: Ensayos sobre el teatro popular andino.* Lima: Editorial Horizonte, 1992.

Montes Camacho, Niver. *Proceso íntimo del carnival de Oruro.* Oruro, Bolivia: Editorial Universitaria, 1986.

Moreno, René. *Nicomedes Antelo.* Santa Cruz de la Sierra, Bolivia: Universidad Mayor Gabriel René Moreno, 1960.

Murillo, Josermo, and Antonio Revollo. *La Virgen del Socavón y su carnival.* Oruro, Bolivia: Centro Diocesano de Pastoral Social, 1992.

Nava Rodríguez, Ascanio J. *Referencias sobre el carnaval del Oruro.* Oruro, Bolivia: Editoriales Latinas, 2004.

Oleszkiewicz, Malgorzata. "El ciclo de la muerte te Atahuallpa: De la fiesta popular a la representación teatral." *Allpanchis* (Cuzco) 39 (1992): 185–220.

Paredes, Manuel Rigoberto. *La Altiplanicie.* La Paz: Ediciones Isla, 1965.

―――. *La elección de convencional en la provincia de Muñecas: Fraudes de la mesa escrutadora de Mocomoco.* La Paz: Imprenta Richter, 1899.

―――. *Provincia de Inquisivi: Estudios geográficos y sociales.* La Paz: Taller Tipo-Litográfico, 1906.

―――. *Los Siñani: Tradiciones y crónicas del pueblo de Carabuco.* La Paz: Ediciones Isla, 1968.

―――. *Tiahuanacu y la provincia de Ingavi.* La Paz: Ediciones Isla, 1955.

Platt, Tristan. "The Andean Experience of Bolivian Liberalism: Roots of Rebellion in 19th-Century Chayanta (Bolivia)." In *Resistance, Rebellion, and Consciousness in the Andean Peasant World, 18th–20th Centuries,* edited by Steve Stern, 280–318. Madison: University of Wisconsin Press, 1987.

―――. *Estado boliviano y ayllu andino: Tierra y tributo en el Norte de Potosí.* Lima: Instituto de Estudios Peruanos, 1982.

―――. "Liberalism and Ethnocide in the Southern Andes." *History Workshop* 17 (1984): 3–18.

―――. "Simón Bolívar, the Sun of Justice, and the Amerindian Virgin: Andean Conceptions of the Patria in Nineteenth-Century Potosí." *Journal of Latin American Studies* 25, no. 1 (1993): 159–85.

Poole, Deborah. *Vision, Race, and Modernity: A Visual Economy of the Andean Image World.* Princeton, N.J.: Princeton University Press, 1997.

Posnansky, Arthur. *Tihuanacu: La cuna del hombre Americano/Tihuanacu: The Cradle of American Man.* Vol. 1. New York: Augustin, 1945.

―――. "Tiahuanacu y la civilización prehistórica en el altiplano." *Boletín de la Sociedad Geográfica de La Paz* 31 (1911): n.p.

Post, Charles Johnson. *Across the Andes: A Tale of Wandering Days among the Mountains of Bolivia and the Jungles of the Upper Amazon.* New York: Outing, 1912.

Qayum, Seemin. "Creole Imaginings: Space, Race, and Gender in the Making of Republican Bolivia." PhD diss., University of London: Goldsmiths College, 2002.

―――. "Nationalism, Internal Colonialism, and the Spatial Imagination: The Geographic Society of La Paz in Turn-of-the-Century Bolivia." In *Studies in the Formation of the Nation-State in Latin America,* edited by James Dunkerley, 279–98. London: Institute of Latin American Studies, 2002.

Rasnake, Roger Neil. *Domination and Cultural Resistance: Authority and Power among an Andean People.* Durham, N.C.: Duke University Press, 1988.

Rivera Cusicanqui, Silvia. *Oppressed but Not Defeated: Peasant Struggles among the Aymara and the Qhechwa in Bolivia, 1900–1980.* Geneva: United Nations Research Institute for Social Development, 1987.

Rowe, John. "El movimiento nacional Inca del siglo XVIII." In *Tupac Amaru II—1780: Sociedad colonial y sublevaciones populares,* edited by Alberto Flores Galindo, 11–66. Lima: Retablo de Papel Ediciones, 1976.

Saavedra, Bautista. *El ayllu.* La Paz: Imprenta Artística Velarde, Aldazosa, 1903.

Salmon, Josefa. *El espejo indígena: El discurso indigenista en Bolivia 1900–1956.* La Paz: Plural, 1997.

Sans, Rafael. *Novena de la milagrosa virgen de Copacabana.* Translated into Aymara by Wenceslao Loaiza V. La Paz: Imprenta Yungas, 1891.

Scott, James. *Weapons of the Weak: Everyday Forms of Peasant Resistance.* New Haven, Conn.: Yale University Press, 1985.

Seed, Patricia. "Failing to Marvel: Atahuallpa's Encounter with the Word." *Latin American Research Review* 26, no. 1 (1991): 7–32.

Soria Choque, Vitaliano. "Los caciques-apoderados y la lucha por la escuela." In *Educación indígena: Ciudadanía o colonización?*, edited by Roberto Choque Canqui, Vitalino Soria, Humberto Mamani, Esteban Ticona, and Ramón Conde, 41–78. La Paz: Ediciones Aruwiyiri/Taller de Historia Oral Andina, 1992.

Stepan, Nancy Leys. *The Hour of Eugenics: Race, Gender, and Nation in Latin America.* Ithaca, N.Y.: Cornell University Press, 1991.

Stephenson, Marcia. "Forging an Indigenous Counterpublic Sphere: The Taller de Historia Oral Andina in Bolivia." *Latin American Research Review* 37, no. 2 (2002): 99–118.

Stern, Steve, ed. *Resistance, Rebellion, and Consciousness in the Andean Peasant World, 18th to 20th Centuries.* Madison: University of Wisconsin Press, 1987.

Taylor, Diana, and Sarah Townsend, eds. *Stages of Conflict: A Critical Anthology of Latin American Theater and Performance.* Ann Arbor: University of Michigan Press, 2008.

Thomson, Sinclair. "Bolivia's Turn-of the-Century Indian Problem: The Case of Manuel Rigoberto Paredes." Master's thesis, University of Wisconsin, 1987.

Thomson, Sinclair, Adolfo Gilly, and Forrest Hylton. *Revolutionary Horizons: Past and Present in Bolivian Politics.* New York: Verso, 2007.

Tiahuanaco: Datos para la defensa de la segunda sección de Pacajes. La Paz, 1897.

Ticona Alejo, Esteban. *Los Andes desde los Andes: Aymaranakana, Qhichwanakana, Yatxatawipa, Lup'iwipa.* La Paz: Ediciones Yachaywasi, 2003.

Torrico Zas, Martin Gabriel. "El mito que reactualizó el racismo y reavivó una guerra heredada." In *Observando el racismo: Racismo y regionalismo en el proceso constituyente*, edited by Luis Bredow and Defensor del Pueblo, 72–98. La Paz: Defensor del Pueblo, 2008.

Turner, Victor. "Social Dramas and Stories about Them." *Critical Inquiry* 7, no. 1 (1980): 141–68.

Unzueta, Mario. *Valle.* Cochabamba, Bolivia: La Epoca, 1945.

Vasconcelos, José. *The Cosmic Race = La raza cósmica.* Translated by Didier Tisdel Jaén. Los Angeles: Centro de Publicaciones, Dept. of Chicano Studies, California State University, 1979.

Villamil de Rada, Emeterio, and Nicolás Acosta. *La lengua de Adán y el hombre de Tiahuanaco: Resumen de estas obras.* La Paz: La Razón, 1888.

Wachtel, Nathan. *The Vision of the Vanquished: The Spanish Conquest of Peru through Indian Eyes, 1530–1570.* Translated by Ben Reynolds and Siân Reynolds. New York: Barnes and Noble, 1977.

Wachtel, Nathan, and Laura Ciezar. *El regreso de los antepasados: Los indios urus de Bolivia del siglo XX al XVI.* Mexico City: El Colegio de México, Fondo de Cultural Económica, 2001.

Wade, Peter. *Blackness and Race Mixture: The Dynamics of Racial Identity in Colombia.* Baltimore, Md.: Johns Hopkins University Press, 1993.

———. *Race and Ethnicity in Latin America.* London: Pluto, 1997.

Weinstein, Barbara. "Racializing Regional Difference: Sao Paulo versus Brazil, 1932." In

Race and Nation in Modern Latin America, edited by Nancy Appelbaum, Anne Macpherson, and Karin Rosemblatt, 237–62. Chapel Hill: University of North Carolina Press, 2003.

Yucra León, Victor. "Trabajo de investigación: Caracollo como un pueblo plurinacional dentro de la sociedad boliviana." Unpublished manuscript, 1995.

Zárate Willka, Pablo. "Proclama de Caracollo." In *De la revolución al Pachakuti: El aprendizaje del respeto recíproco entre blancos e indianos,* by Filemón Escóbar, 310. La Paz: Garza Azul, 2008.

INDEX